TWO OLD FOOLS IN TURMOIL

NEW YORK TIMES BESTSELLING AUTHOR

VICTORIA TWEAD

Ant Press

CONTENTS

THE OLD FOOLS SERIES
AVAILABLE IN PAPERBACK, LARGE PRINT AND EBOOK

Two Old Fools in Turmoil is the fifth book in the *Old Fools* series by New York Times and Wall Street Journal bestselling author, Victoria Twead.

> *Chickens, Mules and Two Old Fools*
> *Two Old Fools ~ Olé!*
> *Two Old Fools on a Camel*
> *Two Old Fools in Spain Again*
> *Two Old Fools in Turmoil*
> *Two Old Fools Down Under*
>
> *Prequels*
> *One Young Fool in Dorset*
> *One Young Fool in South Africa*

Latest Release:
Dear Fran, Love Dulcie: Life and Death in the Hills and Hollows of Bygone Australia

FREE PHOTO BOOK
TO BROWSE OR DOWNLOAD

For photographs and additional unpublished material to accompany
this book, browse or download the

FREE PHOTO BOOK
from
www.victoriatwead.com / free-stuff

THE ENCHANTED POOL

When the phone rang very late in the evening or early in the morning, it was usually my daughter, Karly, ringing from Australia.

"Hi Mum! How are you both? What's the weather like in El Hoyo?"

"Karly! Lovely to hear from you! Joe's fine and you know what Spanish summers are like, sunshine every day. How are you? How's Cam? How's my gorgeous granddaughter?"

"Indy's fine. We're all fine. Actually, we were thinking of getting a pet to join the family."

"Lovely! Like a guinea pig or rabbit?"

"Well, no…"

"Oh, a cat. Or dog?"

"No…"

"What then?"

"We thought it might be nice to get a pig."

"Wow! Do you have enough space in your new garden?"

"Yes. Plenty. Pigs are very intelligent and affectionate, apparently. Anyway, this weekend we're going to visit the farm where they're for sale."

"Keep me posted! I wish Australia wasn't so far away!"

"I will. Can't wait for you both to come out to Aus this Christmas.

You won't believe how Indy's grown, and I can't wait to show you our new house. We love it!"

"We can't wait either!"

It was the summer of 2014 and life was almost perfect. I say 'almost' because one thing was bothering me. I couldn't talk to Joe about it. He wouldn't let me.

But for now we were soaking up the Spanish summer. We hoped to spend Christmas in Australia but that seemed a long way off.

As a child, I used to love the feeling I had on the first day of the school holidays, when I knew I had six whole weeks stretching out ahead of me. It was the same in El Hoyo in June. Hot weather was guaranteed. Barbecues would never be rained off. The Spanish sun was so big, hot and heavy that it barely managed to heave itself over the mountain range. But it did, and as the day progressed, it rolled in a giant arc across the sky until it hung high, burning all within its reach.

While the villagers hid from the sun, Joe and I drove out of the valley to a neighbouring small town where a cool, sparkling, public pool awaited us. We loved it. Only mad dogs and Englishmen go out in the midday sun so we often had the pool to ourselves until later in the afternoon.

A waterfall cascaded down the mountain slope above the pool, fed by warm natural springs. Sometimes we saw wild goats cropping the dry grass on the crags above us. As they grazed, they stood silhouetted against the gigantic blue sky. Bright red dragonflies whizzed to and fro, often settling on the edge of the pool to rest.

To us, the pool was enchanted.

"Pah!" said Paco, our next door neighbour. "You go to that pool so much, you should get yourselves an *abono*."

Joe nodded sagely. I had no idea what an *abono* was and made a mental note to ask Mr Know-It-All later.

"Have you heard about the King of Spain?" asked Carmen, her eyes wide with disbelief. "I can hardly believe it!"

"Yes, we watched the news last night."

I didn't know a great deal about Spanish history, but I knew that Juan Carlos became King on the 22nd of November, 1975, two days after the loathed dictator, Franco, died. Juan Carlos introduced reforms and gently guided Spain back to democracy. Ordinary people like our neighbours, Paco and Carmen, adored their King who they believed to have delivered them from evil.

"¡*Madre mía!*" exclaimed Carmen, her double chins shaking. "When Prime Minister Rajoy called that emergency press conference, we didn't expect King Juan Carlos to step down."

"Pah!" shouted Paco. "He was a good king! Exactly what we needed after that *bastardo* Franco."

"Paco!" chided his wife. "We have company."

"Pah, Joe and Veeky know what kind of a man Franco was. But Juan Carlos is only 76 years old, he did not need to step down!"

"It's a shock," agreed Carmen, "but perhaps it's time the young ones took over. Soon Spain will have a new king and queen in Felipe and Letizia."

Carmen was right. Less than three weeks later, Spain had a new king and queen.

"What's an *abono*, then?" I asked Joe when we were back home.

He looked at me blankly.

"You know, the thing Paco suggested we take to the pool. You nodded as though you knew exactly what it was."

"I have no idea. I guess it's some kind of inflatable or a sun lounger or something."

I sighed and settled in front of the computer. I didn't know it at the time, but the *abono* quest had just begun.

I typed *abono* into Google Translate and read the results.

"Fertiliser? Manure? Why *on earth* would Paco suggest taking fertiliser or manure to the pool?"

Joe looked blank.

"Oh, wait. There's more. It also means season ticket."

"Ah."

"Now that would make more sense. We'll ask about that."

The next day we arrived at the pool. Apart from the lifeguard, nobody was there.

We were familiar with all the lifeguards who worked at the pool. Lorenzo was our favourite and we'd already decided he should get the EPLGY, or Enchanted Pool Life Guard of the Year award. Lorenzo was almost square-shaped, and although he didn't look the athletic type, he took his job very seriously.

He never stopped working. Even if there were no swimmers or sunbathers, Lorenzo busied himself. Using his net, he skimmed off invisible floating leaves, or polished the sun loungers with a soft cloth. When children arrived, he watched them with narrowed eyes. Woe betide them if they were over-excited, too boisterous, or threatened to endanger themselves or others. Picnickers were welcomed, but firmly instructed where to find the garbage bins and where to set out their meals.

Our least favourite lifeguard was Alberto. Alberto was tall, handsome and bronzed by the Spanish sun. He rarely wore a shirt and his oiled six-pack and biceps gleamed. Girls stuttered when they spoke to him, and, believe me, even grandmothers found themselves staring in his direction.

We would have awarded the WEPLGY (Worst Enchanted Pool Life Guard of the Year) to Alberto without hesitation because he did almost nothing. Alberto sat on a folding chair under a parasol, tapping out texts or playing games on his mobile phone. This took all his attention, and he rarely looked up from the task. New arrivals were forced to wait at the gate until he was ready and dozens of small children might have drowned before he had even noticed.

Occasionally he would put his phone aside and stretch theatrically, thus attracting maximum female attention. He then strolled to the edge of the pool, poised and dived in like a harpoon, cutting through the water with hardly a ripple. After several lengths, he climbed out, water streaming from his muscular torso. Girls averted their eyes, trying not to stare. He would then resume his seat and take up his mobile phone again.

Alberto was on duty that day, in the loosest sense of the word.

"Ahem."

No response. Joe tried again.

"¡Buenos días!"

The game Alberto was playing on his mobile must have been enthralling. At last his eyes flicked up at us.

"Four euros," he said, resuming his game.

"Thank you," said Joe, placing the coins in a tidy little pile on the table. "Um, we were wondering if we could buy *abonos*, please."

"Not here," said Alberto. "You can buy them at the bank."

Joe and I looked at each other. *The bank? Really?*

Alberto's dark head was bowed as he tapped away at the little screen on his phone. Unwilling to continue talking to the top of his head, we walked away.

We'd been given the clue, and the second phase of the *abono* quest had begun.

"Honestly! Alberto doesn't deserve that job! How can anyone be so unhelpful?"

"Never mind," I said. "Let's not bother today, it's too hot. Tomorrow we can come earlier and go to the bank first."

We shrugged off our outer clothes and slipped gratefully into the cool waters of the pool. Bliss.

The next day, we parked the car at the far end of the town, near the bank. It was late morning and the bank was busy with queues at every counter. My heart sank, and I remembered why I avoided shopping with Joe at all costs.

Running errands and getting groceries was Joe's task. Curious friends often asked me why I didn't accompany him, and the answer came easily. I didn't go with him because I valued my sanity. In fact, I'd rather have my brains pulled out through my nose than go shopping with Joe.

Nobody *enjoys* queuing, although most of us accept it as a necessary evil. However, queuing and Joe are like cats and water; he *detests* it. At first he just grumbles loudly, and scratches himself, which is bad enough. If things don't improve, he will begin to heckle, making me shrivel with embarrassment as people turn to stare. It amazes me that no stores have banned him from entering their premises.

"I'll sort this, why don't you wait outside?" I suggest sweetly, but he ignores me, preferring to stand with me and complain at the top of his voice.

I have to admit that I prefer the polite British attitude to queuing. You know exactly where you are, who is in front and who is behind. This concept is usually ignored in Spain and the person with the sharpest elbows gets served first.

Our local chemist, or *farmacia*, had recently adopted the ticket system. Simple, take a ticket from the machine and wait for your number to show on the screen. Even Joe was pleased.

"How did you get on at the chemist?" I once asked, when Joe returned from a shopping trip.

"It was frightful, you won't believe what happened."

I groaned. *What had annoyed him this time?*

"Go on, what happened?"

"I pulled ticket #63, and when it was my turn, this dreadful old goat pushed in front of me. I jumped forward, showed her and the assistant my ticket, but the old goat still got served before me! Can you believe it? So I stood back and waited. By the time she's finished, #64 is being called and *another* old goat barges past me."

"Oh dear."

"This one flashes me her #64 ticket, and points to the screen showing #64, so the assistant serves her!"

"So what did you do?"

"Do? DO? I exploded!"

What a surprise.

"I went up and down the queue and showed everybody my ticket and told them what I thought of their queuing system. When the number changed again, I marched up to the counter, but so does another customer! The assistant looked at both of us, from one to the other."

I winced, imagining the scene.

"Everybody is watching now. I waved my ticket at the crowd, pointing at the number: ticket #63. The assistant looks again at the screen, and the other man's ticket. Then she raised her eyebrows, not sure who to serve. So she looked at the other waiting customers in question. "Who's next?" she asks."

"And?"

"All the other customers swung around. "Serve him! Serve him!" they said, pointing at me, knowing I would erupt again."

I had to laugh at the story, but I was very glad I hadn't been there.

No, Joe is not at his best shopping, or waiting in queues, but he behaved himself quite well as we made our way closer to the bank teller that day. When it was our turn, I did the talking.

"Good day," I said, in Spanish. "We would like to buy two *abonos* for the public swimming pool, please."

The girl behind the counter smiled and ignored my Spanish.

"Good morning! I speak English very nice."

"Oh, thank you!" I said brightly. "We'd like two season tickets for the public swimming pool, please."

"I have no problem."

"Oh, that's good news. You sell *abonos* here at the bank?"

"Yes. How much you want pay?"

"Pardon?"

"You must say to me how much you want pay."

Was this a game? A strange Spanish tradition? Was she trying to catch me out?

"But we don't know! We don't know how much a season ticket costs. Don't *you* know how much it is?"

Joe's foot was starting to tap the floor dangerously. Other bank customers were beginning to stare.

"No, I do not know how much euros. You must go and find out, then come back and say me and give me money."

"But who will know? Where do we go?"

"This is like some stupid treasure hunt," growled Joe at my side. "Let's go and find a gypsy. I'm sure she'll tell us if we cross her palm with silver."

"Gypsy? I am apologetic. I do not understand. What is gypsy?"

"Shh, Joe!" I said. "I'm sorry," I said to the girl, "we just weren't clear about who could tell us how much the season ticket will be."

"Ah, they will tell you how much euros at the, (*pause*) I don't know how you say, *ayuntamiento*."

"Town hall," growled Joe.

"Yes! I had not remembered the words! Town hall! Yes, please asking the mens at the town hall. Is there any more one thing I can kindly help with?"

"I think not," said Joe.

"Thank you, no," I said, "but we'll be back."

I followed Joe who was already marching out of the door.

"Where's the town hall?"

"I don't know. It's probably near the Police Station. We know where that is."

"But that's right on the other side of the town!"

"Never mind, good exercise."

We set off on our mission in the baking heat, eventually standing in front of the building marked *Policía*.

"I can't see the town hall," said Joe, panting and scratching himself in annoyance.

Neither could I.

"Excuse me," I asked an old lady dressed in black. "Can you tell me where the *ayuntamiento* is, please?"

She looked alarmed, so I repeated my question more slowly. The local dialect is very strong, in fact so thick that many Spanish people from further north struggle with it, so it was hardly surprising that this local ancient couldn't understand my Spanish. She peered into my face, watching my lips move. This time she caught the word *ayuntamiento* and her face broke into a toothless smile.

BREADED ROLLED JAMÓN AND CHEESE
FLAMENQUINES

Traditional *flamenquines* are a slice of pork, covered with a slice of *jamón*, rolled into a tube, breaded and fried.

Ingredients (serves 2)

4 pork cutlets

4 slices of *jamón*

4 slices of cheese

2 eggs

2 fistfuls of flour (doesn't matter which type)

2 fistfuls of breadcrumbs

Oil for frying

Method

Break the eggs into a shallow bowl and whisk lightly.

In a separate bowl, sprinkle the flour.

In another shallow bowl, sprinkle the breadcrumbs.

Pound the meat, or roll with a rolling pin, until the pork cutlets are as thin as you can get them.

Layer each cutlet with a slice of *jamón* and a slice of cheese.

Roll into a fairly tight tube and shove a toothpick or two through to secure it.

Dip into the flour to coat it, then the egg, then the breadcrumbs.

Fry in hot oil until golden brown. You can deep fry or just use an inch of oil, turning as it browns. Fry in batches so you don't crowd the pan.

Serve hot.

2

VALENTINA

"Do you know where the *ayuntamiento* is?" I repeated.

"*Arriba,*" quavered the old lady and pointed her walking stick in the direction that Joe and I had just come. "Up there!"

"You're joking," growled Joe, but she wasn't.

"The town hall is near the bank," croaked our new friend.

"But of course it is," said Joe.

Luckily the irony was lost on the old lady and she hobbled away with a cheery wave.

"I think I know a short cut," announced Joe.

Why do I always fall for that one? Why do I listen? Joe has an appalling sense of direction and his shortcuts are invariably disastrous. Perhaps it was the onset of heatstroke that made me agree to trudge after him through the back streets of the town.

"Unfortunately we have to go up this steep road first," said Joe, "but it should curve round and then it'll be Ski Sunday."

"Ski Sunday?"

"Downhill all the way."

It was too hot for jokes. The street climbed, and so did we, then wound round just as Joe had predicted.

But then the street stopped without warning. A brick wall had been built across the road, from one side to the other. Why, we had, no idea, but there was no passing it.

Sweat streamed into my eyes and I was panting. I was disgusted at how unfit I had become. However, it wasn't me that I was concerned about, it was Joe. The effort had stolen all his breath and he was bent double, gasping. His skin wasn't a good colour.

"Joe…"

"Give me a second…"

"Joe, this isn't normal. We have to find out why you become so short of breath."

Joe was beginning to recover.

"I don't…(puff)…want to talk about it…(puff). I'll be fine…(puff). I'm just unfit."

I didn't believe that. Unlike me, who was always the last to be picked for any teams, Joe is the sporty type. He used to run marathons, play football and squash. So why was he gasping after the slightest bit of exercise?

It took much trekking, with plenty of wrong turns and numerous pauses for Joe to regain his breath, but we finally found ourselves back at the bank where we had started. If I hadn't been so worried about Joe, I'd have enjoyed seeing the backstreets where old ladies sat outside their houses shelling peas, or sweeping their doorsteps until they gleamed. I loved seeing the scarlet geraniums bursting from window boxes. I would have preferred not to see so many caged finches and canaries hanging in windows, but their songs were a delight to hear.

"So where's the town hall?" Joe groaned.

I asked a passing shopper, who pointed at a plaque on the wall beside a shadowy staircase.

"Look, Joe! It's up these stairs! No wonder we couldn't find it!"

Upstairs, at the counter, we asked for swimming pool *abonos*.

"For one week? Or for one month?" asked the young man.

"*Un mes*," we chorused. "One month, please."

"That will be twenty euros each," said the young man, stamping a sheet of paper with the town hall logo. "Take this paper to the bank and pay them."

So we did.

"We'd like two season tickets for the public swimming pool, please," I said to the bank teller, and received the response I expected.

"Of course. How much would you like to pay?"

"Forty euros for two," I said confidently and handed her the sheet of paper.

"Thank you, here are your cards."

Smiles all round.

Quest completed.

Happily, we headed off to the pool to use our season tickets for the first time, and to cool down. The rest of the afternoon was uneventful. Alberto, who was on 'duty', accepted our season tickets without comment, and our swim was peaceful.

At precisely two o'clock, we looked up to see one of our favourite sights. On the pavement outside, two rather overweight labradors were taking an elderly Spanish man for a walk, as they did every day at that time. When they reached the Enchanted Pool entrance, the dogs strained and pulled.

"No, you can't go in there!" the man said loudly, as he did every day.

He dragged them away to continue their walk.

"Poor things," I said to Joe. "I bet they'd love to jump in the pool for a swim."

That evening, Joe and I sat outside under the vine with a bottle of Paco's homemade wine. In the street, our neighbours, the Ufartes, were out in force. We could hear Papa Ufarte's guitar and I knew that Mama Ufarte and the twins would be whirling and stamping, arms held high in exuberant flamenco moves.

"Did you know the Ufarte twins are winning awards for their flamenco dancing?"

"No, I didn't, but I'm not surprised. I think flamenco is in the Ufarte blood."

"Yup. They told me they may be performing at the village *fiesta* this year."

We fell into a companionable silence.

"Any plans for tomorrow?"

"Yes," I replied. "You are going to start your book."

Joe groaned.

"Come on, you've been talking about it for years. I think you should call it, *One Young Fool in South Africa*."

"Yes, you're quite right. I know it's not a pretty story but perhaps it's time to get it all off my chest."

"Talking about chests," I said, "I'm worried about yours. You get out of breath so quickly. Why don't you let me make an appointment for a check up?"

"No way! I'm perfectly okay! Now listen, I forgot to tell you what Marcia at the shop told me today."

I sat up, all ears. I confess that hearing gossip is one of my many vices.

"Hello, Mum! Australia calling!"

"Hello Karly! I was just thinking about you all. How did you get on with your pig-viewing at the farm?"

"Indy loved it. She was fascinated by all the animals. Completely changed our minds about getting a pig though..."

"Oh, really? Why?"

"Well, the piglets were beyond cute, but we met the mother and father and they were HUGE! Pity, because we'd already thought of some great names, like Hammy Davis Jr or Swinona Ryder."

Receiving mail, whether letters or parcels, often posed a problem for us in Spain. Parcels frequently arrived on the fish van, or we'd collect them from Marcia at the shop, or the petrol station at the bottom of the mountain. It was one of those quirky things we just learned to live with.

"Well? What's the news?" I asked. "What did Marcia tell you?"

"It seems that our fishy postal deliveries are going to be a thing of the past," Joe replied. "El Hoyo has entered the 21st century at last."

"How do you mean? Is our mail going to be delivered by drones?"

"No. Not *that* high tech, but close. We've got a new postie. Marcia introduced me."

"Oh, really?"

"Yes, a very nice young lady by the name of Valentina. She's going to be delivering our mail by moped in future. Starting next week."

"Wonderful! Any more news?"

"Yes, well, I think so. Marcia was itching to tell me something but when Valentina arrived, she stopped."

"Oh? I wonder what that was about?"

"I don't know, you'll have to ask her."

I was disappointed, but resolved to chat with Marcia and find out what she had nearly divulged to Joe. Meanwhile, I had something else on my mind.

Joe's health worried me, but I wasn't sure what I could do about it. On the other hand, there was plenty I could do about my own expanding waistline and lack of fitness.

The night before, I had looked at myself in the mirror, something I don't enjoy. I mean, *really* looked. Where had all that extra weight come from? Reluctantly I climbed onto the scales, ashamed of the layer of dust I disturbed, evidence of how seldom I weighed myself.

No!

That figure couldn't be right! I tried leaning forward a little, then jumped off and tried again. It didn't make any difference. Even when I moved the scales to a different place, they still insisted on that awful number.

So I made myself a promise. I vowed I would lose a significant amount of weight by December, in time for our visit to Australia.

It felt good having made the decision.

I chatted with my daughter online about it.

"Get yourself a FitFirst," she suggested. (It wasn't really called that, but I don't want to advertise.)

"What's that?"

"It's a device you wear on your wrist. It counts your steps throughout the day, and there's an app online that keeps a record of everything, and tells you all sorts of stuff."

"Perfect! How many steps should you do a day?"

"Ten thousand."

"Gosh. That sounds like a lot."

Carmen rolled her eyes when I told her about the FitFirst.

"*¡Madre mía!*" she exclaimed. "Whatever next? I'm sure I do more than ten thousand steps a day running after Paco and the rest of the family. And with the wedding of Sofía and Alejandro next summer, I will be running around even more."

I believed that, but Carmen's ample curves spoke of a fondness for food. Hardly surprising as she was a wonderful cook.

Joe also rolled his eyes when I told him I'd ordered a FitFirst online.

"I bet you can't do ten thousand steps in one day."

"Bet I can!"

I waited impatiently for the device to arrive.

"Joe," I announced a few days later, "I'm just popping down to Marcia's to see if my FitFirst has arrived."

Joe looked up from his computer. He was busy at work on his book.

"You really just needed an excuse to go and chat with Marcia, didn't you?"

I pouted and flounced off down the street towards the village square and Marcia's shop. Joe's taunt was partly true. I wanted to collect my Fitfirst, if it had arrived, but I was also curious to hear the village gossip.

Lizards darted up the crumbling walls as I passed, and the weeds, so lush a month ago, were dry and crisp, no longer thrusting through every crevice. In the distance I could hear the buzz of a bee, the only sound to break the sultry silence apart from my footsteps on the dusty street.

Before I reached the shop, I looked up, shielding my eyes from the sun's glare. The buzzing had intensified and I soon realised it wasn't a summer bee busy pollinating at all. It was a yellow moped descending into the valley.

The young lady rider and I arrived at Marcia's door at exactly the same time. I smiled at her as she switched off the engine and unclipped the chinstrap of her helmet.

"*¡Buenos días!*" I said. "You must be our new postlady!"

"Yes," she said, pulling off her helmet and shaking out masses of wavy black hair that gleamed in the sun and fell like a waterfall down her back.

Somebody behind me gasped. I spun round. I hadn't realised there was anybody there.

"Geronimo, I didn't see you," I said. "Where are your dogs?"

"Over there, resting," he said, pointing, but he never tore his eyes from Valentina.

Geronimo's dogs lay panting under the shade trees in the square, floppy tongues lolling. Swallows dived low, snatching flies, their shadows darting like high-speed arrows across the baked ground.

"I am Valentina," said the young lady, seizing the initiative and shaking my hand.

"Very pleased to meet you," I said.

"And how are you, Geronimo?" she asked, amusement dancing in her eyes.

Geronimo reddened and he appeared to have difficulty meeting her gaze.

"Geronimo, stop gawking like an idiot and help Valentina carry the mail inside," said Marcia, appearing at the shop doorway.

Geronimo, never one to say much unless it was to sing the praises of his beloved football team, Real Madrid, was silent as Valentina opened the back pannier on the moped and pulled out a bag marked *Correos*. He stepped forward, took it from her and carried it into the shop.

"You are *senõra* Twead, yes?" asked Valentina, as we followed.

"I am, yes," I replied.

I wasn't surprised she knew who I was as Joe and I were the only foreigners in the village, and she'd already met Joe.

"I have a packet and some letters for you. If you would like to take them now it will save me putting them in your mailbox."

She took the mailbag from Geronimo, brushing his hand ever so slightly with her own. Geronimo jumped as though an electric charge had sparked, and I heard Valentina draw a tiny breath.

I looked at old Marcia behind the counter. She'd missed nothing. Our eyes met and she twitched one silver eyebrow ever so slightly.

"Here is your mail," said Valentina quickly, after a brief rummage in the mailbag.

"Thank you," I said.

"Did you come for anything else?" Marcia asked me.

"No, just a chat as I haven't seen you for a while, Marcia. I'll pop back another time. Thank you for these, Valentina, nice to meet you and I'll see you again soon. See you, Geronimo."

I took my mail and left the highly charged atmosphere.

"Did you find out Marcia's news?" asked Joe as he carried two cups of coffee out to the table under the vine.

"No, not yet, but I met Valentina, the new postlady."

"What did you think of her?"

"Seems very nice. And I think I may have witnessed something significant."

I told him about Geronimo's unexpected appearance, how he'd been struck dumb by Valentina, how I'd seen them accidentally touch, and the effect it had had on both of them.

"Honestly, Vicky, you never cease to amaze me! Only you could create such romantic nonsense out of absolutely nothing. I'm sure you're imagining things."

"I'm not! Any female would agree with me. Even Marcia saw it. I can't help it if you men have absolutely no idea of what's going on right in front of your noses. I won't say another word about it, but just you wait and see. Right, now I'm going to open my mail."

I handed Joe the bills and concentrated on opening the FitFirst device.

I spent a happy half hour setting it up. Ten thousand steps, how hard could that be?

I walked round the garden a few times and checked it.

Six hundred.

Okay, how about if I climb the stairs and do a few circuits of the roof terrace?

Determined, I began walking again. It was more tiring than I thought it would be, particularly with the sun beating down on me. I rested, leaning my elbows on the wall and looking down on the street. Neither the Ufartes or Paco's family were outside their houses; it was too hot. In fact, the village looked deserted except for a couple sitting together on a bench, under a shade tree in the square. The yellow moped was parked nearby. At their feet lay Geronimo's three dogs and Valentina was absentmindedly fondling one dog's ears.

How nice! I thought. Geronimo deserved a little love in his life. Perhaps his luck had changed at last. If only he could curb his drinking a little, then ladies would appreciate what a good sort he was.

I glanced down at my FitFirst. One thousand four hundred.

Right, so this was going to be a little harder than I had thought. Never mind. No pain, no gain. I set off again.

"How many steps have you done?" asked Joe as I marched past him for the third time.

"Four thousand."

"I told you you'll never do ten thousand a day."

I guess it was at that point that the step obsession began.

GRILLED ASPARAGUS WITH HAM AND CHEESE
ESPÁRRAGOS GRATINADOS

For this recipe you can use whichever type of cheese you prefer, just make sure that it isn't too strong and overpowers the asparagus.

Ingredients

Asparagus, fresh or bottled - 4 or 5 spears per person

Sliced ham, or *jamón* - enough to wrap each spear

Cheese - a fistful to sprinkle on top.

Method

Preheat the grill to a medium high heat.

Pat the asparagus spears dry. Wrap each stick of asparagus with the *jamón* or ham leaving the tip bare.

Lay the wrapped asparagus in a shallow oven dish.

Sprinkle your chosen grated cheese over the top.

Grill until the cheese is golden and bubbling.

Serve hot.

3

STEPS

"Well, Mum, we've done it!"

"What?"

"I'll email you a photo. Looks like this little guy might be joining our family! He's a Staffy/husky cross, ten weeks old and was abandoned along with his brother. He's coming for a home visit on Tuesday to see how we all get along."

"Wow! Does the shelter know you have a toddler?"

"Yep, we were totally honest. I told them that Indy was totally mental and runs around like a mini drunk. They don't think it's a problem at all. They said he's playful but placid and very gentle. He comes on Tuesday night so they can check our house at the same time, then if we're all happy he stays for two weeks to see how it goes. Their rules are very strict."

From the day I buckled the FitFirst onto my wrist, I became obsessed by the number of steps I walked and wasn't content until I'd reached my target of ten thousand.

The pattern of my days completely changed. As soon as I woke, I had steps on my mind. While I waited for the kettle to boil, I marched up and down. If I was writing, instead of gazing at the view for inspiration, I organised my thoughts while marching round the garden. When I went shopping, to give myself extra steps, I parked as far from the entrance of the supermarket as possible.

I marched round the village, up the road, out of the valley and back again. The villagers became accustomed to seeing me stride past. I'd explained the FitFirst to some of them, and they clearly thought the whole concept was completely insane, but they humoured me.

"Veeky!" called Carmen as I marched past her front door. "Stop and have a coffee with me. I have just made *churros*."

"Thank you, but I can't! I've only done five thousand today."

And off I went, one foot in front of the other, step after step after step.

"Pah!" called Paco. "You will wear your shoes out!"

Actually, he was right. It was too hot to wear closed-in shoes, I only ever wore flip-flops, and I *did* wear them out. In the past, when my flip-flops had aged, the toe-piece usually snapped or pulled out of the sole. Now, after continuous walking, the sole of the flip-flop became compressed and wafer-thin. So thin that I could feel every tiny stone underfoot, which made walking very uncomfortable. A new pair of flip-flops lasted about a month.

"Beaky!" Pancho the mayor called out from the village square. His nasal tones were unmistakeable, and I had long since become resigned to being called Beaky. "Beaky! I have not seen you for a while. We must talk about those English lessons you were going to give me…"

"I'm sorry, Pancho, I can't stop…" and I pointed at the FitFirst on my wrist by way of explanation.

I tried hard to look disappointed but was glad of the excuse. The mayor never gave up attempting to get me on my own. I left him gaping after me as I strode past and disappeared up a side street.

I couldn't go to bed until I'd hit my target of ten thousand. At eleven-thirty, if anybody had looked up, they'd have seen me silhouetted against the night sky, walking round and round and round our roof terrace.

Oh, the relief and sense of self-satisfaction I felt when the FitFirst finally buzzed and vibrated, signifying that the target had been reached.

"Did you do it?" asked Joe sleepily as I finally climbed into bed.

"Yup!"

And then the next day it began all over again.

Anxious to add to my steps, I marched to Marcia's shop.

"Good morning," she said. "Come into the back, I have cake for you and you will take some for Joe."

"Thank you," I said, as her black cat stared at me with big green eyes from the counter. "Just a tiny, tiny piece. Are you celebrating something?"

"Yes! Today is my birthday. Today my sons and their families will drive up to El Hoyo and come to see me."

"That's wonderful," I said. "Happy birthday! May I ask how old you are?"

Marcia smiled, then frowned in thought. Her hand ran through her silver hair and a hair pin slipped out and bounced on the tiled floor.

"¡Madre mía! Do you know, I am not sure! When you have lived as many years as I have, you forget to count. I think I am eighty-six years of age today, but I will check with my family."

We both laughed.

"My eyes are not so good now, but I can still bake a perfect cake."

She cut me a generous slice and passed me the plate. I tried not to think of all the evil calories lurking in that cake, waiting to turn into fat and increase my waistline.

"You must have seen so many changes in El Hoyo," I said, taking a bite.

"Many changes. It seems like only yesterday that I was a young girl running barefoot in the village with my cousins. Of course the lead mine was busy then. All the families here had something to do with the mine in those days."

"Why did it close?" I asked, thinking of the now-silent mine at the other end of the village.

Joe and I had once strolled there and climbed the steps up the mountainside. At the top we discovered an open shaft. Looking down, we marvelled at the blackness, and man's determination to hack valuable minerals from the most inaccessible of places. We were also astonished at how the shaft had been abandoned, left open, a dangerous, gaping wound in the mountainside.

"I think it was a combination of reasons. Lead became unpopular because they discovered it had harmful properties. The lead was already beginning to run out in the mine of El Hoyo, and it became too expensive to extract. So the decision was made to shut it down."

"What happened to all the miners and their families?"

"They went back to the cities to find work. Most families kept their cottages though, and their descendants still come back for weekends and the summer holidays."

I nodded. Paco and Carmen were perfect examples. They lived in the city during the week, but on Friday night they returned to El Hoyo for the weekend, and spent all summer in the village. Both Paco's and Carmen's fathers and grandfathers had worked in the lead mine.

"Enough of the past," said Marcia. "How is Joe?"

"Between you and me, I'm a bit worried about his health, but I don't really know if anything is wrong, and he won't go to the doctor to find out."

Marcia nodded.

"¡Madre mía! Men are their own worst enemies," she said. "Look at Geronimo, if he would just stop drinking, some nice girl would fall in love with him."

"What about our new postlady, Valentina?"

"I think she likes him. But I think she will soon find out how much he drinks. I don't think there will ever be a future for those two unless he stops."

I sighed. That was unlikely to happen.

"But I have other news that will interest you. News about one of your neighbours."

"Really?"

Marcia gave a wry smile and nodded.

"Which one?"

"I have been told that Lola Ufarte is returning to the village this summer."

I gaped at her.

Marcia's black cat walked into the room and swished her tail with disdain. I was sure most of the villagers would feel the same.

"Are you sure?"

"Quite sure."

My mind shot back over the years to when Lola Ufarte, Mama Ufarte's younger, beautiful, feisty sister had first swayed into El Hoyo. She'd worn micro skirts and jangly gypsy bracelets and every male in the village had been captivated. She had left a trail of broken hearts before leaving in disgrace.

We thought we'd never see her again, but she returned. Spanish families are close and it appeared she'd been forgiven. This time, however, she brought an unwholesome young man with her and yet again, left in disgrace.

"Has her family forgiven her again?" I asked, astonished.

"It is normal in Spanish families. Blood ties are very strong."

I reported back to Joe, who, although he insists he doesn't approve of gossip, was all agog at the news.

"So Lola is coming back, is she? I wonder what havoc she will wreak this time? Vicky, I wish you'd stand still when I speak to you."

"Sorry, doing steps."

I was actually very pleased with my progress. The weight was dropping off, and I felt great. Most days now I reached my target of ten thousand with ease, but if I didn't I wasn't averse to a tiny bit of cheating. Unfortunately, the FitFirst seemed to detect underhand shenanigans.

At eleven-thirty one night, I noticed I had another thousand steps to go before I reached my target. Our washing machine was beginning its spin cycle. I whipped off the FitFirst and taped it to the vibrating machine, hopeful that it would clock up lots of steps for me. It didn't.

No choice but to dash up to the roof terrace and trot in circles under the stars until the FitFirst registered ten thousand. Any villager spotting my orbiting silhouette against the night sky probably thought me crazy. At midnight, the Fitfirst would revert to zero. There was no time to lose.

Another day I felt particularly lazy. Catching sight of Yukky, Paco and Carmen's dog, I had an idea. Yukky (probably named Jacky but it sounded like Yukky to us when Paco called him) was a springer spaniel with boundless energy. Seeing him race up and down the street, chasing his tennis ball, gave me an idea.

"Yukky," I called, unclasping the FitFirst from my wrist.

Yukky bounded up to me and I grabbed his collar, quickly attaching the FitFirst.

"Fetch!" I cried, throwing his ball down the street.

Off he galloped, retrieved the ball and brought it back for me to throw again.

"Fetch!" I cried again, and again.

"You're having a good game with Yukky," remarked Joe from our doorstep, unaware of my sneakiness.

"Yes."

I was confident this would work. When Yukky was out of breath, he flopped down to rest, panting. Checking first that Joe had gone back inside, I swiftly repossessed the Fitfirst, eager to find out how many steps Yukky had clocked up for me.

None.

Not one.

I guess the gadget was calibrated to recognise only my own paces.

Completing those steps had become part of my life. When I cleaned my teeth, I walked on the spot as I brushed. In the evening, when I watched the TV, I jumped up and marched round the room during every commercial break. Joe became accustomed to holding conversations with a moving target.

I changed my goal to eleven thousand steps, then twelve thousand. The scales gave me good news every time I stood on them, and I loved it. I'm not the type who enjoys working out or attending gyms, not that there were any nearby gyms to join. Walking daily suited me much better.

"I must say, I'm surprised at how well you're doing," commented Joe, as we sat on the edge of the Enchanted Pool, dipping our feet in the water. "How do you feel?"

It was one o'clock, and the place was deserted apart from Alberto, the lifeguard, who sat in the shade playing games on his phone.

"Fantastic!" I replied, and meant it. I felt really well. "I feel so much more comfortable, and fitter. I can't wait to go to Australia and..."

I stopped as I followed Joe's gaze. He was staring down at his ankles.

"Joe? Have your ankles always looked like that?"

"No."

"They look a bit blue, and swollen and puffy."

"I know."

"What do you think is the matter with them?"

"I don't know."

"Are you still getting headaches?" I asked.

"Yes, sometimes."

"Do you think your blood pressure medication needs adjusting?"

He paused and sighed before responding.

"Yes, maybe. Vicky, I wasn't going to say anything yet, but I've made up my mind."

"About what?"

"I've come to a decision because I think there is something very wrong with me."

TUNA WITH ONIONS
ATÚN ENCEBOLLADO

Tuna is a very versatile fish with a hardier consistency that enables it to handle strong flavours.

Ingredients (serves 2)

Half a kilo of fresh tuna, cut into bite-sized cubes

2 medium size red onions, white will also work

2 medium garlic cloves

1 bay leaf

¼ teaspoon of sugar

100 ml water

A good pinch of paprika

A good pinch of dried oregano

Salt and pepper to taste

A good splash (about a tablespoon) of sherry vinegar

Olive oil for cooking

Method

Drizzle a little olive oil into a medium / hot, deep frying pan.

Throw in the tuna cubes and cook until they start to turn golden.

Remove the tuna and set aside.

Finely slice the garlic and onions, then fry on a medium heat, adding a little more oil if necessary.

Add the sugar, a pinch each of salt and pepper and stir well.

Lower the heat so it is barely on and cook the onions very slowly until they brown, taking care not to burn them. Stir regularly.

When the onions are soft, add the sherry vinegar and water and bring the heat up to medium.

Leave cooking for another couple of minutes before adding the tuna back into the pan and stirring well.

Remove from the heat and stir in the paprika and oregano.

Serve hot.

4

A BAD PENNY

"You need a check-up, that's all."

"Yes, I do need a check-up."

"I'll make an appointment for you."

"No, that's what I'm trying to tell you. I want to be completely checked out. I want to talk to the doctor in English and I want to be able to understand everything if they *do* find anything wrong."

"Lots of Spanish doctors speak English."

"No, Vicky. I want to go back to the UK and get checked out there. If I have to go into hospital for tests or something, I want it to be in my own country."

"But there's probably nothing wrong with you!"

"I know, but just in case."

"When?" I had a feeling I knew the answer.

"In December. I want you to go to Australia as planned, but on your own. Meanwhile, I'm going to the UK."

"You're joking!"

"No, I'm not."

"Why don't we go now? We don't have to wait, then we can both go to Australia."

"No, it's going to need some setting up, and whatever happens, I don't want you to miss out on the trip to Aus. I know how much you've been looking forward to seeing Indy again."

"But..."

"I want us to enjoy the remainder of the summer together here in Spain, then we'll go our separate ways. Not for long. If all goes well, I'll join you out there after two or three weeks."

I gaped at him but recognised that set expression on his face, that granite look in his eyes. That told me his mind was made up.

"But don't you want me to come with you to the appointments?"

"No need for us both to be there for those. We'll keep in close contact. I don't want to spoil your trip to Aus and I won't be able to relax until I've had myself checked out."

"But, Joe..."

"Oh no! Look who's just arrived."

Clearly, Joe was not prepared to discuss it further.

I looked up and groaned. A large Spanish lady was bearing down on us. She was a regular, like us, and I recognised her immediately. Joe and I called her the Metronome.

The Metronome had two most annoying habits, both of which upset our British sensibilities. She was inconsiderate, and she invaded our cherished personal space.

Looking neither left nor right, she marched towards us and dumped her belongings on the lounger nearest ours. Although she had any number to choose from, she always selected the one that was closest. Why she did this baffled us because, apart from Joe and myself, there were no other bathers.

She then began to disrobe, preparing to enter the pool. Her routine never wavered and we knew exactly what she would do next. It was why we called her the Metronome.

She entered the water via steps halfway along the pool and, having launched herself, began swimming slowly and deliberately across the width. At the far side, she turned and swam back, never looking to her right or left. She always swam breaststroke, backwards and forwards, backwards and forwards, for exactly thirty-five minutes.

More often than not she arrived when Joe and I were already in the pool. We preferred swimming lengths but were now forced to dodge the width-swimming Metronome. She would stop for nobody, not even, I suspect, a great white shark if one had suddenly appeared.

My new fitness regime dictated that I must swim twenty lengths. But now I had to adjust my pace either to slow down and allow the Metronome to cross in front of me, or speed up so that I was not caught in her path. It spoiled the rhythm of my swim. However, concentrating on the Metronome's exact location allowed me no time to brood over Joe's decision not to join me on the trip to Australia.

We love the Enchanted Pool, but perhaps we should go to the beach instead, I mused.

Then I dismissed the idea.

The Enchanted Pool was just too delightful, and going to the beach was downright embarrassing. I winced at the thought.

Why embarrassing? Because Joe has this irritating habit of wearing his mask, snorkel (including mouthpiece) and flippers long before he reaches the water's edge. Then he makes his way down to the water, lifting his knees high in the air like *My Little Pony* so he doesn't trip over the flippers. His actions made me think of a duck stepping over invisible obstacles. All this is accompanied by loud heavy breathing because his mask and snorkel are already in place. I always follow at a distance, trying to look nonchalant, hoping nobody will think we are together.

But the embarrassment doesn't finish there. Oh no. Joe is not the type to walk straight into the water. Instead, one teeny-weeny baby step at a time, he inches forward, however warm the water is. He squeals through the snorkel whenever an over-enthusiastic wave laps his sun-warmed skin. He walks on tiptoes (not easy when wearing flippers) and his elbows point to the sky. It can take a long time before he submerges himself, and when he does, his muffled bellow of, "Wesh tryfig Farkinoñfeezm!" which I choose to interpret as "Goodness, it's freezing", can be heard by seagulls on the next beach.

And the beach was fraught with other hazards, like jellyfish. Sometimes dead jellyfish are strewn along the beach, delivered there by the waves that hide many more. They lurk in the shallows, waiting to brush their tentacles against sensitive skin, causing indescribable pain and a rash. Some people blame over-fishing. Man kills the fish or turtles that normally prey on the jellyfish, thus the jellyfish thrive and increase in vast numbers.

No, I conclude, swimming at the Enchanted Pool was much less stressful, even if we had to share the space with the Metronome.

That afternoon, as we drove home, I tried to broach the subject again, but Joe refused to talk about it. Other than repeat that he wanted tests done in the UK, and that it was pointless for me to be with him, Joe refused to talk about it.

I watched the mountain scenery flash past. I loved it all. The gnarled, ancient olive trees clothed in silvery leaves. The wild fig trees with leaves like giant hands, their fruit ripening in the sun. The little streams, now dry, that meandered through the rock. We always looked out for wild goats, and were often rewarded with a glimpse of a family group. Once, we saw a whole group grazing in olive trees. There is something very strange about seeing goats in treetops, but of course they are magnificent climbers.

As we crested the mountain and swung down the road into El Hoyo, we had an excellent view of the village from above. I always looked for our house. That day I saw something a little unusual.

"Joe, there's a car parked outside the Little House."

The Little House, as we called it, was a tiny cottage across the street, opposite our garden gate. It was always empty, apart from *fiesta* times, when the owners, two elderly brothers and their sister, arrived and stayed for the weekend. Now a car parked outside, and I was curious.

We waved to Marcia as we passed the shop, then turned the corner into our own street.

The car parked outside the Little House was a rusty and rather dented model. It had its doors open, revealing all manner of suitcases and bundles. A young lady, probably in her thirties, was carrying an infant into the house. The lady's hair was short and not styled. Her clothes were unremarkable, sensible, even dowdy, right down to her worn, open-toed, flat sandals. As they entered the house, the infant's eyes stared over its mother's shoulder.

"I wonder who that is?" I asked, not expecting any answer from Joe.

We parked the car in our garage and walked up the street, past the Ufarte house to our front door. The Ufarte house was quiet and Grandma Ufarte's armchair stood empty outside in the shade.

Just as Joe was putting the key in our lock, a head popped out from the front door on the other side, making me jump.

"Pssst! Veeky!" hissed our neighbour, Carmen, her double chins shaking with excitement.

Joe raised his eye-brows in question. Carmen shot out of her house and leaned in close to me. Her breath smelled of cinnamon. She didn't greet me with the customary kisses so I knew she had something urgent to impart.

"Did you see who is moving into the Little House?"

"Um, yes, a lady with a baby. She was unpacking, by the looks of it. Has she come to stay for the summer? Do you know her?"

"Yes, she is renting the house and has come for the summer, or maybe permanently... Do I know her? Of course I know her! So do you!"

"Do I? Why, who is she?"

"It is Lola Ufarte!"

I was grateful for the technology which had made it increasingly easy to stay in touch with distant family. It allowed Karly and I to chat frequently, either by instant messaging, or video calls. I am old enough to remember when one had to book telephone calls to other countries.

"Hi Karly. I'm up writing at stupid o'clock again and just wondered how you all were. My weather app tells me it's raining in Sydney. How's Indy? How's the puppy?"

"It is raining, yuk! LJ has started puppy classes and he's easily the most obedient dog there."

"LJ?"

"After the hotel at Lake Jindabyne where Cam and I met. He hasn't learnt how to wee outside yet though. LJ, I mean, not Cam. And he's in a spot of trouble with Cam's parents for leaving a puddle on their Isfahan Persian rug. LJ, not Cam."

"Oh. And how's Indy?"

"Indy's fine. Her favourite word is 'ROW' which she says loudly and insistently until you sing 'Row, row, row, your boat' with her."

"Oh, you used to love that song!"

"Well, it's attraction has rather worn off recently."

"I can't wait to meet LJ and see Indy. And you and Cam, of course."

"Won't be long now. Wish you were both coming, but I do understand."

According to the Oxford English Dictionary, a 'bad penny' is 'the predictable, and often unwanted, return of a disreputable or prodigal person after some absence'.

That was a very fair description of Lola Ufarte.

Carmen had invited me in for a coffee. The house was quiet and cool. Paco was busy in his *cortijo* up the mountain, and we rarely saw little Paco who was now nineteen years old and had a car of his own.

"I can't believe she would come back," I said, "but it's good that the Ufarte family has forgiven her again."

"I was talking with Maribel, her sister," said Carmen, spooning sugar into her coffee. "She says that Lola is a changed woman."

"How so?"

"The way she dresses, for instance."

"Well, I must say, I didn't recognize her. She looks quite different. In fact she looked quite, um, ordinary."

"Yes, Maribel says that since the baby arrived, she is more sensible. She has toned down her behaviour and is very sorry for all that has happened in the past."

"Really? Is Lola married now? Who is the baby's father?"

"I do not know. I do not think she is married and I do not know who the father of the baby girl is. Maribel has forgiven her sister for trying to steal her husband. She says Lola would never do such a terrible thing now and just wants to be a good mother and respected member of the village."

"That's good to hear," I said, but was not totally convinced. I was thinking of Geronimo. I remembered he was one of the many men who had fallen under Lola's spell in the past. "I hope she doesn't spoil anything between Geronimo and Valentina. They seem to be getting on so well."

"Yes, I hope all will be well. Maribel told me that she and her husband discussed it for a long time and they decided that they would give Lola another chance for the sake of the children."

"Ah, I can understand that."

"The new little girl should get to know her cousins and aunt and uncle, and the twins will adore looking after her."

I nodded and crossed my fingers. I really hoped this would turn out well.

Every summer the *ayuntamiento*, or council, showed a family movie in the square. Everybody brought their own chairs and settled down with friends and family to watch. It began when the sun dropped in the sky and the sound of the evening cicadas filled the air. Geronimo, his Real Madrid scarf absent for once, set up the big screen as the villagers gradually took their positions and the sun hid behind the mountains.

As usual, Marcia had parked one of her dining room chairs by her shop doorway, and was settled nicely, knitting needles clacking. Every now and then, Geronimo would smile from across the square at Valentina who was sitting beside Marcia, holding her ball of wool.

Other adults had also brought their own chairs, while the youngsters preferred to perch on the low wall that surrounded the square. Paco and his old friend, Alejandro, sat together, heads bowed, probably discussing politics. Carmen and Alejandro's wife were equally occupied and I imagined they were discussing the forthcoming wedding of daughter Sofía to son Alejandro Junior. Little Paco sat on the wall, his arm round his girlfriend.

The Ufarte family was there in force. Grandma sat on a folding chair and beside her on the stone bench sat Papa and Mama Ufarte. I was pleased to see them holding hands and felt relieved their marriage was still strong in spite of Lola's return.

Lola Ufarte was seated on another chair, a little distance away. Her baby squirmed on her lap. Lola looked at nobody, unless she was greeted, then she smiled and ducked her head. Her behaviour was impeccable.

The Ufarte boys played football with a crowd of other village boys. They had grown tall, and Carlos, the clingy toddler we named Snap-On so many years ago, was unrecognisable. Now he was about eight and no longer glued to his mother, but just as football crazy as his big brothers.

The Ufarte twins waved to us from across the square. They remained identical and I hoped they didn't know that neither I nor Joe could tell them apart.

"*Tía* Veeky! *Tío* Joe!"

We waved back. The twins ran over to us.

"The movie is called *Buscando a Nemo*," said Twin #1.

"It's all about fish," said Twin #2.

We smiled. We had already watched the movie *Finding Nemo*, but hoped that watching it again in Spanish might further improve our language skills.

"But now we are not *buscando a* Nemo," explained Twin #1, shaking her head, her palms upward.

"No, we are *buscando a* Pollito," said Twin #2, sighing.

"Oh no!" I said. "Has your little brother gone missing again?"

FISH WITH LEMON
PESCADO AL LIMÓN

Ingredients

If you like fish with crispy skin, then just prepare the sauce separately. Omit the capers if you wish as they're not vital.

2 medium to large white fish fillets, skin optional, any firm white fish will do, such as cod or hake

One lemon

1 garlic clove

1 teaspoon of capers

A pinch each of coarse sea salt and cracked black pepper

A pinch of dried fennel (optional)

1 glass of dry white wine

Olive oil for frying

Method

Fry the fish in a little olive oil to your personal preference.

Meanwhile, grate the rind of the lemon and crush the garlic clove.

Mix the grated lemon rind, the salt and pepper and crushed garlic into a paste.

Add the lemon juice and glass of wine.

When the fish is cooked, add the wine/lemon/garlic mixture to the pan and simmer for 5 minutes.

Add the capers and dried fennel and leave simmering for another minute or two.

Serve the fish with your favourite accompaniments, perhaps potatoes or rice.

Drizzle any remaining sauce on top.

5

VISITORS

The Ufarte twins' little brother was affectionately known as Pollito, which means 'little chicken'. Unlike his older brother, Snap-On, who remained glued to his mother for years, Pollito had been blessed with an adventurous spirit. Although only four and a half years old, he would wander off to explore whenever the opportunity arose.

Luckily, El Hoyo was a very safe place. Traffic was sparse and all the families were either related or had known each other for years. Older children looked out for younger ones, and although Pollito's exploring had often earned him scraped knees and grazes, he had never really come to any harm.

"Yes, but this time we think we know where he is," said Twin #2.

"He is looking at the kittens."

"Next to the shop."

"In the old ruin."

"Mama told him not to."

"Because the mama cat is wild."

"And the kittens will scratch him."

"Oh dear!" I said. "Would you like me to help you find him?"

Before they could answer, we all heard a howl coming from the direction of Marcia's shop.

"¡*Madre mía!*" chorused the twins.

A grubby little urchin emerged from the shadows, his mouth wide, preparing for another bawl.

"Pollito! Over here!"

The little boy raised his head and saw his sisters. His howls grew in volume for their benefit and his clenched fists rubbed his eyes.

The girls galloped over to him and enveloped him in their arms, dabbing his scratches with their hankies and kissing the pain away.

Pollito was a brave little fellow and soon quietened. His sisters took a hand each and led him back to their parents, passing us on the way.

"We told you the kittens would scratch you."

"If you tried to pick them up."

"Mama brought some candies."

"To eat while we watch the movie."

"If you're good, I expect she'll give you some."

"Look! The film is starting now."

"You'll like it, it's about fish."

Music flooded the square. Pollito forgot his scratches and settled with his family to watch the film. His big brothers stopped kicking the ball and sat on the wall, legs swinging as they sucked on candies.

Geronimo, satisfied that his job was done for the moment, returned to Valentina's side. She smiled up into his face and reached up to run her fingers through his long hair as he bent to kiss her.

"Joe!"

"What?"

"I don't think Geronimo is drinking! Look, he's not clutching a beer bottle and I can't see one poking out of his pocket."

"That's good. Perhaps Valentina is a good influence."

I hoped so.

As the movie played, my mind wandered.

So much to think about.

I'm an optimist so I was positive that Joe's checkups would reveal nothing too sinister. Of course, I was relieved that he'd finally agreed to be examined, but I was bitterly disappointed that he wouldn't be joining me on the trip to Australia.

Never mind, if he gets the tests done quickly, then he can join me Down

Under for a few weeks.

That thought cheered me.

Felicity, the village cat who considered our garden to be her personal territory, was raising kittens. We only fed them the occasional scrap because we didn't want them to be dependent on us. Felicity, never as tame and trusting as Sylvia and Gravy had been, watched us warily, but allowed her kittens to snatch up the scraps and run for cover.

In the evenings, Joe and I often sat outside and watched the kittens at play as the night closed in.

"Becky will enjoy watching these little tykes," I said, as Kitten #1 dived on Kitten #2 from a plant pot where he had been lying in ambush.

"Oh, have you heard from her? Is she visiting us as usual this year?"

"Yes, I was chatting to her online today. You'll never guess what!"

"What?"

My niece, Becky, visited us quite often, always alone. She wasn't married, but she had a fairly busy social life and was frequently dating.

"You know you can bring whoever you like," Joe and I repeatedly told her.

"Nah," she had replied every time, "I like coming out here on my own. I'd have to meet someone *really* special before I considered bringing him with me."

"Well," I said, enjoying the news. "Becky asked if she could bring her boyfriend!"

"Really? That's a surprise!"

"Yes! I reckon this may be a serious relationship."

"What's his name? Do you know anything about him?"

"His name is Gresh. I don't really know anything about him except that he's never been married. And, like Becky, he doesn't have any children."

"Sounds perfect. I shall look forward to meeting him."

At the airport, we picked out the couple easily. Becky was holding hands with a tall man.

"This is Gresh," said Becky.

Gresh grinned. He had warm, friendly eyes and an easy smile.

"Good to meet you," he said. "Thank you so much for having us."

We exchanged kisses and handshakes.

"It's a real pleasure," Joe and I chorused.

We loaded their luggage into the car and drove home along the coast as Becky pointed out various sights. Then we turned off into the mountains, following the meandering roads we knew so well. Soon we were descending into our valley.

"Welcome to El Hoyo," said Joe. "I hope you won't be bored, it's very quiet here."

"Perfect!" said Gresh. "A whole holiday with nothing to do. Just what I need to unwind."

Becky snorted. I looked at her in question.

"Gresh doesn't know how to unwind!" she said. "He never stops! He's always doing something, and if there's nothing that needs doing, he'll find something."

She was right. Gresh didn't know how to relax. Becky was soon horizontal on a sun lounger with a cold drink in her hand, but Gresh couldn't sit still.

First he explored the house, then the roof-top terrace. Next, he walked round the village, calling "*¡Hola!*" to the bemused villagers. He introduced himself to Geronimo (using sign language) and peered inside Marcia's shop waving cheerily at the old lady behind the counter.

Then he headed for the new bar and poked his head in the door. A number of Spanish heads swivelled. They were all men aged over seventy, and every one of them gawked at him. Gresh beamed and called out another cheery "*¡Hola!*".

Having run out of things to explore, he looked around. He heard a mule bray somewhere. It was probably old Uncle Felix's mule grazing higher on the mountain.

"Gosh, you look a bit hot and bothered," said Becky when Gresh eventually returned home. "What have you been doing?"

To be perfectly honest, Becky looked equally hot and bothered, but we must blame the sun and chilled wine for that, not exercise.

"I heard a donkey braying, so I climbed the mountain to look for it," said Gresh.

"Ah, that was probably a mule," I said. "Her owner died, but she's well cared for. She's often tethered somewhere on the mountain to graze, usually with a horse. Did you find her?"

"No, I didn't," Gresh admitted. "I could hear her, but I couldn't see her."

His answer came as no surprise. The valley has a peculiar effect on sound. Sometimes, especially at night, one could clearly hear conversations emanating from the other side of the valley.

"Never mind," said Becky. "Come and sit down and have a drink."

So he did.

But only for two minutes.

Then he was up again, sorting out our winter firewood, or some such task that he imagined was desperately in need of doing.

Not only did Gresh carry out useful jobs round the house and garden, but we soon discovered that he loved to cook. Lucky us! He insisted on a daily drive down the mountain, accompanied by Becky, to shop for fresh ingredients. He cooked splendid dinners every evening, and we were completely spoiled.

One particularly hot day, Joe suggested we should drive to the Enchanted Pool. Gresh hadn't brought any swimming trunks with him, so he purchased some especially for the occasion. They were bright red and matched his English sun-scorched skin.

A number of people were at the Enchanted Pool when we arrived, but I was pleased to see the Metronome wasn't among them. I recognised an elderly couple, regulars at the pool. They never swam, preferring to stand and chat in the shallow end, doubtless there just to cool down.

Becky was already wearing her bikini under her shorts and top.

"Can't wait to get in!" she said, flinging off her clothes and jumping into the water. I thought her olive green bikini looked a little strange, but I didn't have time to look properly, so I didn't say anything.

When she climbed out of the pool, I stared at the bikini again. Then

I understood.

"Becky, that's a lovely bikini," I said, laughing, "but I think you may need to adjust it."

Joe and Gresh heard me and swung round to look, then roared with laughter.

Bewildered, Becky stopped towelling her hair and looked down at herself, then turned the same colour crimson as Gresh's new swimming trunks.

"Oh no!" she squeaked, wrapping the towel around herself and fleeing to the changing rooms. She was wearing the bikini bottoms inside out and the white gusset was on the outside for all to see.

The rest of our guests' stay went without a hitch, except for one night when Gresh organised a barbecue. After a few beers, he dropped nearly every uncooked sausage and burger onto the ground. He laughed so hard, he promptly dropped a chicken piece.

"You've found a good one there," I said to Becky privately. "We really like Gresh."

Becky smiled and her eyes sparkled.

When their holiday ended, we drove the couple back to the airport. They were the most undemanding of visitors and Gresh proved to be a great cook. He served up delicious meals every night and, despite its gritty taste, the barbecue was a highlight.

"Gresh, you and Becky are welcome to come back any time you like," we told them as we hugged at the airport.

And we meant it.

How quickly that summer flashed past! The village emptied of families and children began a new term at school.

Before we knew it, the fig leaves had puckered into brown, crisp, shrivelled misshapes. The leaves on our vine yellowed and loosened, dancing crazily in the wind until they lost their hold and drifted away. Unpicked grapes rotted, attracting wasps. The Enchanted Pool's gates were locked.

It was hard to believe I would be jetting off for another summer in

Australia, while poor Joe would be heading for the freezing temperatures of a British winter. I was already making lists in my head of the things to be done before we locked up the house for the winter.

But first, the village was preparing for the annual *fiesta*. At the weekends, ladies cleaned their homes from top to bottom. It was common to see the entire contents of a house turned out onto the street, room by room, while walls were being whitewashed. Men were banished to stock up on winter firewood and the buzz of chainsaws could be heard all over the mountain. Next weekend, each house would be crammed full with family and friends, to celebrate the *fiesta*.

Girls showed each other new outfits and little boys chatted about the firecrackers they would buy from the African stallholders.

By now, we were very familiar with the expected routine. Friday noon would see Geronimo lighting rockets in the square to celebrate the opening of the *fiesta*. Vehicles would begin to arrive. Later, the streets would be choked with parked cars as would the road winding down into the village. Our car would be in our garage, and there it would stay until the conclusion of the *fiesta* on the Sunday evening.

"Hi Mum, how are you?"

"Good, thank you! Are you all okay?"

"Yes, we're fine. Summer's coming and we've had some amazingly hot days already. Just thought I'd tell you our latest plan."

"Oh yes?"

"We have this funny little room off the garage. The previous owners laid wooden floors. We're going to make it into a writer's retreat for you."

"That sounds amazing!"

"We're going to paint all the bricks white, and we'll get a desk. And a sofa, perhaps one of those that folds down into a bed. Always useful. And a TV, Internet, coffee-making stuff…"

"Gosh! My own writing lair! I've never had one of those! How fabulous!"

It was all so exciting. But first we must survive the village *fiesta*.

CATALAN SPINACH
ESPINACAS A LA CATALAN

This is superb with a little blue cheese crumbled over the top at the time of serving. Cook to your liking, depending whether you prefer it wilted or crisp.

Ingredients (serves 2 as a side dish)

A medium shallot

A fistful of pine nuts, or almonds, or walnuts

A fistful of raisins

500g (18 oz) baby spinach leaves

Some blue cheese to crumble over the top

Olive oil for frying

A couple of pinches of sea salt

Method

Pour a healthy glug of olive oil into a large frying pan. A wok is perfect for this.

Bring the heat to medium/high and throw in the nuts and raisins. Stir a little and cook for about 90 seconds.

Add the spinach.

Sprinkle with the salt.

Keep tossing the spinach, ensuring it all gets covered in the olive oil, and the ingredients are well mixed.

6

A LOST CHICKEN AND
OBSERVATIONS

Not many folk turned out to watch the opening of the *fiesta* at noon on Friday. Joe and I were there, and Marcia sat outside her shop, her silver hair-pins glinting in the autumn sunshine. Valentina sat beside her. She must have finished her mail round early and come to support Geronimo, I concluded.

Another lady sat by herself in the square, an infant on her knee. It was Lola Ufarte. I saw Valentina steal a curious glance at her. Did she know that Geronimo and Lola Ufarte shared history? Probably. I was sure Marcia would have told her.

A few other people were dotted around, but the vast majority would arrive later that night. The stage had already been erected, and Geronimo stood at the side of it, his strong arms encircling some outsize fireworks that he clutched to his chest. A priest in full regalia climbed the steps up the side and took centre stage.

"Who's that?" I asked Joe.

"The new priest's assistant," Joe hissed. "Marcia told me that the church has appointed him to help Father Rodrigo with his duties. Poor old Father Rodrigo is in his eighties now and Marcia says he has terrible rheumatism."

The new priest was young and tall, and looked rather splendid in his robes. His crisp, dark hair had a tendency to wave, and his jawline was strong and masculine.

The priest crossed himself and smiled at the people below. He said a few words, then pressed his palms together, closed his eyes, tilted his chin heavenwards and began the *Padre Nuestro*, or Lord's Prayer.

"*Padre nuestro,*
que estás en el cielo.
Santificado sea tu nombre…"

The villagers stood, or sat, with bowed heads, allowing the familiar chant to wash over them. I sneaked a look round and was surprised to see one other person who was clearly not praying. Somebody was staring at the young priest.

I nudged Joe and flicked my eyes at Lola Ufarte. He looked too, but Lola had seen my movement or had suddenly remembered she was supposed to be behaving herself. Now her eyes were downcast and she was mouthing the last words of the *Padre Nuestro* in time with the priest.

"*No nos dejes caer en tentación y líbranos del mal.*
Amén."

The priest said a few more words. I caught the words 'Santa Barbara', the patron saint of El Hoyo, and then the priest declared the *fiesta* open.

Geronimo stepped forward, and tumbled the fireworks into a pile at his feet. Then, picking up a giant rocket, he lit the touch paper and sent each soaring, one by one, into the blue sky. Soon, grey smoke trails criss-crossed each other and muddied the blue of the sky.

The villagers *oooh-ed* and *ah-ed* as the rockets exploded. I did too, but my exclamations were more of horror as I never got used to Geronimo's utter disregard for health and safety precautions.

Only one face wasn't upturned. One rather dowdy-looking lady with a small child wasn't watching the firework display. Instead, she stared, almost hungrily, at the priest.

Lola Ufarte.

"Vicky, you're imagining things," said Joe when we got home.

"I'm not! I promise you, Lola Ufarte was staring at that young priest as though she planned to eat him on toast for breakfast."

"Well, she's not going to get any joy there. Catholic priests aren't allowed to marry."

Something was happening in the street outside our house so I broke off the discussion to investigate. The whirl of polka dots made me smile.

"Hello *Tía* Veeky!"

"Do you like our costumes?"

"They are real flamenco dresses."

"Tomorrow we are performing."

"On the stage."

"With lots of people watching."

Twin #1 wore a wonderful flounced dress of red and white polka dots, while Twin #2 wore the same in blue. Their black hair shone, swinging with each step, and their heeled shoes matched their dresses perfectly. Even though no music accompanied them, their steps were perfectly synchronised and I clapped with delight as they swirled and tapped.

"Joe! Come and see!"

Joe appeared beside me on the doorstep and smiled.

"*Tía* Veeky! *Tío* Joe! We will teach you some flamenco steps!"

"It's very easy!"

"No, no, I'm sorry," said Joe. "I'd love to, but I get too out of breath. I'll watch."

"*Tía* Veeky, the steps are easy."

"It's just Toe, Heel, Heel, Toe, Flat."

"Tap your toe."

"Then tap your heel."

"Like this!"

"Tap your heel again."

"And keep it on the floor."

"Stop!" I begged. "You are going too fast!"

"We will start from the beginning."

"Watch!"

"We'll do it slowly."

"Like a snail."

"Tap your toe."

The sad truth is that I am particularly uncoordinated when it comes to dancing. Trying to teach me flamenco steps was a complete waste of time and I failed to pick up even the most basic moves.

Joe, however, was hugely entertained and I blocked out his guffaws as I concentrated. When I finally admitted defeat, I looked up, to see Paco on his doorstep also enjoying the show. The pair of them found my two left feet hilarious.

"Thank you for the lesson, girls," I said. "I shall look forward to seeing you performing on the stage tomorrow."

I marched past the men with my nose in the air. I may not be able to dance the flamenco, but at least I tried.

That evening, the band struck up on the stage in the square, but we didn't join in. The big dance would be held on Saturday night. We strolled around the square and waved at a few people we knew. Elderly couples waltzed near the stage as the girl soloist warbled Spanish songs, and the backing group kept up the rhythm. The next day's dancing and music would be much more energetic.

Saturday was always filled with *fiesta* events. There would be organised games for the kids, with clowns and fairy princesses. There would be flamenco dancing, and I looked forward to seeing the Ufarte twins performing. There would be a baby show, and talent contest. A procession would tread along the winding path up the mountainside to the shrine.

Then, when the tired sun slipped behind the mountain, the coloured lights in the square would twinkle, the band would strike up again, and the *fiesta* dancing would begin in earnest.

At first, just a few couples or family groups with children would take to the floor, but gradually more couples and families would appear, until, by midnight, the square would be a throbbing mass of colourful dancers.

Years ago, Joe and I had made the mistake of arriving at around nine o'clock, wondering why so few people had turned up. We soon learned that Spanish parties rarely begin before midnight. For this reason, we always had a siesta in the afternoon. Even so, we never saw the end of any *fiesta* dance as they often continued until four or five o'clock in the morning.

Saturday dawned and El Hoyo welcomed another beautiful autumn day. On stage, the Ufarte twins danced their flamenco beautifully, keeping in time with the other girls in their troupe. I didn't know the baby that won the baby show, but he was a lovely little chap who produced a broad smile for everybody. The talent contest was won by a budding young magician who extracted an egg from behind the mayor's ear. We also joined the procession that slowly wound its way up to the shrine where cups of hot chocolate were being served.

At midnight, Joe and I sauntered towards the square. Lights blazed in every house and voices and laughter could be heard from within. Young footsteps ran behind and overtook us.

"Hello *Tía* Veeky! Hello *Tío* Joe!"

The twins, still in their flamenco outfits, scarcely paused as they swerved past us.

"We've lost Pollito again."

"He was at home."

"But now we can't find him."

"He's probably in the square."

And away they ran down the street, their flamenco dancing shoes tapping with each step.

There were plenty of dancers already in the square, and the band was in fine voice. Stall holders had set out their wares: hot dogs, neon sticks, glass coolers and the inevitable firecrackers. Two long tables had been set out as a bar, although the only drinks on sale were beer, red wine and Coca Cola.

"Can you see Pollito?" I asked Joe.

"Nope, but look, I think the twins have found him."

I followed his gaze in time to see flamenco dancer #1 hauling her reluctant little brother out from under a firecracker stall. Flamenco dancer #2 took a firm hold of his other hand.

"Pollito! What were you doing under there?"

"We were worried about you."

"You must not disappear."

"You must tell us if you want to go somewhere."

"Mama was very worried."

"We found him," said Twin #1 as we drew up.

"So we see," said Joe, smiling.

I smiled too. It was past midnight, and this little urchin and dozens of others of around the same age were still wide awake and part of the celebrations. This would never happen in England. It was just *so* Spanish.

Marcia sat outside the shop, under a lamp-post, fingers busy with her knitting. Everybody wore their best to the *fiesta*, and I noticed that Marcia's customary black dress had been adorned with a black lace collar. Geronimo and Valentina stood beside her, Geronimo's hand on the back of the old lady's chair.

Although not related, Marcia and Geronimo enjoyed an extremely close bond with each other. Geronimo helped her with everyday tasks and sometimes watched the shop if she was away. They were very comfortable with each other, and Marcia scolded him when she didn't approve of his behaviour. Marcia already had two fine sons, who lived in the city, and I felt that Marcia regarded Geronimo as another.

Pancho, the mayor, and his wife stood in a group chatting with Father Rodrigo and the new priest.

I waved to Paco and Carmen who were dancing at the edge of the throng. Not far away was their daughter Sofía with her fiancé, Alejandro Junior.

Little Paco danced with his girlfriend, and Mama and Papa Ufarte stood some distance away, holding hands. I couldn't see Lola Ufarte anywhere.

"Would you like to dance?" asked Joe, uncharacteristically.

"Why, thank you, kind sir," I replied as he swept me onto the dance floor.

Thankfully, at that moment, the band slowed down the tempo and the lead singer began to croon a plaintive song. I had plenty of time to peer over Joe's shoulder and indulge myself in one of my favourite hobbies: observing. Joe may call it 'nosy-parkering' but I maintain that there is nothing wrong with being a keen observer.

People were still arriving, mostly in family groups or as couples. My eyes were drawn to a beautiful girl who appeared to arrive on her own. She walked tall on high-heeled strappy sandals that made her hips sway. Long tanned legs were barely covered by her shocking pink mini-dress. She tossed her head and her short, dark hair caught the light.

I happened to glance at Geronimo and was surprised. He stood with his mouth open, staring at the new arrival as though mesmerised. Valentina, at his side, stared at him, then back at the newcomer. There was a shocked expression on her face.

I frowned. Who was this girl? Why was Geronimo reacting like that? Of course, I should have worked it out immediately, but it was the gypsy bangles on the girl's wrists that confirmed it.

Lola Ufarte.

That is, the *old* Lola Ufarte, as she used to be, was back.

Dressed to kill.

I briefly wondered where her little girl was and guessed that the elderly *abuela*, Granny Ufarte, was probably on babysitting duty at home.

To be fair, Lola didn't even look in Geronimo's direction, but the harm had been done. I saw Valentina pull Geronimo into the shop, and I had no problem reading her body language. She was not happy.

Oblivious, Lola Ufarte made her way to the rest of the Ufarte family. The twins were delighted to see her, and dragged her onto the dance floor.

The band began another energetic number and Joe and I admitted defeat, preferring to watch instead of dance. I found it interesting that Lola was writhing and undulating to the music just feet from where the young priest stood. Was he her quarry? He didn't appear to notice her, but she wriggled and her hips swayed as though the whole of Spain was watching her dance.

I didn't see Valentina again that night.

Sadly, I watched as Geronimo emerged from the shop, a bottle of beer in his hand. Marcia caught his sleeve as he passed her chair but he shook her off.

At around one o'clock, the church clock probably struck, but the music was too loud for anyone to hear it. Geronimo dived into the shop, and emerged with another load of fireworks. He looked a little unsteady on his feet but that didn't stop him signalling to the band who finished their number and moved aside, allowing him to take centre stage. He set down his bottle of beer, flicked a lighter and lit the first of many touch-papers. Rocket after rocket exploded into the sultry night sky, sending forth showers of multicoloured sparks that crackled and boomed around the valley.

"Good fireworks show," remarked Joe, as we walked home.

"It was."

"It all went very smoothly, I thought."

"Except for Geronimo and Valentina."

"What on earth are you talking about?"

"I think they've probably broken up. And Geronimo is drinking again. And Lola Ufarte is up to her old tricks."

"Vicky, we've been together all evening. How can you possibly know all that?"

"Just observing."

We slept soundly that night, in spite of the music which continued to throb for hours. And nobody was allowed to sleep late on Sunday morning because at nine o'clock, Geronimo set off more fireworks and a marching band from a neighbouring village stamped up and down the streets.

Then the churchbells clamoured, summoning the villagers to prayer. I noticed Lola Ufarte hurry past our house, pushing a baby stroller, heading for the church. She wore white jeans and a top, but the tightness of the jeans, the scoop of the top's neckline, and the jangling of the gypsy bangles were designed to turn men's heads.

"Was that Lola Ufarte walking past?" asked Joe.

"It was."

"Gosh, she looks different somehow…"

"Yes. She does."

Nobody could accuse Joe of being observant.

Sunday was packed with more activities, including the wine tasting event, which Paco always refused to enter. Joe and I had heard the reason why many times.

"Pah! It would not be fair," Paco argued. "If I entered my wine, I would win every year. Ask anyone, they will tell you that Paco makes the best wine in El Hoyo."

There was the Pudding Contest, judged by the mayor and his wife, won again by a delicious-looking *arroz con leche*, or rice pudding, complete with cinnamon, vanilla and lemon peel shavings.

But the main event was the procession. It passed our front door so we didn't need to watch the beginning that emerged from the church, but waited for it to pass our doorstep. The procession was headed, as always, by the clergy. Father Rodrigo hobbled along, supported by the new young priest. Their colourful robes reflected the joyousness of the occasion. They were followed by a statue of Santa Barbara who was borne on a flower-bedecked pedestal, supported on the shoulders of Paco, Geronimo and six other male villagers. Then came the statuette of the Virgin Mary, seated on her bed of flowers, carried by the village ladies. This year, Carmen, Sofía and Mama Ufarte were supporting the platform on one side, while another three ladies took the weight on the other, one of whom we easily recognised.

"Isn't that Lola Ufarte?" hissed Joe.

"Yup!"

"I had no idea she was the religious sort."

"Hmm... Neither did I."

The marching band followed and the trumpets drowned out any further conversation.

MURCIAN SALAD
MOJETE MURCIANO

This recipe requires no cooking and is fast and simple to put together.

Ingredients (serves 2)

1 standard tin of chopped tomatoes

2 standard tins of tuna (in oil, brine or vinegar – your choice)

2 hard boiled eggs – quartered

½ medium onion – coarsely chopped

Fistful of black olives – pitted

Good quality extra virgin olive oil

A pinch or two of coarse sea salt (omit this if your tuna came in brine)

Method

Place all the ingredients in a bowl except for the olive oil and salt. Mix if you like, or just layer them.

Refrigerate for half an hour to let the flavours absorb.

Finish off with a good drizzle of olive oil and a sprinkle of salt.

Serve.

7

CHIMNEYS

"Hi, Mum, how are you?"

"Great, can't believe how fast the time is flashing by now. Only a few weeks until I'm with you in Australia!"

"Indy and I've been painting your lair."

"Oooh! Exciting!"

"And you are the proud owner of a TV aerial."

"Lovely! What's the weather like?"

"Sydney is warming up nicely. It'll be beautiful by the time you get here. How's Spain?"

"The *fiesta* was as crazy as usual, and the weather is still good, but it's getting cooler."

The *fiesta* was over for another year and temperatures began to drop. Soon Marcia would go down the mountain to spend winter with her sons in the city where it would be warmer. We, too, began to plan for the weeks ahead. Days were still pleasant and sunny, but cold nights were tiptoeing in.

"We still have plenty of firewood," said Joe. "I reckon as we'll be away most of the winter, it isn't worth ordering any more."

"That's good," I said, "but we haven't cleaned the chimneys for a long time, do you think we should?"

"No, I'm sure they are very clean, they won't need doing yet."

"I'd be happier if we just tested them."

"Honestly, Vicky, you do worry about nothing! Okay, if it puts your mind at rest, we'll just light a quick paper fire in both fireplaces and make sure all is well."

"Thank you."

We had two wood-burners, a stove in the kitchen and fireplace in the living room. We were in the living room at the time and I turned to look at the fireplace in question. It had a glass door and should have been empty, apart from a few dusty cobwebs that may have appeared over the summer months.

"Joe!"

"What?"

"There's something in the stove!"

"Don't be ridiculous!"

"There is! Look! It's moving!"

Old Spanish houses are not like modern houses. Windows were built small in an effort to keep out the heat in summer and preserve the warmth inside in winter, but the reduced natural light made rooms darker.

Joe bent down and squinted into the blackness of the stove.

"I wish you'd admit you need glasses!"

"I can see perfectly well, thank you."

"Look! It's moving again! It's some kind of animal…"

Joe reached to open the glass door.

"Wait!" I cried. "Don't open it, let's see what it is first! We may need to catch…"

Too late.

Something black shot out, swooped round the room and clung sootily to a picture frame.

"Aaaagh!" I yelled. "It's a bat!"

I'm not at all frightened of bats outside in the fresh air. I think they are wonderful creatures, and they certainly did a grand job of devouring El Hoyo's flying insect population. I loved the way they flitted round the lamp posts, catching moths.

But I have to admit, I don't like the idea of bats flying round my head indoors. Especially scared, sooty bats.

"Quick, open the front door," Joe ordered.

I flung the door open but the bat was too frightened to move, and merely blinked.

"Perhaps we should throw something over it," I suggested, using the royal 'we' as I had no intention of doing it myself.

"Hmmm… Good idea," said Joe, grabbing my favourite white T-shirt which I'd foolishly left lying around.

He hurled it at the poor creature, but the bat sat tight, its tiny hands gripping the picture frame, its eyes regarding us over its shoulder. My T-shirt slid to the floor, soot-smeared.

"I know, I'll get the little fishing net," Joe suggested, "if I can find it. Stay there and watch the bat. We don't want it hiding somewhere in the room and coming out later."

"Can't I go and look for the net?" I argued, but Joe had already gone.

"Right, Batty," I said quietly. "Just you hang in there and behave until Joe comes back with a net. We'll soon have you outside."

But the bat was restless. To my horror, it looked around, twitched, then sprang into the air.

"Aaaagh!" I yelled, crouching down and covering my head, trying hard to follow its flightpath as it circled the ceiling.

"Beaky!"

I must have jumped a foot in the air.

"Beaky! What are you doing?"

A figure stood in the doorway, blocking out the light. I knew that voice. It was Pancho, the mayor.

I half-straightened up, my eyes searching the ceiling, but during that fraction of a second when I'd been distracted, the bat had disappeared.

"Poor Beaky!" said Pancho, walking into the room. It didn't matter how good his English, his nasal voice still made my name sound like Beaky. "Are you sick?"

"No, no!"

"You must not be afraid, there is nothing here."

"But…"

"Why were you crouching on the floor, poor Beaky? And why do you keep rolling your eyes to the heavens?"

"I'm not rolling my eyes!"

"Poor Beaky," said the mayor, taking my hand and raising it to his lips. "You look pale. I am thinking your husband does not look after you properly. Perhaps he would let me take you out for a soothing drive. Or a quiet drink in my office at the town hall."

My mouth dropped open. Where was Joe with that wretched net?

"Pancho, there is *nothing* wrong with me. There was a …"

Try as I might, I couldn't think of the Spanish word for 'bat'.

"A what, dear Beaky?" he asked gently. "You can tell me anything…"

I snatched my hand away.

"Bat!" I said in English.

"But what, my dear?" he asked, following my lead and speaking in English.

"Not 'but'! I said 'bat'!" I flapped my arms. "Bat!"

Pancho raised his eyebrows. I could see concern in his eyes.

I shook my head in exasperation.

"You know, a little mouse with …" Now I couldn't remember the word for 'wings'.

"A leetle mouse with clogs on?" he smiled. "This song I have heard the children sing in the English class at the school."

A movement behind his head caught my eye. The bat! It was clinging to the curtain rail, staring balefully down at us.

"*Allí arriba,*" I said, pointing triumphantly. "Up there."

Pancho looked up, and the bat chose that second to launch again.

"*¡Madre mía!*" squealed the mayor, his eyes huge, all chivalry and counselling forgotten. "*¡Es un murciélago!*"

Oh! I thought. *So that's the Spanish word for a bat!*

In that moment, I forgot to be afraid of the bat and watched the proceedings with fascination. The little creature flapped round the ceiling, searching for an exit.

"*¡Madre mía!* Go away!" gibbered Pancho, covering his head and backing out of the front door into the street. His fear far outstripped mine. A casual observer might be forgiven for thinking that a giant mutant vampire had invaded our home, not merely a small, harmless, common, Spanish bat.

Unfortunately, the bat spotted the escape at exactly the same moment as Pancho and swooped out after him.

"*¡Ayuda!* Help! Help! It's chasing me!" yelled the mayor as he galloped down the street.

I sank onto the sofa, unable to stifle my giggles as I heard Pancho's footsteps receding.

"Oh!" said Joe, coming in, clutching our shrimping net. "Where's the bat? Am I too late?"

"It went out by itself."

"Did it? Oh, good. Funny thing, I just saw the mayor pelting down the street shouting something. No idea what he was yelling."

"I think I might know," I said, and started laughing again.

Joe crumpled up an old newspaper and threw it into the stove. He struck a match, allowing the little flame to curl around the paper until it burst into life. Smoke poured from the burning paper, but instead of being drawn up the chimney, it swept back into the room.

"Blast it," coughed Joe, scratching his nethers. "Looks like you were right. This chimney does need cleaning. And if this chimney needs cleaning, then I suppose the kitchen one does, too."

"Shall we call in a chimney sweep?"

"No, we can do it easily. It won't take a minute."

Huh!

"Shall we go and buy a chimney brush?"

"No need, all we have to do is poke something up there."

"What sort of something?"

"Anything. Like a bundle of rags on the end of a stick, or something. What's this?"

"Well, it *was* my favourite T-shirt, but I guess it's no good now since you used it as a bat catcher."

The irony, and my annoyance, were completely lost on Joe.

"Perfect," he said, and before I could stop him, he'd rolled it into a ball and was poking it up the chimney with the shrimping net.

Soot fell in soft clumps, spraying a fine black dust over everything in the living room.

"Can't you wait until I've covered stuff up?"

"Oh well, I've started now... Oh dear, I can't seem to get any higher. Have we got a longer pole?"

"What do you mean, have we got a longer pole? How should I know? We both live here, you know. Okay, I'll go and look for something."

I stomped off, furious at the way the job was being tackled. I couldn't find a long pole, but I found a couple of bendy bamboo poles and brought them back.

"Is that all you've got?"

"We could tape them together?"

That worked, except the poles went straight past my T-shirt and made no impression on the soot whatsoever.

"Hmm... I think the rag has got stuck," said Joe, stating the obvious. "I'll find some more rags and see if we can dislodge the blockage."

The more items Joe pushed up the chimney, the blacker he got and the more the blockage grew. I almost lost track of what he'd pushed up there. In the old days, he could have climbed up inside, but now the chimney was lined with much narrower metal tubing.

"Looks like I'm going to have to go down the mountain and buy a proper chimney brush," he said.

I wanted to remind him that I'd suggested that at the start, but I graciously held my tongue.

While he was gone, I swept, dusted, and stripped off the covers of the couch and armchairs.

"Honestly, girls," I said to the chickens as they crowded round the fence to watch what I was doing. "You're better off without a husband. If he'd just waited, I wouldn't have to be outside shaking soot off these covers."

Then I dragged out the dust-covers and spread them over the furniture in the living room. Better late than never.

Just as I was finishing, Joe returned with a shiny, new, extendable chimney brush, and this time, the job went smoothly. He went up to the roof terrace and stuck his new purchase down the chimney, giving it a good jiggle as he thrust. Years' worth of soot crashed down amidst the bundle of rags. *RIP, favourite T-shirt.* More black dust floated round the room.

"Stop! I have a question," I said, when Joe had pronounced the chimney clean and I was restoring the living room to normality. He was preparing to attack the kitchen chimney and was kneeling in front of the stove, opening the glass door.

"Yes?"

"Well, why not clean the kitchen chimney from the top, too? I mean from the roof terrace? We can keep the stove door closed, and just wait for the soot to settle before we open the stove door and sweep it out. That way, I won't have to cover everything up again."

"Um… That actually makes very good sense," Joe conceded, and took his new favourite tool up the outside stairs to the roof terrace.

I should have checked.

But I didn't.

I foolishly trusted Joe would have shut the kitchen stove door before he started.

WHUMPH!

An avalanche of soot slid down the chimney tube and landed in the stove, billowing out in black clouds that filled the kitchen and settled in a fine film on every surface.

"Did any come down?" Joe's disembodied voice floated down the chimney, dislodging more pockets of soot that descended to join the slag heap below.

"Yes!" I yelled up the chimney. "Why *on earth* didn't you shut the stove door?"

"Oh, didn't I?"

"No! You didn't! There's soot everywhere."

Both chimneys were clean, but it took me several hours to clean the kitchen and I found soot in crevices for a long time after.

"Good news," I said.

I'd been walking round the village trying to increase my step quota for the day. My daily target was thirteen thousand, and it took dedication to achieve that.

"What good news?"

"I passed Marcia's shop, and I saw Geronimo having an intense conversation with Valentina. Judging by their body language, I think they were making up their differences."

"Honestly, Vicky! As usual, I bet you were imagining things."

"I wasn't! I'm making myself a coffee, would you like one?"

"Well, as you've seriously interrupted my writing session already, I might as well."

Joe's desk was near the window that looked out onto the street. It was a warm autumn day and our front door was open. Just as I was taking Joe's coffee over to him, I happened to glance out of the window.

CHORIZO AND POTATOES

Although this recipe is basically sausage and potatoes, by using good quality chorizo and a pinch of saffron, it will taste very authentic.

Ingredients (per person)

One medium potato, peeled and quartered, or sliced thickly

12 cms (4-5 inches) of chorizo, cut into thick slices

Small pinch of saffron (use a pinch of turmeric if you can't get saffron)

Pinch of salt

Small bay leaf

Method

Put the sliced potato and chorizo into a saucepan with just enough cold water to cover.

Add the saffron, salt and bay leaf.

Bring to the boil.

Cover, and turn the heat down. Leave gently simmering for between 45 minutes and an hour, or long enough for the potato to be tender.

Try not to stir it if you have chosen to slice your potato, as it may disintegrate. Don't top up the water - it shouldn't boil dry if you have the heat low enough.

Remove the bay leaf and serve.

8

PARTINGS

The window by Joe's desk gave a perfect view of the street and I was delighted by what I saw.

"Careful," said Joe, "you'll knock everything off my desk leaning over it like that."

"I was right!" I exclaimed, ignoring him. "Guess who I can see walking down the street, hand in hand."

"Santa Claus and Her Majesty the Queen?" said Joe, standing up and stretching.

"Don't be ridiculous. It's Valentina and Geronimo. Didn't I tell you they were making up? Right again!"

But I was stopped in mid-crow when I spied who was approaching the couple from the opposite direction, hips swinging, gypsy bangles tinkling.

Lola Ufarte.

The couple were staring into each other's eyes, unaware of Lola. No time to lose.

"Joe! Quick! Do something!"

"What are you talking about?"

"Distract Lola so she doesn't disturb Geronimo and Valentina!"

"What? How..."

"You'll think of something."

I shoved him out of the front door, straight into Lola's path. Lola stopped short, her eyebrows raised.

"*Hola*, Lola, I just wondered if..."

Well done, Joe!

"Yes?"

Lola's exquisite eyebrows arched in question, and her hands were on her hips as she waited, bangles resting. I think she always thought Joe a little strange, ever since she'd mistakenly accused him of being a peeping tom, years ago.

"Er, um..." Joe stuttered.

Joe was struggling. I knew his brain was racing, and Lola's hostile stance wasn't helping. Then he said the first thing that came into his head.

Unfortunately, it sounded very random.

"I have a brand new chimney brush."

Lola stared at him for a long moment, as though he'd just crawled out from under a stone.

"You have a new chimney brush?"

"Yes."

I watched from the shadows. Joe had that rabbit-caught-in-the-headlights expression on his face.

"If you have a blockage in your chimney, I can push it out for you," he said at last.

Lola's eyes widened as she continued to stare at him.

"Thank you, I will remember that offer," she said, and marched past.

Geronimo and Valentina had turned off down a side street, and Joe's delaying tactic had worked perfectly. I was delighted, but I sensed Joe was not pleased with me. I decided I needed to check the roof terrace. Urgently.

"Vicky? Vicky, where are you?"

Much later, when Joe had calmed down somewhat, we were discussing the incident.

"You can't meddle in other people's business," said Joe. "If Lola Ufarte is going to come between them, you can't stop that happening."

"I know," I admitted sadly.

"Hi Mum, how are you?"

"Good, thank you! Guess what I unearthed from the garage today!"

"What?"

"You remember the musical nativity scene we used to have when you were little? It played Silent Night and you children weren't allowed to open your presents until it had finished."

"Yes! We called it The Dreaded! That tune went on and on for ever. Every time we thought it had finished, it would play another few bars."

"It must be nearly an antique now. We had the same tradition when I was a child, and I decided you kids should suffer the same way as I did."

"Haha! I remember it was sheer torture!"

"The tune's a bit rusty-sounding but it still works."

"You'd also be a bit rusty-sounding if you'd been in a cardboard box in a leaky Spanish garage for ten years."

"Well, I'm going to pack it and bring it with me to Australia. Then you can decide whether you want to continue the tradition and torture Indy in the same way..."

As our departure date drew closer, my thoughts turned to what we were leaving behind.

I wasn't concerned about the village cats. When we spent a year in Bahrain, we had worried about our favourite cats, but they had managed perfectly well without us. Now, Felicity's youngsters had grown and left home. We sometimes left scraps out, but not regularly enough to make it a habit. The truth is, village cats are very capable of fending for themselves, which is why there are so many feral cats in Spain. They catch rodents and lizards and are wonderful opportunists. Villagers avoided leaving food unattended near open windows.

The chickens, however, needed care. Our flock had dwindled to just three elderly individuals and we didn't want to introduce any more. Paco had kindly offered to look after them while we were away. Then one morning, Joe came back from feeding them, looking unhappy.

He placed a single egg on the kitchen table. Being in their twilight years, our chickens rarely laid, so we were always pleased to find an egg.

"One egg," he said, "but I'm afraid one of the girls died in the night."

"Oh, what a shame. I hope she didn't suffer. Do you know which one she was?"

"Not really. Since they've got their new winter feathers, all three look the same to me. I don't think it's Mrs F though."

Mrs F was my favourite at the moment. Unlike the other two who were content to scratch and cluck in their run, Mrs F Chicken dreamed of a more glamorous, exciting life, living alongside us. She was the only chicken we ever had who plotted her escape every minute of the day. Whenever she succeeded, which was surprisingly often, she would come looking for us. Many a time I jumped as she sauntered into the kitchen. Often she'd appear at Joe's elbow as he was typing.

"Vicky! It's that effing chicken again!" he would yell, which was how Mrs F Chicken earned her name.

The next night, another chicken died in her sleep, leaving just Mrs F.

"We can't ask Paco to look after just one geriatric chicken," I said. "Especially Mrs F who will be trying to escape all the time."

"Why not give her to Miguel up the mountain? He's got loads of chickens."

"No, that would be cruel. He has an established flock. She'd be at the bottom of the pecking order and at her age it would probably kill her."

"Well," said Joe, eyeing my casserole dish, "there's always the pot... With bad weather coming, chicken stew would be very nice."

I hoped Mrs F hadn't heard that. We've never been tempted to eat our own chickens and I didn't intend beginning with Mrs F.

The decision was soon taken out of our hands. Within a few days,

Mrs F had also joined her sisters up in chicken heaven. It was sad to see our chicken coop empty, the first time in ten years. I missed the comfortable sounds they made, and I missed their company when I was in the garden. However, we no longer needed to find a chicken sitter.

But it seemed that I was about to share a brand new flock of chickens on the other side of the world.

Emails, Skype conversations and messages between me and my daughter increased in frequency as the departure date, 9th of December, approached.

"Mum! We're bidding right now for a chicken coop on eBay!"

"Really? You're going to get some chickens?"

"Hang on... No! Somebody else is bidding!"

"Oh..."

"Yes, we want to get chickens! If we get the coop, Cam will assemble it all first, and build a nice run and stuff. When you get here, we'll go and buy some chickens together."

"How exciting! Do you have foxes where you are?"

"No, I don't think so, but we have snakes and goannas and other chicken-eating stuff. It'll all have to be enclosed properly. Oh! Yay! We won it!"

"I wonder what LJ will make of chickens!"

"We'll soon find out."

The time had come to begin packing our suitcases. Of course, Joe couldn't be trusted to pack for himself. Left to his own devices, he would have packed an assortment of books, his computer, and a few odd socks. Then he'd ask what all the fuss was about, and why do people take so much stuff when they go on a trip?

Packing felt most peculiar. I had two open suitcases lying on the spare room bed, one for me and one for Joe. Swimming costumes, summer dresses, sandals, shorts and T-shirts were stowed in mine while in Joe's I folded warm sweaters, long trousers, scarves and gloves. He would be staying with family in the UK for three of the coldest months, while I would be in Australia for three of the hottest. He had definitely drawn the short straw.

The two very different suitcases were a constant reminder that Joe and I would be separated for some time. We could only hope that the doctors would find nothing amiss, and he could then book a flight to Australia without having to worry about his health.

"Indy is *so* excited about you coming," said my daughter on the phone. "Whenever we see a lady, doesn't matter what age, she asks her, 'Are you my Nanny?'"

I smiled. Indy was two and a half now. The last time I'd seen her was when she and her parents had visited us in Spain on her first birthday.

Joe and I had been careful to book flights that were departing within hours of each other, despite having destinations to opposite sides of the globe. This would allow us to leave the house and village together and our wonderful neighbour, Paco, had kindly offered to drive us to the airport.

But first, we had to secure the house for the three months we'd be away. Winter in the Spanish mountains can be wet and wild, and we were glad of our recently installed windows and doors, and confident, too, that our roofs no longer leaked.

"Strange to think that when we come back, the vine will be sprouting new leaves," I said.

Joe nodded. The grapevine, in its winter state, looked lifeless, and it was hard to believe that it would ever burst into bud again.

"I feel so torn," I said. "I'm counting the days until I go to Australia, but at the same time I'm missing you already, and I know I'll miss home."

I didn't vocalise my other terrible fear, that the UK doctors might find something seriously wrong with him. I was sure Joe was having the same thoughts, because he seemed to read my mind.

"We'll be back in El Hoyo in no time," he said. "And if we get any unexpected bad news, we'll cope. We always do."

We hugged, and a million unspoken words hung in the air.

"I think it's very likely that I'll be pronounced fit, in which case I'll jump on the next plane to Aus."

"That's what I'm praying for," I said.

In December, the village was almost empty of inhabitants, although many families still spent weekends in their cottages. It was easy to see who was home by looking for the smoke curling out of chimneys.

"So you will be coming back to El Hoyo in March?" asked Marcia.

"Yes, we'll be away for exactly three months."

"I shall tell Valentina to give me your mail. I will keep it safe for you."

"Thank you," I said. "Talking of Valentina, how is the romance?"

Marcia tossed her head and a silver hairpin slipped out of her hair.

"I'm afraid that romance flew out of the window last week," she said, shaking her head and sending more hairpins flying.

"Oh, I'm sorry to hear that," I said. "What went wrong?"

I had asked the question, but I think I'd already guessed the answer.

"Somebody in the village rather enjoyed getting between them, I think," said Marcia.

I nodded.

"Enjoy your trip," she said, kissing me on both cheeks. "Safe journey."

An hour later, Carmen, Joe and I watched Paco lift our suitcases into his Range Rover as though they were filled with feathers.

"Are all the doors locked? Water turned off?" I asked Joe.

"Yes, all done, stop worrying."

I handed our spare keys to Carmen.

"Have a wonderful time, and we'll see you in three months," she said.

"Pah! They'll be back before you know it!" said Paco.

Suddenly I was transported back to the last time he took us to the airport when we'd just signed the contract to teach in the Middle East for a year. Back then, we had no idea what shocking events lay in store for us, and I felt as though the same thing was happening now. What would the British doctors find when they examined Joe? How would it affect our lives? Would my stay in Australia be eventful? Would Joe join me?

We drove through the village and past the square. It was early afternoon, but I saw Geronimo sitting on his own, an empty beer bottle standing beside him on the bench. His eyes stared at nothing, and no expression played across his face. One hand was pushed deep into his coat pocket, and the other gripped a full bottle of beer. He lifted it to his waiting mouth.

We all have different problems, I thought, and squeezed Joe's hand, grateful that we still had a little time together.

The next hours remain rather a blur to me. At the airport, we thanked Paco, and waved him goodbye, promising to let him know when we were coming home. We bought coffee, and sat holding hands as the precious minutes trickled by. Neither of us wanted to prolong the agony, so we hugged and whispered our goodbyes, then set off in different directions, heading for our respective boarding gates.

People milled around me.

Where are they all going? I wondered. *And why? Are they leaving family behind?*

I have very little recollection of my twenty-seven hour journey to Australia. I can't remember who I sat next to on the flight to Madrid, or on the flight from Madrid to Dubai. I remember killing time in Dubai airport by walking briskly, trying to reach my daily steps target.

I attempted sleep on the long trip from Dubai to Sydney, but only managed short naps as I sat next to a Russian couple who'd had a manners by-pass and insisted on climbing over me at unreasonably regular intervals.

Joe will have arrived hours ago, I thought.

I had strange, disturbed, distorted dreams that I'd arrived and my daughter didn't recognise me, then announced that I wasn't as good as she remembered. I woke sweating and scared.

And then the plane's engine changed note, the air hostesses prepared for landing and our wheels finally bumped down on the tarmac of Sydney's airport. It was nighttime, but the airport lights blazed. I'd left Spain on a winter's day, and arrived in Australia on a balmy summer night.

BEEF STEW
ESTOFADO

The real trick to this recipe is to cook it as slowly as possible so that the cubes of beef are ultra soft and tender.

Ingredients

1kg (2.2lb) of stewing beef, cut into 3cm (1 inch) chunks

1 tablespoon of flour

200 mls (7 fl oz) of beef stock

1 glass of red wine

2 leeks, trimmed and sliced into 1cm (¼ inch) slices

6 to 8 garlic cloves, peeled and finely sliced or chopped

2 medium onions, finely chopped

1 large carrot, finely sliced

1 celery stick, finely sliced

1 tin of chopped tomatoes

¼ teaspoon of ground cumin

1 teaspoon of paprika

Olive oil

Salt and pepper to taste

Method

Heat two good glugs of olive oil in a large saucepan or casserole dish.

Brown the beef, then stir in the flour, cumin and paprika.

Stir in the wine, then throw in all the veggies and stir well.

Add the beef stock and bring to the boil. Reduce the heat down really low, cover it and leave for at least a couple of hours.

Season to taste.

Serve when the meat is tender, with rice, mashed potato or fresh bread.

9

BIRDS AND SPIDERS

I found my luggage and passed through Customs without drama, although I felt light-headed from travelling and lack of sleep. Along with dozens of other weary travellers, I trundled my trolley to the Arrivals gate. My daughter and son-in-law sprang out from the crowd, and suddenly, the long journey was history.

We hugged and all talked at once.

"There you are!"

"How was the journey?"

"You look wonderful!"

"Mum! I'm so pleased you're here!"

"I can't believe I'm here!"

"Are you tired?"

"Where's Indy?"

"She's staying with Cam's parents. It's a bit late for her, and we thought it'd be nicer if you see her tomorrow when you've rested a bit. Today she asked the cashier in Woolworths if she was her Nanny."

"Oh, bless her heart! I can't wait to get my hands on her!"

"Did you manage to get any sleep on the journey?"

"A bit, but I had awful dreams."

"So did I last night! I dreamt that you didn't approve of my parenting!"

"Haha! As if! And I dreamed that I was a terrible Nanny!"

Cam took charge of my luggage and we walked outside. Even though it was nighttime, everything seemed exotic, different. I looked up to see a million stars studding the clear sky.

"It's so warm," I exclaimed.

"The weather forecast is great, prepare to get very hot this week!"

"We've decorated the house Griswold-style."

"You've what?"

"You know, like the Griswolds! The movie, *National Lampoon's Christmas Vacation*? They decorated the house with so many Christmas lights that they caused a city-wide power cut."

"I keep forgetting it's Christmas!"

"Wait until you see our lights, they are *awesome*!"

And they were awesome. They lit up the lovely house that I had only seen in pictures. Tiny, white fairy lights ran along the eaves, dangling like icicles. More sparkled in the bushes.

"I love it!"

"Yes, we keep adding to it. Now, come and meet LJ."

I knew LJ was no longer a puppy, but I must admit to being rather taken aback when this giant hound bounded up and jumped up on me, putting his paws on my chest. He looked extremely threatening as his face was on a level with mine. I was to learn that he was a very gentle dog, and a perfect example of not judging a book by its cover.

"Get down, LJ! LJ, get down!"

But LJ wanted to play.

"He'll soon get used to you, he's always like that with new people. He gets over-excited. Come and see everything else."

Tired as I was, I loved the guided tour. Everything was sparkly clean and smelled of polish. I could see how hard they'd worked to have everything perfect for my arrival, and when they flung open the door to my lair, I gasped.

"It's absolutely perfect!" I said. "I just love it!"

The brick walls were painted white. I had a desk, TV, sofa, fridge, kettle, and unlimited Internet access. It was the ideal retreat, a place to sit and write during spare moments.

It was too dark to see much outside, but I could see the silhouette of the new chicken coop.

"We've got loads of things planned," said Karly. "Tomorrow, don't get up until you're ready. I expect you'll need to catch up a bit after that journey. I'll go and collect Indy in the morning. Cam will be at work, then he has to put some finishing touches on the coop and perhaps later on we'll go out and choose some chickens. And this weekend we've been invited round to Cam's parents for a meal. They've got a lovely boat, and they're going to take us all out for a sail sometime. Oh, and did you know this area of Sydney has a hundred beaches? Let's see how many we can visit during your stay!"

I crawled into bed, dog-tired, but my heart was singing. Images of chickens, a hundred beaches, my new writing retreat and fairy lights, whirled around in my exhausted head.

I hope Joe comes out soon, I thought, and tapped out a quick text to him.

Arrived safely, all well. House is beautiful. xxx

Then I lay back and fell into a deep sleep.

Next morning, I was woken up by a most unexpected sound. Somebody was playing the tune of Happy Birthday right outside my window. Not singing, but playing the first few bars, over and over again.

Imagine an orchestra comprising strange unworldly instruments tuning up. Imagine shrieks, caws and whistles, with the occasional crack of a whiplash. That's a typical Australian dawn chorus.

Then add an instantly recognisable tune into the mix. The strains of Happy Birthday were unmistakable, although I couldn't identify what instrument was producing it. It sounded a little like pan pipes.

But it's not my birthday. I'm dreaming.

I opened my eyes and sat up, suddenly remembering where I was. Of course, Australia! And this dawn chorus was an event that took place every morning and so unremarkable to Australians that few ever even noticed it.

I remember the birds in Britain for their beautiful songs, but they sang sweetly, politely. The birds in Spain were too heavily hunted to be very evident. However, in Australia, the birds are prolific and super-noisy. When Joe and I visited Queensland in 2008, we stayed in a house on the edge of a golf course. We delighted in the crazy dawn chorus, and this was exactly the same.

I was not yet able to distinguish the different birds, so I couldn't tell the difference between the sounds of the rainbow lorikeets, the Indian mynah birds, the cockatoos, and the magpies. (I soon learned of the existence of the whiplash bird, and heard it often, but I have yet to see one.)

And then the tuneful rendition of Happy Birthday began again, and I understood. It was a *bird* singing it, but which bird had learned to reproduce the notes so perfectly? I had no idea.

I lay back on the pillows with my eyes shut, listening to the wonderful sounds of nature, waiting for the house to wake up. It didn't take long because most Australians are early risers. Their habits are in stark contrast to the Spanish who rise quite late, siesta in the middle of the day and don't go to bed until the early hours of the morning. The Happy Birthday bird sang again, and I smiled. Three months in this lovely house with my family and surrounded by wonderful Australian birds was going to be heavenly.

"Mum, I'm just off to collect Indy. Help yourself to coffee and toast."

I poured myself a coffee then prowled round the house, getting my bearings. From the back garden, LJ watched me through the windows. I explored the front and saw that we were at the bottom of a leafy cul-de-sac. Tall trees stretched up, while colourful shrubs and bushes jostled each other beneath them. I've always enjoyed gardening, but I recognised none of the plants and flowers that grew so abundantly here.

I sat on the doorstep, sipping my coffee. Everything was so exotic and strange, bordering on the slightly crazy. Gigantic spiders' webs hung in the trees, giant beetles with outsize horns like antlers scuttled past, scaly lizards basked in the early sun, ants of every size laboured, while the birds, none of which I could actually spot, sang as though auditioning for concerts.

The Happy Birthday bird was just repeating his song for the hundredth time when Karly returned. In the back, I saw a little face framed by a cloud of golden curls. I ran round the car and flung the rear door open.

"Indy! Where's Indy?" I asked. "This big girl can't be Indy!"

Indy gurgled.

"Where's Indy?" I asked again, pretending to look for her.

"I'se Indy."

"Are you sure?"

Indy nodded earnestly.

"And how old are you?"

"Two!"

By now I'd unbuckled the straps to her carseat and released her.

"So you're quite sure you're Indy?"

More earnest nods.

"Well, then, come here, gorgeous girl!"

I grabbed her and smothered her with kisses, making her giggle.

"Look, Nanny!"

She was holding up her wrist to show me. I wasn't sure what I was supposed to be looking at.

"What is it?"

"Oh," said my daughter, "she's showing you her freckle."

I didn't even have time to admire it before Indy remembered something else to show me.

"Nanny, Nanny! Chick-uns!"

I set her down and she tugged me by the hand, leading me to the new chicken coop.

"She can't wait to get the chickens," said my daughter. "We're planning to get some from the garden centre but as you're a chicken expert, you can help us choose."

"Well, I'm hardly an expert…"

Indy stuck her head into the empty coop.

"Chick-uns! Where are 'ooo?" she yelled.

"Did you have a coffee and a look round the house while we were gone?"

"I did, thank you. I love the house, and the garden, and everything! And how cool to have a Happy Birthday bird!"

"A what?"

"You know, the bird that sings Happy Birthday."

"Pardon?"

"The Happy Birthday bird. Stop teasing me!"

"Mum, I have *no* idea what you are talking about."

I checked her face to see if she was joking. She wasn't.

"There's a bird round here that sings the first few bars of Happy Birthday. I heard it when I woke up, and lots of times since."

"Ha! I think I would have heard that! Perhaps you're suffering from jet-lag or something."

"You *must* have heard it! Listen, it's probably singing now."

I put up my hand for silence, and we stood still and listened.

Nothing.

Plenty of other random birdsong and trills. But no Happy Birthday bird.

"I did hear it, honestly."

"Of course you did, Mum."

She had the same expression when she caught me wearing odd shoes, or trying to unlock the front door with the car key. Yes, I am absent-minded, particularly when I'm writing a book, which is most of the time.

I sighed. There comes a point when one must admit defeat, and I had reached it. She hadn't ever heard the Happy Birthday bird's song, but I was positive she soon *would* hear it and when she did, she would eat humble pie and regret her scepticism. I was prepared to wait.

"Let's take LJ to the off-leash dog park. He needs a good run, and there's a kids' playground there which Indy will like," suggested my daughter. "Then we'll have some lunch."

LJ cantered round the park like a pony, Karly following him, while Indy and I concentrated on the playground's offerings.

"Pider!" said Indy, and showed me how to remove the webs with a long stick. Australian spiders are prolific, and the slide, seesaw, climbing frame and swings were all draped in cobwebs, no doubt constructed overnight.

I was pleased to see that Indy was developing a healthy respect for spiders. I didn't want her to be frightened of spiders, like her mother and I were, but Australian spiders should be avoided as many will deliver a painful bite, and there are some that are downright dangerous.

Lunch was uneventful until Karly handed me a little pot.

"Can you give that to Indy, please?"

I stared at the stuff.

"You give your daughter frogspawn to eat?"

"It's chia seeds with yogurt."

I stared blankly at her.

"They're great for her digestion and give her energy. She loves them."

"Really? How come I've never heard of chia seeds before?"

"I guess you can't get them in Spain?"

"Maybe. Can I have a look in your cupboards, see if there are any other edible surprises that may have passed me by?"

"Be my guest."

I should explain that when she was eighteen months old, Karly refused to eat any food apart from sausages.

No vegetables. No fruit. No meat.

Just sausages.

I tried everything, then in despair, I went to the doctor and explained the problem. It was 1982, and the doctor was unconcerned.

"Is she healthy?" he asked. "Happy? Sleeping well?"

"Well, yes…"

"Then I wouldn't worry," he said. "Keep giving her things to try, but don't upset yourself, or her, by trying to force her. It's a phase, she'll pass though it."

It proved to be a very long phase that lasted many years. Unlike her big brother, who ate everything and had become quite the little gourmet, Karly only ate sausages. Every day she had sausages for dinner. If we ate out at a cafe or restaurant, she'd ask for sausages.

At Christmas, while we enjoyed turkey and all the trimmings, Karly's plate sported a sausage decorated with a piece of holly in an attempt to make it look a little more festive.

Gradually, she began to eat other things, but not particularly healthy foods. She'd eat sweet things, then bread, potatoes, and cheese. The big breakthrough came when she was about twelve and went to stay with a friend in Hong Kong. She returned having discovered she liked chicken, fish and lots of other foods. I guess she had no choice but to try these things while she was a guest in somebody else's house.

As the years went by, she began to eat more variety of foods, and I knew she had developed a passion for cooking. But I didn't know how far she'd come. I didn't know she was cooking and consuming health food items I'd never heard of. Heck, I couldn't even spell or say them.

"What's this? Psyllium husks?"

"Ah. Yes. That's a digestion aid, extremely high fibre."

"What do you do with them?"

"You can add to flour, or pasta, or whatever."

"And this?" I peered at the label. "Quinoa?"

Of course I pronounced it as I saw it, 'quin-oa', but was sharply corrected.

"Mum, it's pronounced Keen-wah."

"Really? Why?"

"I don't know! I can't believe you've never come across these basics."

"Now, hold on, Mrs I-only-ate-sausages-until-I-was-twelve-years-old. And what's this? Shouldn't it be in your gardening shed?" I squinted at the label. "Diatomaceous earth? Fossil shell flour? You must be joking! And this? Green banana starch?"

Karly shrugged.

"All good stuff," she said.

I abandoned my scrutiny of the pantry, feeling out of my depth. It was more like an apothecary's workshop than a cook's larder.

Something on the floor moved into my line of vision and I instantly forgot all about health foods.

I froze. It was the biggest, blackest, hairiest spider I had ever seen, and it was heading straight for me. I opened my mouth to scream.

"My pider!" said Indy, pointing, her finger slimy with chia seeds.

Just a second, spiders don't hum, I thought. Karly's grinning face appeared round the corner.

"Did I get you?" she asked, showing me the remote control in her hand. "How scared were you, out of ten?"

"That was a very robust eleven," I said, as my heart retuned to its normal pace.

That was the day that the Spider War was waged.

There were no rules. The aim was to hide the spider in unexpected places and scare the skin off each other. The higher the scare factor out of ten, the more satisfaction for the prankster.

After lunch, Indy was allowed to watch a little of her very favourite DVD before her afternoon nap.

"I'm secretly quite pleased she's chosen this as her favourite," said Karly. "You couldn't get anything more British!"

"What is it?"

"Noddy and Big Ears. She loves it. Can you sit with her for a minute?"

"Of course."

She gave me the DVD which I slid into the player. I fumbled with the remote control but Noddy refused to pop onto the screen.

"Indy do it."

My granddaughter, age two, knew exactly how to control both the TV and DVD player. Soon Noddy was driving his little red car into Toytown.

As I sat with my arm around my little granddaughter, I couldn't help being transported back nearly sixty years. Of course, we didn't have a TV when I was little, but I remembered the Noddy books I had as a child. I may have changed a great deal over the years, but Noddy hadn't aged a day.

What with playing with Indy, catching up with family news, and watching Cam finish the chicken coop, the day slipped away delightfully.

I was tired, but before I went to bed, I tiptoed into the kitchen, looked around, then popped the spider into an empty saucepan.

I climbed into bed at eleven o'clock that night, and wondered whether Joe, in the UK, was awake enough for a chat. To my delight he was.

SPICY PRAWNS
GAMBAS PIL PIL

Gambas Pil Pil is a really simple dish to make, plus it is extremely fast to cook.

Ingredients

Olive oil

3 or 4 cloves of garlic - finely sliced

A good teaspoon of paprika (smoked or sweet)

A handful of raw prawns per person, shelled and de-veined if you prefer

1 fresh chilli, very finely sliced, you choose whether to include the seeds for extra heat, or not

Method

Pour about 1 cm (¼ inch) of olive oil into a pan on a high heat.

Sprinkle in the paprika and stir well.

Throw in the garlic, chillies and prawns.

They will cook very quickly, so keep turning until the prawns turn pink. It will only take a minute or so.

Serve with fresh bread for mopping up that awesome chilli/garlic oil.

10

CHICKENS

"So how was your first day in Australia?"

"Lovely. Indy is just gorgeous, bright as a button. She loves imagining. We read her pretend books that all start 'Once there was a little girl with blonde, curly hair whose name was Indy. She was a princess...' and so on, and she turns all the pretend pages."

I went on to tell him about the house, the Christmas decorations, the warmth, the wonderful Australian light, the plan to get chickens, the spider game, and the Happy Birthday bird.

"Are you telling me you heard a bird singing Happy Birthday?"

"Yes."

"Vicky..."

"It's okay, Karly and Cam don't believe me either. Now do you have any news?"

"Actually, yes. As soon as I arrived, I phoned the surgery and they happened to have a cancellation with Dr Holland, so I took it."

"Gosh! That was quick!"

"It was."

"What's he like?"

"Scottish, gingerish hair, middle-aged, kindly. I liked him."

"Okay."

"So I told him we live in Spain, and I hadn't had a proper medical since I was fifty, and that I felt I needed one. He agreed, and sent me for all sorts of tests."

"Like what?"

"Well, he took my blood pressure, I had a blood test, a chest X-ray, urine test, you know the sort of thing."

"That sounds pretty thorough."

"Yes. Anyway, I made another appointment with him for later this month to discuss the results."

"Good! Let's hope they find absolutely nothing wrong, then you can come out here and sample Karly's fossil shell flour cupcakes."

"Pardon?"

"Never mind.

"Well, that was a good solid eight."

"What was?"

"The spider in the saucepan."

"Haha!"

The garden centre that we visited had everything a family could wish for. It had a play area with little cars for Indy to drive, a stall serving coffee, more plants and shrubs than you could shake a stick at, and chickens. Many of the chickens roamed free which delighted Indy.

"Where are 'ooo, chick-uns?" she called as she chased the poor creatures round a row of potted palms.

The chickens for sale were in a large pen. They were much younger, with stubby combs, than the ones roaming free. There were brown ones, and a few other, more showy ones.

I had a memory flashback of the chickens we had bought over the years in Spain, and the horrible chicken shop where the hens were stuffed into tiny cages, five in each. Thank goodness, Australia seemed to be a great deal more humane in its treatment of the hen population.

"How many do you think we should get?" asked Karly.

"I think maybe four would be good," I said. "That would give them plenty of room in the coop, and three or four eggs a day is plenty. Enough to eat and some to give away."

"Which sort should we choose?"

"Well, we always found the brown ones to be more sensible, and reliable layers. The fancy ones were often a bit neurotic."

"Okay, let's have three brown ones and that gorgeous black one over there."

The black chicken was much bigger than her brown sisters, and her glossy, black wings nearly touched the floor. The assistant caught the hens we had chosen and put them into two big boxes with big air holes cut in the side.

We bought a sack of grain and Indy chose some feeders to hang in the coop. As we drove home, the chickens in their boxes remained quiet.

"What shall we call them?"

"Let's see if they develop personalities, then we can think of names."

"Good idea."

At home, Cam carefully lifted the two brown chickens out of one box and set them down in their new home. At first they seemed a little bewildered and stood still, absorbing their new surroundings. Then they spied the new feeder and made their way over to it, happily tucking in as though they'd always lived there.

The third brown chicken was next, and she behaved in the same way as her sisters. Cam concentrated on the last chicken, the black, flamboyant one.

"Oh my goodness! Indy, come over here! One of the chickens has laid an egg!"

In the box was a warm, perfect egg. The black chicken must have laid it during the journey on the way home. I drew on my rather sketchy chicken knowledge bank, and assumed it was the black hen because she was the oldest, judging by her larger comb.

"Look, Indy, the chicken has laid an egg in the box!"

"Look, Indy, our first egg! Feel how warm it is."

"Clever chicken! Thank you for laying a lovely egg."

"Indy do it," demanded my granddaughter, holding out her little hands.

"You must be *very* careful," said her father, gently placing the egg in her outstretched hands, "because it will break."

Indy stared at the egg in her hands, then, without warning, she ran forward to the chickens and threw the egg.

"Chick-uns! Ere y'are, chick-uns!"

The egg smashed open and spread over the ground. The chickens jostled each other to suck it up.

"Oh!" said Karly.

"Oops!" said Cam. "That wasn't the plan."

"Oh dear," I said. "Never mind, they'll all be laying eggs soon."

The black chicken stretched her neck upwards and crowed.

"I thought only cockerels crowed, not hens," Karly remarked.

"Me too! How very odd!"

But the black hen was definitely female because she continued to lay eggs as the days went by. But she didn't cluck, she crowed.

"Perhaps she's a transvestite," suggested Karly. "We'll call her Tranny."

"Okay, but what about the other three?"

"I can't tell the difference between them, can you?"

"No, not really."

"Actually, they all remind me of Margaret Thatcher."

"Do they?"

"Yes. I think we should call them Margaret."

"All of them?"

"Yes."

"Good idea. No mix-up then."

It reminded me of when Karly and her brother were small. We used to have three goldfish which we couldn't tell apart, so we named them Wet Wet Wet, after a popular 1980s band. Poor Wet died, but we had Wet and Wet for years afterwards.

Visiting the Margarets and checking for eggs became an enjoyable daily ritual, although only Tranny produced eggs. I knew that the Margarets would lay soon, but Karly was impatient.

I was in my writing lair when Karly stuck her head round the door.

"I'm off to the gym, can you check the Margarets' food and water, please? Oh, and see if they've finally decided to lay an egg. Indy's coming with me, she loves the gym creche."

"No problem. Don't pull any muscles."

I read the last few paragraphs of what I had written the day before, then pulled my desk drawer open.

An enormous black spider crouched in the corner.

Just for a nanosecond, I was terrified, but reason took charge as I recognised the monster my beloved daughter had placed carefully in my drawer. I had reached an eight on the Fear Scale.

I no longer felt like writing, and went on the prowl instead, looking for the perfect place to conceal the spider, unexpected enough to scare the heebie-jeebies out of her.

Broom cupboard?

No, she might not go in there for a couple of days.

Fridge?

No, somebody else might come across it. I finally decided on her underwear drawer, but looking in the fridge had given me an idea.

I took out a box of eggs and transferred them to a bowl. Then I went back to my writing lair, taking the eggs with me. I went back to work but listened out for Karly. Soon she drew up in the drive, and I was ready.

I went out to meet her, carrying the bowl of eggs.

"Hi, Mum."

"How was the gym?"

"Good. Tiring, but good. Everything okay here?"

"Yep, all good. I did a bit of writing, and I checked the Margarets, and look what I found!"

Karly swung round and saw the bowl of eggs for the first time. Her eyes grew large.

"You are *kidding!* The Margarets laid all those today? Wow!"

"Yes, they did really well, didn't they?"

"Are the eggs still warm?"

"No, I don't think so. Have a look, though, they're perfect."

"But there are *loads* of them! I thought they laid just one a day."

"Yes, it's rather unusual to get so many at once," I agreed, but I was struggling to keep my face straight. "And I'll tell you what else is unusual."

"What?"

"It's unusual for chickens to stamp the date and 'Farm Fresh' on each egg."

Karly stared at me, then at the eggs piled in the bowl.

"Mum!"

The relief of being able to laugh out loud was enormous. I had tears running down my cheeks.

"Don't listen to Nanny, Indy, she's being silly," said my daughter haughtily, and stalked into the house.

"Silly Nanny," said Indy, and rolled her eyes.

"You're going to have to try harder than that, you know."

"Pardon?"

"The spider in my underwear drawer."

"Ah."

"Barely a six on the Fear Scale."

That weekend we were invited to Cam's parents' house for lunch. We'd met many times before so it was good to catch up. When we arrived, the sky was overcast, but didn't give us cause for concern.

Their lovely house is in a wonderfully leafy suburb, with wide tree-lined streets. The kitchen window had a gorgeous outlook over the garden, and our hostess clearly had green fingers. (I learned later that Australians say 'green thumbs'.)

"It looks so beautiful," I said, admiring the lawn, the pool and the masses of delicate white flowers with their backdrop of glossy, deep green leaves. "It looks very cool in this heat."

"Ah, I struggle," said Cam's mother. "We have so many rabbits round here, and they eat everything. And if the rabbits don't eat it, the wallabies do. Whatever I plant, shrubs, roses, whatever, the rabbits and wallabies come and destroy it."

"Well, I think the garden looks amazing. You must teach me about the plants out here. I loved gardening when I was in England, I had a greenhouse and everything, but I'm a complete novice when it comes to Australian plants. I don't recognise any. What's that, in the big pot?"

"Ah, that's one of Australia's most popular plants, the lilly pilly. Flowers in summer and has berries in winter."

Suddenly, the sky blackened as though a light switch had been flicked.

"I think we might be in for a storm," somebody said as a sudden, violent gust of wind tore through the garden.

The sentence had hardly been uttered when we were deafened by missiles pummeling the roof. Giant hailstones, larger than golfballs, pelted down from above.

We stood in a row, pressed to the window, watching the unbelievable scene outside.

Like countless white cannonballs, the hailstones pounded down, snapping off branches, twigs and leaves in their path. The swimming pool water danced and splashed and lumps of ice floated with the debris. The beautifully swept patio turned grey with ice which began to pile up in dirty heaps, driven by the wind. We watched the garden being destroyed before our eyes. The delicate blossoms I had admired just minutes ago had already been hammered into the ground by the hail.

"We've put on an event to welcome you to Australia," Cam's father joked.

We'd all been staring out of the window overlooking the back garden, but somebody thought to open the front door and look out on the front drive. Karly's car was being pounded, and even from that distance we could see the pits forming in the bodywork as the vehicle was bombarded. A tiny part of me felt relief because I had been given permission to drive her car, and I was quite nervous about it. Perhaps if I dented it now, it wouldn't show.

Those gigantic hailstones did much damage that day and it was my first personal experience of Australia's sudden and unexpected extreme weather. But it wouldn't be the last.

We were well into summer now, and approaching Christmas. It still felt strange to see houses, malls and streets decorated for Christmas, and Christmas carols being played as background music in shops while we sweltered in the heat.

One evening we visited a nearby street renowned in Sydney for its extravagant Christmas decorations. Every house was draped in Christmas lights. Inflatable Santas, snowmen and reindeers stood on every roof, swaying slightly in the warm breeze. A dozen different Christmas songs could be heard. One house and front garden had even been covered in fake snow.

Cam was carrying Indy and her eyes were huge as she pointed at all the wonderful sights. Me, I was just pleased I wasn't footing the electricity bill.

My daughter and I fell into step.

"That was a fairly weak six, you know," I said. "You're losing your touch."

"What was?"

"The spider in my sponge bag."

"Ah. You found it."

"I did."

"Has Joe had his test results back?" asked Cam.

"He's going to the doctor today. We'll know everything very soon."

"Are you nervous?"

"Yes, a bit. I guess we just need to know if there's anything wrong, then we'll know exactly what we have to face."

Karly and Cam nodded.

To be perfectly honest, I wasn't looking forward to my next chat with Joe.

FRIED GOATS' CHEESE
QUESO DE CABRA FRITO

These are fine on their own as a starter or a *tapa*, but you could also serve them with a leafy salad for a light lunch.

Ingredients (per person)

1 large egg yolk

Teeny dribble of milk

Handful of breadcrumbs

2 slices firm goats' cheese (take it out of the fridge at the last second) about 1½ cm (½ inch) thick

Olive oil for frying

Some honey, jam or cranberry sauce for drizzling

Method

Whisk the egg yolk and teeny amount of milk in a shallow bowl. Just a gentle whisk - you don't need to put too much air into it.

Put the breadcrumbs on a plate.

Heat the olive oil in a pan over a medium to high heat.

Dip the slices of goats' cheese in the egg/milk mix.

Roll them gently in the breadcrumbs - this can be a little messy.

Place straight into the pan. Don't disturb much as they can be fragile.

When the underside is golden, flip carefully. They'll take only a couple of minutes to cook.

Meanwhile, heat some honey in the microwave or in a small pan.

Serve immediately, drizzled with the warmed honey or jam.

11

DARK SHADOWS AND DUCKS

"How's everything with you?" asked Joe.

"Never mind me, everything is great here. How did *you* get on? Did you have your appointment with Dr Holland?"

"I did."

"Well? Did he have the test results? Don't keep me waiting!"

"Slow down, Vicky. I'm going to tell you the whole story."

"Okay. I'm listening."

I could hear him take a breath, while on the other side of the planet, I held mine.

Everybody else in the waiting room seemed to be absorbed by their mobile phones. Joe was just thumbing through an ancient National Geographic magazine, when Dr Holland's door opened.

"Joe Twead?"

"Yes, that's me."

Joe stood up and followed Dr Holland into his room. The doctor plonked himself behind his desk and Joe settled himself on the chair he indicated with a wave of his hand. Dr Holland was a man of few words.

"The test results are in. Let me see..."

Joe waited and found himself staring at the eye test pasted on the wall, seeing how far he could read down the chart. Dr Holland was absorbed by, what Joe presumed to be, his chest X-rays. He was right.

Dr Holland spoke, without preamble.

"I see that there are a few dark areas on your lungs, but nothing to worry about. It's not cancer."

Joe's brain attempted to process this information.

Is this good news?

Yes! I don't have cancer.

But, dark areas? What does that mean?

What is the doctor seeing?

"Do you have any trouble breathing?"

"Yes, actually I do a bit. I think I'm just unfit."

"Your ankles look swollen."

"Yes, they are. They've been puffy for quite a while."

"Hmmm. I'll make an appointment for you to see the nurse who will give you a spirometry test. It will measure your lung capacity. It only takes a few moments."

"Thank you, doctor. Is my blood pressure acceptable?"

"It's a bit high. I will prescribe some tablets to keep it under control."

"Thank you."

"Let's look at your blood test results. Cholesterol is normal, good. What's this?" he said, peering at another sheet. "Hmmm, it seems your PSA level is slightly higher than normal. Yours is 5.1 and it should be lower."

"Sorry doctor, what's PSA?"

"Prostate Specific Antigen. It's an enzyme found in the blood produced by prostate cells. Normal levels of PSA in the blood are small amounts between zero and three, at the most four. Higher levels can be caused by cancer or non-cancerous conditions such as an enlarged prostate. All high readings of PSA should be checked."

"Actually I did want my prostate checked. My father was diagnosed with prostate cancer but luckily his was caught in time."

"Well, Mr Twead, there's no time like the present," he said cheerfully. "Drop your trousers and underpants and lie down on the bed on your side."

Joe gaped at him for a moment, then did as he was told. Nervousness made him attempt humour.

"This is a bit...um...sudden, Doctor!" Then, "Is it going to be painful?"

"Not at all. You may feel a slight discomfort, but that's all. Draw your knees up. That's it. Now lie still."

The good doctor inserted a finger into Joe's rectum and Joe could feel it touching parts of his body that nobody had ever touched before. It wasn't painful, just uncomfortable. The investigation lasted only a few moments.

"Your prostate is slightly enlarged," the doctor announced, snapping off his rubber glove, "so I am going to refer you to a specialist for a digital rectal examination..."

"What do you mean by digital, Doctor?" Joe asked, expecting a high-tech explanation.

"This," he said, holding up his forefinger, "is the digit we use."

"Oh!"

"You will get a letter in the post about the appointment. In the meantime, I want you to see Louise, our respiratory nurse here at the medical centre. She is here on Fridays, so do be a good chap and make an appointment."

"Did you make an appointment?"

"Yes, I see Nurse Louise this Friday."

"Good."

"So what else have you been doing apart from playing with Indy and scaring Karly with fake spiders?"

"She started it!"

"What about your steps? Have you been keeping them up?"

"Yup! Actually, I've set my daily target to thirteen thousand now. It's not too difficult, what with chasing round after Indy. Or Indy chasing after us. I'll email you a little video of us thundering round the house. Cam sneakily filmed us on his phone."

"Right, I'll look forward to that."

(*If any readers would like to view this rather silly video clip, you'll find it here: http://www.victoriatwead.com/running-round-in-circles/ I've password protected it, as it wouldn't make sense to anybody who hasn't read this book. If you type STEPS into the box, it should open.*)

"And LJ needs walking every day. We usually go to the local showground where there's an off-leash park, and LJ has a good run with Karly while I play with Indy in the children's area."

It was true, thirteen thousand steps a day wasn't too difficult a target to reach with a toddler and large dog in the house. And we reached it easily the day we visited Narrabeen lake.

I highly recommend Narrabeen for a visit. It has four sandy beaches, a wonderful shallow lagoon and an extremely picturesque lake. Narrabeen has two very different claims to world fame. It was mentioned in the Beach Boys' song, *Surfin' U.S.A*, and in January 2005, workmen excavating beside a bus shelter found a skeleton, which turned out to be the 4,000-year-old remains of a man. He has become known as Narrabeen Man.

But it isn't surfing or ancient skeletons that spring to my mind when I think of Narrabeen.

I think of ducks.

Menacing ducks.

As we drove into Narrabeen, pelicans sat above us, perched on lamp posts, observing the activity below. Parking was easy and we took Indy's hands.

"We're going to feed the ducks," Karly told her.

My mind jumped back more than thirty-five years to when I used to save our stale bread and took Karly and her brother to feed the ducks near our house in Sussex.

"And you can go on the swings, Indy."

We headed for the nearest playground.

"I can't see any ducks," I commented.

"Ducks! Where are 'oo!" shouted Indy.

It didn't matter. We finished in the playground and carried on walking along the lakeside path. Trees shaded us and twigs snapped underfoot. The flat water of Narrabeen lake sparkled.

"Well, I think we wasted our time bringing bread for the ducks," I said.

"Wait, there's one!" said Karly.

A single white duck emerged from the bushes alongside the path.

"Duck!" said Indy. "'ere y'are, duck-duck!"

She flung a piece of bread towards it. Two-year-olds are not renowned for their overarm throwing ability, and the bread landed just in front of her shoe.

The duck, with a gleam in its eye, charged forward. It snapped up the piece on the ground, then launched itself at the bread Indy still held in her hand.

Indy stepped back. Another duck popped out from nowhere. It was at that moment I realised that the bushes lining the path were alive with ducks.

To our right, leaves parted, and ducks pushed their way out. On the other side, more ducks emerged. A huge army of white ducks was gathering, and they were all waddling in our direction.

Indy froze. Her eyes grew large and her expression changed to one of fear. She turned and bolted. Karly sprang after her daughter, snatching her up in her arms.

"They're just ducks," she said. "They won't hurt you."

But her tone lacked conviction.

She was walking backwards with Indy in her arms, but the ducks were beginning to gather round her feet, matching her speed, jumping up to reach the bread.

"Mum!" she squeaked. "Help!"

"Drop the bread!" I said and tried shooing them away.

Karly emptied the whole bag and Indy dropped her piece. In seconds the bread disappeared in a feeding frenzy of snarling ducks.

Bushes in front of us began to spit out ducks. More ducks appeared from behind trees and dustbins, from everywhere. On the lake, flotillas of ducks were paddling over to us, their formations drawing giant Vs in the water.

I tried to reason with them.

"We don't have any bread!" I yelled. "It's all gone!"

The bread may have been long gone, but the ducks were still coming, clearly convinced we had loaves concealed about our persons.

We turned and started walking quickly back the way we had come, but the ducks were not to be put off. However fast we walked, the ducks kept up. They were always right behind, cackling, heads down, webbed feet pumping as they waddled after us.

"Have you seen behind us?" I panted.

Karly turned her head, and saw what I had just seen. Almost the entire ground behind us was covered by a bobbing sea of white ducks, waddling as fast as they could to keep up with us.

"Mum, run!"

I didn't need telling twice.

We ran.

The ducks soon accepted defeat, apart from a few determined individuals that took off and flapped after us for a few feet. Then they, too, gave up and began to melt away. We didn't stop running until we were back in the car and had closed the doors behind us.

"That was surreal!"

"I've never seen so many ducks!"

"I never knew ducks could be so menacing."

"I hope we haven't given Indy a duck phobia."

I still recommend Narrabeen lake for a lovely, tranquil walk.

But I don't recommend feeding the ducks.

Early mornings were a good time to catch Joe for an online chat because it was his evening. I always awoke around six o'clock when the birds were at their noisiest. I would lie still, listening to the birdsong, tempted to wake Karly so that she, too, could hear the Happy Birthday bird. Then my iPad would ping, and I knew Joe was free for a chat.

"Did you go and see Nurse Louise today?"

"I did."

"What did she say?"

"Well, she made me blow into a mouthpiece which was attached to a machine. She said the machine recorded how much air was left in my lungs after I had exhaled. Then she looked at the printout and said, 'Oh dear, I'm afraid you have COPD.'"

"What on earth is that?"

"Chronic Obstructive Pulmonary Disease."

"Is it serious?"

"That's what I asked. She said it can be but if I manage it properly, with medicines and exercise, I should be fine."

"So it's nothing to worry about?"

Pause.

"Joe?"

"I'm afraid it's not good news."

"Wait a minute! Is there any cure?"

"No. I'm sorry."

"Don't be sorry! But what does that mean? I don't understand!"

"It means I will always struggle to breathe."

"Oh no!"

"I know. Like I said, it's not good news."

"But what exactly is COPD?"

"It's an umbrella term, really. It's the name they give a collection of lung diseases. People with COPD have trouble breathing, due to damage done to their lungs. In my case, the air sacs around the lungs that normally expand and contract during breathing are breaking down, making it hard for me to carry air in and out of my lungs."

"That sounds terrible. Will it get worse?"

"Yes. I'm afraid so. It's up to me to eat properly, and exercise regularly. That will help, so Nurse Louise said. And take all the medicines and inhalers they prescribe for me."

The Happy Birthday bird could have been singing Queen's *Bohemian Rhapsody* and I wouldn't have noticed. This was the worst news.

It was a good thing neither of us could see into the future, because there was more bad stuff heading our way.

FABULOUS SHELLFISH STEW
GUISADO DE MARISCOS

This hearty fish stew is great when you have company. You can do all your preparation beforehand, which leaves you free to spend time with your guests.

Ingredients (serves 4)

A good handful of shell-on prawns

A good handful of shell-off prawns

3-4 large fillets of firm white fish (raw) chopped into 2cm (1in) cubes

Enough mussels (in shells) to allow 3 or 4 for each person

2 tins of chopped tomatoes

1-4 cloves of garlic

Crushed chilli flakes, or chopped fresh chillies – to taste

Mixed herbs - about a heaped teaspoon

1 medium onion, finely chopped

Method

Cover the base of a large saucepan with olive oil, and heat gently.

Chop the onion finely, and cook it slowly until it turns translucent.

Add the garlic, the mixed herbs and chilli.

Stir for a couple of minutes, taking care not to burn it.

Add the tinned tomatoes.

Keep it simmering (stirring occasionally) for about half an hour until it resembles a sloppy sauce.

Pour in about half a litre (1 pint) of water and bring to the boil. As soon as it hits boiling point, add the white fish first, then five minutes later, all the shellfish.

Bring back to the boil, then lower the heat to simmer for another 5 minutes.

Serve with plenty of crusty bread.

12

GIVE ME YOUR BLOOD

Australia's homes and gardens are packed with wildlife. One only needs to know where to look. Some examples one may not wish to encounter, like the deadly funnel-web spider who hides himself in tunnels, waiting for his dinner to walk past.

In the hot summer months, male funnel-webs often wander, searching for a mate. Unfortunately, they are attracted to water and frequently fall into swimming pools where they can survive for many hours. It's not a good idea to stand on one with bare feet, and should one choose to rescue a submerged spider, beware. Funnel-webs defend themselves vigorously if threatened. Their fangs are large, and the toxin they deliver will probably send you to hospital, if not the morgue.

Much more welcome is the aptly-named blue-tongue.

One day I was working in my lair when I heard the Margarets sending out frantic alarm calls. They were clearly agitated.

"Come and see!" called Cam, who had also been disturbed by the excited Margarets.

I walked round and found the cause of the excitement. An amazing, prehistoric creature squatted in the sunshine in front of the Margarets' run, his long blue tongue flicking as he tested the air.

"What is it?"

"It's a blue-tongue, a kind of skink."

What an amazing creature he was! The word 'skink' comes from *Scincidae*, which means shiny-scaled, and this skink's scales positively gleamed in the sun. The blue-tongue didn't seem at all put out by my scrutiny as I stared at his large body, stumpy arms and legs and diamond-shaped head.

The Margarets didn't trust this visitor, but in spite of his size (blue-tongues often reach sixty centimeters, or two feet in length) he wouldn't have done them any harm. Blue-tongues feed primarily on plant matter, beetles, slugs and snails and although their teeth are ferocious-looking, they are blunt. Indeed, blue-tongues only bite under extreme provocation, and their primary defence strategy is bluff.

They may hiss and open their mouths wide to reveal a shocking pink mouth edged with teeth, contrasting with a blue tongue. But usually they just sit quietly, even allowing humans to pick them up. Small wonder that they are popular pets. Blue-tongues can live to be twenty years old and I imagine this particular fellow had called this garden home long before my family moved in, certainly long before Indy was born.

The Margarets alerted me to another reptile stalking their coop. I was alone at the time, and when I investigated, at first I saw nothing. The Margarets were so upset that they had leapt up onto their roosting perch, peering through a high, meshed window whilst sending out hysterical alarm calls.

And then I saw it, probably at the same time as it saw me. I caught the movement, and just for a second, I thought it was an enormously thick snake. But it wasn't, it was a goanna, or monitor lizard. It was on the ground not far from the coop and we eyed each other.

And it was big.

Commonly, goannas average around 140cm (four and a half feet) in length and are great opportunists. They'll eat just about anything, so the Margarets were justifiably upset by this one's presence, although they were probably too large a meal for this particular goanna to tackle.

I felt quite nervous, but the goanna was even more wary of me and clambered up the nearest tree. It was the same colour as the bark, and I did attempt to photograph it in case I was doubted. Still nobody believed me about the existence of the Happy Birthday bird so I felt I needed proof. Unfortunately, that photo no longer exists for reasons I'll explain later.

Each day the temperature rose a little as Christmas drew closer. In the UK, the days were chilly and brief, but in New South Wales it was midsummer, and hot. It was a relief to take LJ for bush walks where the trees and plants blocked out the sun and kept the temperature cool.

Unfortunately, this damp, dark environment is paradise for other Australian wildlife hazards.

My daughter worked from home, which fitted in nicely with looking after Indy. I wasn't totally sure what she did, something to do with co-ordinating labour and materials.

"Let's go for a bush walk when Indy wakes up," she said one day, stretching. "I need a break and LJ will appreciate a walk."

We strolled down the street, then cut between two houses, reaching rough ground, a firebreak separating the houses from the bush. These firebreaks are omnipresent, the gap in vegetation vital for slowing the progress of a potential bushfire.

Beyond the firebreak, the Australian bush was dense. Palm fronds and creepers knitted together overhead, and scrubby plants grew in all directions alongside the winding trail we walked along.

Mosquitoes were so plentiful that they drifted in little clouds, their high-pitched whine unbearable as they flew round our heads.

"Did you bring any insect repellent?" I asked.

"No!"

"Me neither."

We were being eaten alive.

"Okay, let's get out. This isn't fun."

Rubbing our bites, we hurried out and back into the sunshine, then headed home. However, mosquitoes weren't the only things determined to suck our blood.

"Do you mind watching Indy while I make a few important work calls?" Karly asked when we returned. "I need to speak to a new contractor I'm taking on."

"Of course not," I said, and she disappeared into her office.

Indy and I settled down to playing mermaids, Indy's favourite game of the moment. It involved wearing tiaras and 'swimming' in the ocean (actually the wood floor) and was perhaps a little more gymnastic than I would have chosen.

As we swam past Karly's office, I could hear her speaking.

"So you've been allocated another P5? Wonderful. ... Yes, yes, that's good to hear."

I couldn't help admiring her pleasant, confident businesslike telephone manner, a sharp contrast to my own. I don't like the phone at all, and my sentences always come out wrong.

But it didn't last. Suddenly Karly's voice changed, and I sat up in mid-stroke.

"Nanny, swim!" said Indy at my elbow. But something wasn't right in the office. Karly had begun jumbling her words and was speaking so fast I could hardly understand what she said.

"I believe you have ENOUGH GASKETS. Butyoumight, aaaggh need SOME MORE RISERS!" I heard the phone slammed down, then ...

"MUM!"

White-faced, she nearly tripped over us swimmers as she burst out of her office and headed to the kitchen at a super-fast hobble. I grabbed Indy and followed her.

"Karly? Are you okay? Whatever is the matter?"

"Aaaaaghhh! LOOK!"

"What?"

"Where's the salt? Quick!"

I looked down to see where Karly was pointing. Two dark-red, shiny, pulsating leeches were fastened to the back of her leg, feasting.

"I felt my leg throbbing a bit when I was talking on the phone, so I glanced down and saw them!"

We were aware that the neighbourhood bush is home to leeches because my son-in-law picked up a beauty once before when he took LJ for a walk. For this reason, when we returned this time, we had checked ourselves over.

No leeches.

We can't have been sufficiently thorough, but I guess the hungry leeches were probably too small to notice at the time. Twenty minutes or so later they were well into their blood banquet and had swollen significantly.

We doused the pair of parasites liberally with salt. They shrivelled and fell off.

"Oh," I said looking at the little shrunken worms on the floor. "I should have taken a photo for my next book while they were still huge and feasting."

I won't repeat my daughter's response. She used vocabulary I certainly never taught her.

In Britain, Joe sat in a consulting room at the hospital, nervously waiting for the prostate specialist, Mr Reid, to speak. A nurse appeared.

"I just need a blood sample, Mr Twead," she said and plunged a syringe into his arm.

She labeled it carefully. All the while, Mr Reid was studying a computer screen in the background.

"Right, Mr Twead, pull down your trousers and underpants and lie on your side on the bed," said the nurse. "Good. Now pull your knees up to your chest. That's it. He's ready for you now, Mr Reid."

Joe faced the wall and couldn't see what was coming, but could guess. As Mr Reid began his examination, it occurred to Joe that anybody with a medical qualification now had carte blanche to insert his or her finger where daylight never reached.

"Hmmmmm," said Mr Reid, having a good feel. Then Joe heard him pulling off his surgical gloves. "Right, I've finished, you can pull up your trousers now."

Joe stood up, adjusting his clothing.

"Everything okay, Mr Reid?"

"Your prostate is slightly enlarged, but we'll know more soon. We'll be in touch when we have the results of your blood test."

Joe left the hospital, and tried hard not to worry about the verdict that would arrive in the mail.

He didn't have to wait many days before a letter dropped on the doormat.

"What did it say?" I asked.

It was early morning in Australia and the birds were in full voice. As always, the Happy Birthday bird was adding his song to the concert.

"Well, it seems my PSA level is 9."

"That's not good, is it?"

"No. It looks like I'm going to need a prostate biopsy."

"Oh dear, that doesn't sound very nice. What's involved?"

"Well, it's quite interesting really. They'll give me a mild local anaesthetic, then they'll insert a needle and take ten carefully selected samples, in a circle. Then these will be investigated under a microscope in a laboratory."

"And what will that tell them?"

"It'll show whether my prostate is cancerous or not."

"Oh, I'm sure it won't be!"

"Let's hope."

"When will they do this test?"

"Very soon. Straight after Christmas, I think."

Christmas was upon us. School choirs, the kids dressed in shorts and summer dresses, sang carols in the shopping malls. Cam brought home a beautiful tree and set it up in the living room. We all helped decorate the tree, then Cam lifted Indy up to place the fairy on the top.

"We've got everybody coming here for Christmas," said Karly. "I'm going to make it as English as possible with roast turkey, sprouts, and all the trimmings, but we'll also barbecue prawns and things, the Aussie way."

"Sounds wonderful!"

"Yes, we always have a few drinks and end up in the pool at Christmas. Oh, and by the way…"

"Yes?"

"Apart from immediate family and kids, we've all agreed not to give presents. There are too many of us, and we decided it would just get out of hand."

"Oh, that's a good decision. I'm relieved because I had no idea about what to get anybody."

Christmas Eve arrived. Indy left out carrots for the reindeer and a hefty glass of red wine for Santa. In the morning, the carrots and wine had gone, but a bulging pillowcase stuffed with presents waited on her bed.

Indy unwrapped and examined each with excitement, but it was obvious which was her favourite. As she pulled out a glove puppet from the paper, her blue eyes were as large as Karly's serving platters.

"Noddy!" she squealed.

Big Ears was revealed next.

"Big Weirs!"

Then Sly and Gobo, the bad goblins, joined the group. Indy loved them all but Noddy was her favourite.

More presents were piled under the Christmas tree.

"We'll open them when everybody arrives later," Karly told Indy.

But Indy didn't hear, she was too busy showing Noddy her freckle.

Christmas Day was a blur of kisses, wrapping paper, food, drink, chatter, sunshine and laughter. Indy solemnly showed Noddy every present she opened.

And the adult *No Presents* rule?

Absolutely nobody seemed to have heeded that, and mountains of gifts were unwrapped amidst squeals of delight.

Apart from toys, Indy was presented with her first bed. It was made to look like a pink Lamborghini, and probably satisfied her daddy's passion for flashy cars more than her own. I hoped it would prove easy to assemble. I'd heard that Indy's play kitchen had taken Cam (a carpenter by trade) and a cousin (a qualified kitchen fitter) two days to put up the year before.

Finally, Indy was put to bed, tucked up between Noddy and Big Weirs. It had been a wonderful, memorable, family Christmas. I wished that Joe had been there. I also felt sad at the thought that my time in Australia was limited. Apart from visits, and Internet time, I wouldn't see Indy grow. I wouldn't be there to be part of her future birthdays, Christmases and childhood milestones.

And what if Indy ever became a big sister? I would miss that little one growing up, too. Karly and Cam said they didn't feel ready for a new baby, after the devastating miscarriage they'd suffered, but maybe they *would* feel ready one day? The tiny embryo that had died before it was born would never be forgotten, but perhaps that pain would fade someday.

But today had been a very special day filled with love, laughter and generosity. Perhaps my favourite gift was a ticket to a night concert of 60s music held in the open air at Taronga Zoo, overlooking Sydney harbour and the illuminated Opera House. Between numbers, one could hear the lions roar.

And Karly was very happy too. As one of her presents, I'd made her three Lie-In tokens that she could cash in at will. I promised to look after Indy while she and Cam had a few extra hours in bed.

New Year followed Christmas, marked with another family event. From the comfort of the living room, we watched the fireworks explode over Sydney harbour and welcomed in the new year, 2015.

Did I say comfort? Well, not everybody was comfortable because, in my honour, the family had decided the evening should have a Spanish theme. The wearing of red underwear was compulsory. In Spain, wearing red underwear on New Year's Eve is thought to bring luck for the coming year. However, it isn't always easy to buy red underpants for men, and I know one particular member of the party (who shall remain nameless) had reluctantly squeezed himself into a pair of his wife's, much to all our amusement.

To complete the Spanish theme, we all attempted to swallow twelve grapes, one at each stroke of the clock at midnight. As usual, I failed, choking on the seventh.

What would the new year bring? I hoped it would bring health back to Joe. Only time would tell.

PRAWNS WITH GARLIC AND LEMON

Fresh prawns are always best. Avoid using frozen peeled prawns if you can because they will probably be very watery and need cooking longer.

Ingredients (per person)

A good handful or two of fresh raw or part-cooked prawns, de-veined. Leave the tails on for presentation if you like

Half a clove of garlic, peeled and very finely sliced or crushed

Tablespoon or so of unsalted butter

A squirt of freshly squeezed lemon juice

A pinch or two of paprika

Method

Sprinkle the raw prawns with the paprika.

Melt the butter in a frying pan and add the garlic.

Stir for 1 minute, but don't let the garlic burn or it will become bitter.

Add the prawns and cook (turning once) for just a couple of minutes until they turn pink.

Remove the prawns and pop them onto a plate.

Turn the heat up on the pan which should still contain the butter and garlic, and squeeze in the lemon juice.

Cook for 30 - 45 seconds

Drizzle the sauce all over the prawns.

13

HOPS AND SPIKES

One of the many things I adore about Australia is the outdoorsy life that is the norm for the population. Public sports fields, or 'ovals', are rarely empty. They are used by everybody, whether for family keep fit sessions, organised events, joggers, dog walkers or youths who simply want to kick a ball around. Nature reserves abound and visitors are welcome.

Eating outside is standard. A barbecue is an event in England, but in Australia the barbie is merely an extension of the kitchen, and used all year round. Councils provide free gas or electric barbecues at beauty spots, lookout points, parks and nature reserves, and they are well used.

"Hey Mum, let's have breakfast at the wildflower park," Karly suggested one morning.

Of course I readily agreed and we packed a hamper with bacon, eggs and bread rolls.

The wildflower reserve we visited was green and lush, with clearings offering children's climbing frames, shaded seating and barbecues. We dumped our hamper on a table and joined Indy in the children's play area. Indy has inherited her father's daredevil gene so we needed to supervise her climbing. When she reached the top of the frame, she pointed at something over our heads.

"Wobbly!"

I looked blankly at Karly, hoping for a translation, then in the direction of Indy's pointing finger.

Bouncing over to our seating area was a wallaby. Remembering that we had left food unattended, I made my way over, but I doubted that the wallaby would be interested in our breakfast ingredients.

For me, it was a magic moment. The wallaby was unafraid, and allowed me to come extremely close. Indy came running up, and still the wallaby stood its ground, as though aware we meant it no harm.

"Wobbly! Look!"

"I don't know if wallabies are interested in freckles," said Karly, approaching from behind.

But the wallaby was polite. He solemnly studied Indy's wrist for a few moments, then slowly hopped away into the bush.

Joe entered the hospital and found the Acute Services Division of the Urological Department. This was not an appointment he relished. Kindly nurses divested him of his clothes, exchanging them for a gown that covered his front, but left his back woefully bare.

"I must have looked very fetching in my socks, slippers and gown," he remarked later.

He was shown into a darkened room where flickering green computer screens served as the only illumination. It was all very space-age and could easily have belonged in a scene from *Star Trek*. A male voice floated out of the darkness.

"Do lie on the bed on your side, Mr Twead."

Joe's eyes had not yet adapted to the dark and he feared that, should he move, he might step on something expensive. Also, he was not too enthusiastic about the procedure he was about to endure.

Best I buy myself time with a little meaningless conversation, he thought.

"Um, thank you um...Mr..." said Joe, searching the dark for the owner of the voice.

"Reid," said he from just behind, making Joe jump.

"Ah, Mr Reid! Fine room you have here. All these marvelous computer monitors and ..."

"Thank you. Now be a good chap and lie on the bed."

Joe was reluctant, but his arm was seized firmly by a nurse who appeared from nowhere.

"I'm Anna," she said, steering Joe towards the bed.

Generally speaking, I believe hospital beds come in two sizes. The ward bed can be machine adjusted and is fairly comfortable. The other is found in doctors' surgeries, operating theatres and diagnostic rooms, much like the one Joe was in now. These beds are more like boards and are elevated, narrow and extremely uncomfortable.

Joe patted the bed and ran his hand over it.

"It's ... um... very ..."

"Up you get," urged nurse Anna, ignoring his reluctance. "Now, lie on your side with your back towards me. That's it. Bring your knees up to your chest. Don't worry, I know it probably feels like a knife edge, but you won't fall off the bed."

Joe doubted that but eventually he found the position that seemed to satisfy her. He lay perfectly still, convinced that the slightest movement would send him crashing to the floor. With a mighty effort, he clenched his muscles, not daring to move. His entire concentration was centred on staying on the bed, rather than on the activity behind him.

"Right," said Mr Reid, "I am now going to administer the anaesthetic which will sting a little, but that's all."

He inserted something narrow into Joe's rear, and Joe heard a click. He felt a brief but mild pain, then nothing.

"We are now going to take the samples from around your prostate," said Mr Reid.

The nurse and doctor set to work collecting the material for the lab. Apart from clicks, buzzes and a spattering of medical terminology intelligible only to the medics, Joe was aware of very little else.

Half an hour later, Anna helped him off the knife edge. The procedure was over.

"Now, Mr Twead," she said, "you must urinate before you leave. Please don't be concerned if there is a little blood, that's normal. We need to make sure that your waterworks are okay and that you feel no pain when you pee. Take these two tablets, please."

"What are they for?"

"In case you picked up a little infection during the procedure. It's highly unlikely but we must take precautions. Now would you like a nice cup of tea?"

Joe knew this was a ploy to encourage his waterworks but the cup of tea was welcome nonetheless. Anna's ruse succeeded and he soon felt the need. He entered the adjoining bathroom and nervously began to do what came naturally.

"Nurse!"

"Yes, Mr Twead?"

"Is this normal?"

"What, Mr Twead?"

"There's no wee, just blood!"

"Do you feel any pain, Mr Twead?"

"No."

"Well, then all is well."

"But there's so much blood!"

"Don't worry, that's quite normal and it will only last a few weeks before disappearing altogether."

Emerging from the toilet, Joe imagined he would be a whiter shade of pale and require a blood transfusion. But Nurse Anna had heard and seen it all before and continued as if nothing untoward had happened.

"We will write to your doctor who will prescribe more tablets for you."

"Thank you. When will I know the results of the biopsy?"

"That will take some time but we will contact you."

Shopping malls in Australia are excellent. Although not as decadently glitzy as the ones I remember in Bahrain, in the Middle East, where Joe and I taught for a year, they were far better than those in our corner of Spain. The choice of merchandise seemed endless, especially to me. I am not a natural shopper, so I never pined for sophisticated malls in Spain, but I enjoyed the novelty in Australia.

One particular weekend, we were browsing the shops, when we happened to pass a pet shop. In the window were two tiny kittens. Karly, Indy and I ground to a halt. What female can resist kittens? Meanwhile, Cam marched on, oblivious, and had to double back and search when he discovered he'd lost his entire family.

Pasted on the glass was a sign.

Can you give us a good home?

Karly and I stared at the kittens, then at each other, then back at the kittens. One was a comical little thing with black and white patches that reminded me of Felicity in El Hoyo. The other was a tiny tabby with wonderful stripes.

We read the notice which explained that these were rescued kittens and that the pet shop was displaying them for the day, on behalf of the local animal rescue centre, in the hope that somebody would come along, fall in love with them and take them home.

Yes, we'd come along and fallen in love with them. Well, with one in particular.

"Look at the tabby, isn't she beautiful?"

"She reminds me of Fortnum," said Karly.

As children, my son and daughter had a kitten each. We'd named them Fortnum and Mason after the posh shop in London. Fortie, the tabby, was sweet-natured and delicate, but with the heart of a lion. She was the one who kept neighbouring cats at bay, while her big brother, Mason, hid quivering under the couch.

"She's gorgeous! Indy, would you like a kitten?" Karly asked her daughter.

Silly question.

"Karly, are you seriously thinking of adopting a kitten today?" I asked.

"Yes! Why not?"

"What, just like that?" I asked, open-mouthed. "What about LJ? This kitten would be a tiny snack for him."

"He'll be okay."

"But what about Cam?"

"What about me?" said my son-in-law, appearing from behind, having finally found us.

"Hey, Cam, I think we should adopt this kitten, the tabby one. What do you think?"

"Yes, why not? Go for it. As long as it's never allowed in our bedroom."

I stared at them both. I'm not impetuous by nature and I like to have a good think before I make any decision.

Not so my daughter and son-in-law.

Many of their major decisions are made on the spur of the moment. The kitten, however, was scrumptious and I was very excited.

"Really?" I breathed.

"Yes, really!" said Cam, laughing at my reaction.

"Good! That's settled then. I'll go and find an assistant," said Karly, turning away.

As she spoke, an assistant materialised and unlocked the window. We watched as she reached inside and picked up the stripy ball of fluff.

"Hi!" said my daughter, smiling. "Could we talk to you about that kitten, please? We think we'd like to adopt it."

"Oh! I'm so sorry, but that customer over there has expressed an interest. She asked to see it with a view to adopting it."

Hugely deflated, we watched in dismay as a lady took the kitten and stroked it.

"What about the black and white one?" asked Cam.

"No," said Karly sadly, "I wanted the tabby one."

"Well, she hasn't made her mind up yet," whispered the assistant who had left the lady to bond with the kitten. "It may be worth waiting."

Cam went off to pick up some shopping while Karly, Indy and I waited. We feigned interest in the canaries and goldfish, but it was the woman with the kitten we were watching the whole time. She examined every inch of it and held it up high for scrutiny. Then she stroked it again, while it squirmed and wriggled to be free.

"She's phoned her husband," the assistant told us. "She wants his opinion."

The woman's husband arrived, and together they examined the kitten. But by then, the kitten had lost patience and had became a twisting pin-cushion of spikes.

At last, the woman handed the kitten back to the assistant. We watched, breath held. Were they taking the kitten home?

The assistant spoke to the couple, and then walked over to us, smiling.

"The other customers felt she wasn't right for them. They said they didn't connect with her. She's yours if you still want her."

"Oh yes!" said Karly, holding out her arms.

The instant she held the feisty kitten, a miraculous thing happened. The tiny cat relaxed. She sheathed her claws and transformed from a ball of needle-sharp spikes to a purring ball of soft down. Karly crouched down so that Indy could stroke it too. The kitten sighed, closed her eyes and purred herself to sleep.

"Well," said the assistant, "look at that!"

"Are we having her?" asked Cam, returning.

"Yes," said the assistant. "I think this kitten has chosen her home."

Of course we weren't allowed just to take the kitten there and then. Endless forms had to be filled out, papers signed and a vet's appointment made for a final health check. Then Karly and Cam bought food, toys and kitty litter. While all these matters were being settled, I was delighted to see the little black and white kitten had also found a new home.

"What shall we call her?" asked Cam when we finally drove home with her.

"What about Banjo?" suggested Karly. "LJ is named after a hotel in Jindabyne, where we met," she reminded me, "and Banjo's is another Inn there."

I was trying not to think about LJ at home. His favourite toy of the moment was a squeaky ferret which he had ripped to pieces. This kitten was far smaller than the toy ferret. In fact she was barely the size of LJ's paw.

"Great idea," said Cam. "Indy, can you say 'Banjo'?"

"Bandsaw," said Indy, clear as a bell.

"Say 'Banjo', Indy."

"Bandsaw."

"No, 'Ban-jo'."

"Bandsaw."

The kitten was purring loudly. We all looked at each other.

"Why not? That's a perfect name," we all agreed.

Bandsaw didn't offer an opinion. She was fast asleep.

COURGETTE (ZUCCHINI) AND CHEESE BALLS

BOLITAS DE CALABACÍN Y QUESO

These are simply courgette and cheese balls, covered in breadcrumbs and fried.

Ingredients

One medium courgette (zucchini) peeled and grated

3 eggs, 1 for coating

100-125g (4oz) of grated cheese

Fistful of chopped fresh parsley

Salt and pepper

Soft cheese for filling

Breadcrumbs for mixing

Breadcrumbs for coating

Oil for frying

Method

In a bowl, beat two of the eggs.

Stir in the grated cheese, parsley and a little salt and pepper.

Stir in the grated courgette.

Add a few heaped tablespoons of breadcrumbs until the mix is quite easy to form into balls – wet your hands first if it helps it stop sticking.

Use about a rounded teaspoon of the mixture and form a flat, round shape. Pop a small amount of the soft cheese in the centre and gently form the courgette mixture around it until it is completely enveloped.

Set the balls on a tray and pop into the fridge for at least an hour.

Heat oil in a frying pan, deep or shallow, it doesn't matter.

Lightly whisk the last egg and put some more breadcrumbs into another bowl.

Dip each ball into the egg, then breadcrumbs, and set aside.

Fry in batches until golden brown and serve hot.

14

FOUR, EIGHT AND TWO

I seemed to be the only one concerned about how LJ would react to our new kitten, Bandsaw. When we carried in the box he had a good sniff, then pawed it expectantly. Bandsaw's eyes grew to the size of green frisbees and her fur stood on end.

"I'm going to shut him in the garden," said Karly. "He can see her through the window, but we won't introduce them yet."

We stroked Bandsaw and set her on the floor to explore. But it was all too much for her and she shot under the sideboard and refused to come out. But the shyness didn't last very long. Leaving her to adjust in her own time, we ignored her, and gradually she came out to explore the room, always bolting back to her hiding place at the first hint of danger.

After a few days, she had gained enough confidence to visit every room in the house. She knew her way to the laundry where her food, water and litter tray were kept, and she enjoyed sitting on the windowsill and making faces at LJ outside.

And she already had her favourite sleeping spots. One was on the lap of Indy's big teddy bear. Another was on Karly's laptop keyboard.

"Oh for goodness sake," I heard Karly exclaim. "Bandsaw, if I'd wanted to send an email saying 'yyyyyyyyy tghhhhhh' I'd have sent it myself."

But, of course, her favourite spot was on Cam and Karly's bed.

"Bandsaw, get off the bed!" I heard Cam say impatiently when he got home from work every night. "You're not allowed in the bedroom!"

Naturally, she didn't move and just lay there blinking sleepily. So she was forcibly evicted, but that only made her more determined. By the end of the second week, she had worked out that if she sneaked into the bedroom very late at night and hid, she could later climb onto the bed and spend the whole night with the sleeping humans, who were too deeply asleep to notice her.

"What's Bandsaw doing in here?" asked Cam in the morning.

"I don't know, she must have got in," Karly mumbled.

"I thought we'd closed the bedroom door?"

"So did I."

"But she's not allowed in the bedroom."

"I know. You'd better tell her that."

Cats have an unerring sense of what they shouldn't do, and glory in getting their own way.

As for poor LJ, well, he was no match for the kitten either.

Cam and Karly introduced them, slowly and calmly, always making sure that Bandsaw was never in any danger, and that she had places to escape to, like under furniture, should she need to. They let him sniff her. He was fascinated, but her fur stood on end, and she hissed at him. Undeterred, he pushed his big face closer. Out shot a lightning-fast paw, all claws unsheathed.

LJ retreated, a valuable lesson learned.

Gradually dog and cat became accustomed to each other and shared their home peaceably. The No-Bedroom rule was dismissed as unworkable, and Bandsaw became Indy's best friend.

And so, family life continued.

One day, Cam decided that he'd lay new wood floors throughout the house. As usual, the decision was instant and he began work immediately. First, he needed to jackhammer up all the old quarry tiles in the entrance hall. I cannot begin to describe the noise and dust that caused. Bandsaw hid in the most distant part of the house, and LJ stayed in the garden.

Wise dog.

Next, the carpet needed to come up, both in the dining room and Indy's playroom. Every nail had to be pulled out by hand, and there were hundreds. Karly and I busied ourselves by pulling out nails, trying to keep on top of the dust, and ensuring that Indy's feet never touched the ground. Not an easy task with an active toddler.

At last Cam declared the preparations complete and consulted the company who were going to lay the new floor. No, the floor was not level enough, they said.

So poor Cam went back to work.

Finally, the floor was laid, and it looked stunning, well worth all the effort.

Cam, like Becky's Gresh, is the type of person who has to be doing jobs. Karly and I love to sit in the sun, or read, but Cam likes projects. The result of this is that their home is beautiful and is improved upon every month. And sometimes, his projects are very good for me.

I will explain.

I finally plucked up the courage to drive Karly's car. It was much bigger than anything I'd driven before, and driving on Australian roads was new to me. Nevertheless, I soon got to grips with it and often borrowed the car. Perhaps I became over confident, because one day, as I reversed it down the steep drive and into the street, I misjudged the space, and drove the car over the corner of the front lawn. The big tyres gouged great lines out of the grass. Driving off to correct the mistake made it even worse. It had rained recently and the mud was churned up. It looked terrible and I was mortified.

"Don't worry," said Karly, "Cam won't mind."

I knew he wouldn't but he worked so hard all day, and then laboured on the house every spare moment he had. I really didn't want to add to his workload.

When he arrived home, I rushed down to apologise.

"I'm so sorry! It looks a real mess…"

"Doesn't matter one bit," he said.

"But it looks terrible!"

"I was going to dig that bit up anyway. That was my project for this evening. There's something wrong with the drainage there, the water doesn't seem to run away, so I was going to investigate it."

"You're kidding me?"

"No, really. You've done me a favour, you started digging it up for me!"

Time was screeching past, a fact that tugged at my emotions. I looked forward to being with Joe again and catching up with the village gossip. I wondered if Geronimo and the postlady, Valentina, had patched up their differences. And I wondered whether Lola Ufarte was behaving herself.

On the other hand, being with the family and spending time with little Indy these last months had been amazing. And I'd had breakfast with wallabies hopping around, and typed to the sound of cockatoos screeching and kookaburras laughing. Leaving all this would be hard.

February was my final month in Australia and it arrived too fast. I had always bemoaned the fact that my birthday fell in the middle of February, probably the coldest and most depressing month of the year in England. For the first time, my birthday celebrations would take place in summer.

"What do you want to do for your birthday?" asked my daughter.

"Oh, nothing really. No fuss."

When one reaches one's sixties, birthdays don't seem so important.

But Karly planned a lovely day. In the morning, we had breakfast at a beach cafe and swam lengths of the ocean pool at Mona Vale. At teatime, we met up with family members at another beach. We sat at a picnic table amidst balloons and gifts, and drank sparkling wine and gin and tonics. Karly made me a Tim Tam cheesecake as a birthday cake, but I was relieved she hadn't tried to cram sixty candles onto it. For those, like me, who hadn't encountered Tim Tams before, they are very similar to the British chocolate Penguin.

To me, it all seemed deliciously exotic. How fabulous to be able to frequent so many different beautiful beaches, so close to home. A staggering 80% of the population of Australia lives along the coast, and car parking is rarely a problem. Lifeguards keep watch during the swimming season and flags warn swimmers and surfers of dangerous currents. Picnic tables and seating, plus barbecues if you want them, are all provided. Australians take all this, and their wonderful climate, for granted, but for me it seemed like paradise.

"Seagirls!" cried Indy, breaking into my thoughts.

White seagulls screeched overhead, then landed close, watching to see if we had any scraps on offer.

"One more card to open," said Karly. "It's from me and Cam."

I opened it, smiling. Inside the card was a confirmation of booking letter. I looked at it, puzzled.

"We've booked a weekend at The Entrance," said Karly.

"How lovely!" I said. "Um, a weekend at the entrance of what exactly?"

"It's a place," somebody explained. "A town, a seaside resort called The Entrance."

"How nice, but what a strange name for a town," I remarked. "I wonder why it's called that?"

I had become accustomed to seeing Australian towns named after British towns, like Liverpool, Newcastle and Aberdeen. Also, there were many towns with aboriginal sounding names like Kangy Angy and Wagga Wagga, which apparently means 'the place of many crows'. There is Boing Boing which means 'mosquitoes buzzing' and Humpybong which is in Queensland. There is even a town named 1770.

Poring over a map one day, I'd amused myself at how many comical, often rather rude sounding, place names I could find. I lost count of how many Knobs, like Chinaman's Knob, I found, but there were others, far ruder, that also appealed to my childish sense of humour. But maybe my favourite place-name was simply called Nowhere Else.

"The Entrance is surrounded by water on three sides," Cam explained. "It gets its name because it's also the entrance to Tuggerah Lakes, a big lagoon."

"And they have daily pelican feeding," added Karly.

"Peliquins!" said Indy.

"Sounds marvelous!" I said. "Can't wait to see the peliquins being fed!"

We stayed chatting, watching the waves tumbling up the sand. It was a birthday like no other I had ever had.

Only Karly may have had reservations about the fun we had that day. As she sat on the grass playing with Indy, something bit her. It was most likely a bad-tempered spider that objected to her proximity. Two fang marks were clearly visible and her leg swelled up. We never saw the attacker.

Yes, Australia is paradise, but not without its hazards. At work, Cam once picked up a metre-long pipe, tilted it, and a highly venomous red-bellied black snake slid out and landed on his feet. He was chatting with his boss at the time, and the pair of them fled in different directions faster than speeding bullets.

Of course not all Australian snakes are deadly, and neither are all the spiders dangerous. The huntsman, for instance, is huge, and for those with a fear of spiders, it's the stuff of nightmares. However, it's not aggressive, nor poisonous.

Unfortunately, huntsman spiders have caused many a car crash. They seem to enjoy living in cars and are known to pop up unannounced, resulting in shocked drivers losing control.

Somebody once told me that his father had a 'pet' huntsman that lived in his car, on the back parcel shelf. He named the spider Harold. All was well until his son-in-law borrowed the car one day and wasn't told about the squatter. As they drove along, Harold reared up, probably just to say hello. The son-in-law caught sight of Harold in his rear view mirror and drove into the nearest tree. Neither spider nor driver were hurt, but the car was a write-off.

Karly told me about the first huntsman she ever encountered. She and Cam were living with Cam's parents at the time. As they settled down to sleep one night, Karly was just closing her eyes when she spotted a spider on the ceiling in the far corner of the room. She sat up.

"Cam," she whispered, "there's a spider up there."

"Oh yes, I see it. It's only a small one, go to sleep."

"I can't. I can't sleep knowing it's there."

"But it's tiny! It won't do you any harm."

"I know, but I can't relax knowing it's there. Cam, please, *please* get rid of it."

Cam sighed, knowing there would be no peace until he removed it. He got out of bed and walked over to the corner of the room and looked up.

"I can't reach it. Honestly, it's tiny. Really not worth worrying about."

"There's a can of insect spray on the hall table..."

Cam shrugged his shoulders and stomped off to get it. He returned, and watched by Karly, he sprayed the hapless spider which dropped to the floor and died.

"There," said Cam. "It's dead. Can we go to sleep now?"

He looked over to Karly, who was still sitting up in bed. Then his expression froze as something caught his eye. Above Karly's head, over the headboard, was a framed picture. Probably disturbed by the activity, or by the spray, a huntsman spider came marching out from behind it.

Karly caught his glance over her head and followed his line of sight.

"Aaaah!" she shrieked, and executed a perfect take off, leaping out of bed and the bedroom in one giant bound.

How long had it been lurking behind the picture, just above their heads? They didn't know. Maybe days, or weeks. If they hadn't sprayed the other spider, they would have carried on sharing the bedroom with the huntsman. Karly still shudders at the memory of it.

The long weekend at The Entrance was wonderful and gave me another glimpse of Australia. We stayed in a spacious Airbnb apartment with ocean views. We hired a little boat and chugged around the lagoon enjoying the sea air and views.

In the afternoon we watched the pelicans fly in and congregate on the purpose-built water-front pelican feeding platform. Twenty years ago, the staff at the local fish shop threw scraps for the pelicans. Word soon spread amongst the pelican colonies and more and more of the seabirds arrived. By 1996, the town realised that it had a major tourist attraction on its hands and built the Pelican Plaza expressly for feeding these giant, majestic, almost prehistoric, birds. Thanks to continued donations from fish shops, volunteers and sponsors, these pelicans are fed whole fresh fish 365 days a year, given daily health checks, and the public is enchanted and educated by the spectacle.

I watched and cherished every moment of little Indy staring at the 'peliquins', her blonde curls stirring lightly in the sea breeze.

My time in Australia was nearly over.

TIM TAM CHEESECAKE

For those, like me, who hadn't encountered Tim Tams before, they are very similar to the British chocolate Penguin. I see no reason why Penguins couldn't be used instead.

Ingredients

350g (12 oz) Tim Tams

80g (3oz) butter, melted

375g (13oz) cream cheese, cubed and softened

½ cup caster sugar

1 tsp vanilla essence

1 cup thickened cream

3 tsp gelatine powder

¼ cup boiling water

200g (7oz) white chocolate, melted but cooled

Method

Place 250g (9oz) of Tim Tams in a blender and whizz into fine crumbs.

Add the butter and combine.

Press the mixture into a spring-form baking pan and refrigerate 30 minutes.

Beat the cream cheese, sugar and vanilla with an electric mixer until smooth, then beat in the cream.

Dissolve the gelatine in boiling water, stir in with the white chocolate.

Roughly chop the remaining biscuits, add to the cream cheese mixture, then pour over the Tim Tam base.

Cover and refrigerate until set.

Recipe from

http://www.bestrecipes.com.au/

15

A STORM

"Have you packed?" asked Joe.

"Yes, I'm very glad I took the big red case because I seem to have acquired stuff. I had to sit on it to close it. Indy helped."

"Can you believe that three months has shot past already?"

"Nope."

"In two days, we'll both be back in El Hoyo."

"I can't wait!" I said.

It was true, I couldn't wait to see Joe and the village again, but I was also leaving a large, jagged piece of my heart behind in Australia.

"This is probably the last time we'll talk until we see each other in Spain."

"Safe journey. Can't wait to give you a big hug."

"You too. Safe trip. See you at the airport."

It was March 2nd, 2015, the day I was returning to Spain. We left home in bright sunshine, but as Cam drove us towards Sydney airport, the sky was darkening ominously. Australia's weather is often dramatic, and this day would prove to be no exception. Great clouds like sooty avalanches rolled in and, although only early afternoon, it felt like dusk had fallen.

I sat in the back next to Indy, who was in her car seat, and I played games with her. She had a toy CD player that played nursery rhymes, and every time she switched it on, I would 'dance' to it by nodding my head and waving my hands about. Then she would press 'Pause' and I would freeze. If my attention wandered, she'd exclaim, "Nanny! Dance!" Unfortunately, she never tired of the game but at least it helped take my mind off the painful parting ahead.

At the airport, Cam parked the car and hauled my case onto a trolley. We all hugged and I kissed Indy's blonde curls for the last time.

"Bye, bye, darling, I hope I'll see you again very soon. Give my love to Bandsaw."

Karly took Indy from me. Indy suddenly understood that I was going and burst into tears.

Leaving Karly, Cam and Indy was agony. As I headed to the Departures entrance doors, I could hear Indy's howls in my ears just as the first raindrops fell.

Checking in was straightforward. I was pleased that I wouldn't need to reclaim my luggage until I reached Almería, our little airport in Spain, even though my thirty-seven hour journey included stops at Singapore, London Heathrow and Madrid.

To kill time, I walked round the airport, past the stands selling toy kangaroos and boomerangs, past perfume and duty-free stores, past foreign exchange kiosks and back to the beginning again. I thought it might be a good idea to increase my daily steps total now, because I would be seated for long periods when the journey began. I completed circuit after circuit, noticing that raindrops were now bouncing off the floor to ceiling windows in the waiting lounge.

At last it was time to board the plane, but not before I had performed one little deed that I always do before going on a long journey. I like to leave a copy of my first book, *Chickens, Mules and Two Old Fools* on a seat somewhere in the airport. Inside, I write something like,

Hello,

I am the author of this book, and it's not lost, just roaming. Please feel free

to take it with you. When you've finished with it, it would be awesome if you could then leave it somewhere for somebody else to pick up.

I'd love to know how far this book travels, so do join me on Facebook.

Thank you so much,

Victoria

Usually the books disappear without trace, probably thrown away by a zealous cleaner, but a few have travelled the world. One went to Texas, then Florida, then Sweden, before I lost track of it when it was left in the VIP lounge at Bangkok airport.

We boarded the plane as the rain beat a tattoo on the roof of our walkway. I found my seat and got settled, looking forward to the familiar routine of takeoff. I had a window seat and watched soaked airport staff loading our luggage as the rain drummed down on them.

I made no effort to start chatting with the lady in the next seat. Sometimes it's nice to make a new friend and chatting helps to while away the time, but today I preferred to keep to myself. I wanted to think about my wonderful stay in Australia, and look forward to reuniting with Joe. I thought about the many photos I had taken and couldn't wait to download them from my camera when I got home.

The hostesses checked that we were all wearing our seat-belts, doors were locked and cross-checked, and we were all set to taxi off down the runway.

But the plane didn't move.

I checked my watch. It was already ten minutes past our departure time. I peered outside again in time to see sheet lightning, the flash illuminating the rain that pelted down in straight lines. Then another flash, and another.

The public address system crackled into life.

"Good afternoon, this is Tim Evans, your captain, speaking. We do apologise for the delay, but the weather has worsened in the last few minutes and we are waiting in a queue. Air Traffic Control has not given us clearance to take off. We hope the storm will soon pass so that we can start our journey to Singapore. Thank you for your patience."

Can't be helped, I thought. *I guess a few minutes won't make much difference.*

I peered outside. I could see no movement. No vehicles, no people, no planes rolling by, no activity at all. Because the plane was so well sealed, I could hear neither the rain nor thunder. But I could see the rain pounding down on the tarmac, lit by lightning flashes across the dark sky.

Minutes, then a quarter of an hour ticked by.

"May I extend my apologies," boomed the captain's voice again. "We are all anxious to be leaving, but this storm seems to have dug itself in. I'll keep you posted, but at the moment we are being told to remain here."

A long-haul journey is bad enough in ordinary circumstances. But to be delayed, held captive, forced to remain in one's seat in the plane before the colossal journey ahead has even begun, is almost unbearable. My heart sank to my toes.

It can't be for much longer, I comforted myself.

But it was.

"Hello, this is Tim Evans again. I'm afraid I've just been advised that the whole of Sydney airport has been shut down due to the storm. No planes will be arriving or leaving until further notice. I do apologise, but, of course, safety is our main concern."

For two deathly-slow hours, I watched giant raindrops race across the porthole until finally, the pilot spoke again.

"This is Tim Evans again. I'm delighted to tell you that the storm has now moved on sufficiently for us to take off. Thank you for your patience and we hope you enjoy your journey with British Airways."

"Hooray!" shouted the passengers, and burst into a spontaneous round of applause.

It had occurred to me that the two hour delay would have a knock-on effect. I would probably miss my connecting flights at Singapore, London Heathrow and Madrid. Would Joe think of checking my flight?

There was nothing to be done, and I left my fate in the hands of British Airways.

The rest of the journey was uneventful, thank goodness. Yes, I missed all my connections, but seats were found on other aircraft and I eventually found myself in the familiar airport of Madrid not much later than planned.

Surrounded by the clamour of Spanish-speaking voices, I really felt

I was on the last leg of my marathon journey. I pulled out my phone and tapped a message to Joe, as we had planned.

At Madrid boarding plane now. See you in 1.5hrs xxx

Although tired, I almost skipped onto the little connecting plane. As we soared over the mountains, my heart beat fast.

Just over an hour later, the plane circled over the sea and landed. I was exhausted but it didn't matter because I was home. I had just one last job to do: collect my luggage from the carousel. Then I would be outside and in Joe's arms.

The suitcases began rumbling along the conveyor belt, every shape and size and all colours of the rainbow. Mine was large and red, and I would recognise it anywhere.

"*Aquí está la mía,*" called Spanish voices around me. "Here's mine." They grabbed their luggage, manhandling it off the conveyor belt and heading for the exit.

I waited patiently until every suitcase had been claimed and the hall was empty of people. The carousel continued to rumble round and round, but no more cases were being spat out onto the chute.

A member of staff appeared and approached me.

"You wait for suitcase? All finished. No more suitcase today."

I gaped at her.

"You put suitcase in Madrid?" she asked.

"No, Australia." I showed her my luggage receipt, issued in Sydney.

"Ah. Come with me, we must make paper."

I hadn't slept much on the flight and was so tired I could hardly answer all her questions as she filled out the many forms. At last we were done, and I was free to go.

"I will say to my colleagues in Madrid," she said. "Then perhaps suitcase can come on plane this night or tomorrow."

I was upset, but optimistic. I was far too tired, too excited to be home, and I couldn't wait to see Joe who would be waiting for me beyond the swing doors.

But nobody was waiting for me.

I sighed, not very surprised. I checked my phone. Nothing except a *Welcome to Movistar* message from the telecommunications company. Perhaps Joe had assumed I missed the plane because I was so slow coming out of Arrivals? Unlikely. It was far more likely that he was late.

Joe is always late. I have learned that the only way to keep him on time is to lie to him, add an hour to any appointment. If he needs to be somewhere at twelve o'clock, I tell him the appointment is at eleven. It works, and luckily he always forgets this sneaky trick of mine.

I exited the building, enjoying the bright sunshine. Almería airport is tiny, built on a strip of land with achingly blue ocean on one side, and a terracotta-coloured range of low mountains on the other. The plane I had arrived on took off, no doubt heading back to Madrid. A warm breeze fanned the palm trees. Taxi drivers carried on smoking and chatting with each other when they realised I was not looking for a ride.

I looked out across the car park, and at last, there he was, marching towards me, grinning from ear to ear. Then his warm arms enveloped me and time stood still. I no longer heard the taxi drivers, or the house martins chattering as they built their homes above our heads under the eaves of the airport building.

"How are you?" he asked at last, holding me at arms' length and looking into my face. "How was the journey?"

His cheeks looked a little more hollow than I remembered, but his eyes were the same. He seemed breathless, but I put that down to excitement and the walk across the car park.

"Oh, you know what these long-haul journeys are like. I never get used to them."

"I'm sorry I'm a bit late, I wanted to make sure everything was perfect for you at home. Where's your case?"

"I'd like to know that, too! You didn't keep me waiting too long because I was held up, filling in forms."

I explained about the storm, and the delay at Sydney airport, and how I'd missed all the connecting flights.

"Goodness only knows where my suitcase is now…"

"Your big red case is lost?"

"Yes, but never mind that now. I still have my hand luggage and luckily, my main computer is in that, and not in the lost red case. Come on, I can't wait to get home."

We walked back to the car but I didn't let him carry my hand luggage. I didn't want to tire him out even more. Even so, he needed to rest once before we reached the car.

I had left Australia in autumn and I was arriving in Almería in spring. Already the grass verges looked lush, and early wildflowers were peeping out to smile at the sun.

"It's so good to be back," I said, as we drove past almond orchards, the pale pink-white blossoms clothing the trees, and wafting to the ground like confetti when the breeze tugged at them.

"Any sign of another baby?" asked Joe. "Indy really should have a brother or sister."

"No," I said sadly. "I don't think they want another baby now. I think they were so devastated at losing one, that they don't want to put themselves through it again. And they are so enjoying Indy. Karly's really busy at work, too. I think Indy will be an only child."

It suddenly occurred to me that I had done nothing but chatter about Australia since we'd got in the car.

"Enough about Australia," I said. "I want to hear all about *everything*. You, the village, everything."

CHORIZO SOUP
SOPA DE CHORIZO

This warming, filling chorizo soup recipe is fabulous as a quick lunch, or if you thicken it slightly and omit the rice, it works well poured over pasta.

Ingredients

15 cm long (6 inches) chorizo, sliced or diced into little pieces

2 tins of chopped tomatoes

200g (7oz) of cooked butter beans

100g (3½oz) long grain rice (uncooked)

A finely chopped small chilli (or more if you like it spicy)

Handful of finely chopped fresh basil

Small tub of *creme fraiche* (optional but recommended)

Method

Fry the diced chorizo on a medium heat. No need for oil.

Add the chilli and cook for a couple of minutes.

Pour in the tinned tomatoes, rice and beans, and turn up the heat a little.

Simmer for about 20 minutes, then bring the heat down to low again.

Stir in the *creme fraiche* and basil, and cook gently for another 2 minutes or so, just to warm it through.

Serve with fresh bread.

16

SHOCKS

We sailed down the mountain and into the village.

"No dramas with my journey from the UK," said Joe. "I arrived around midday, took a taxi home, and that was it. "

"And the house was okay?"

"Yes, apart from a cheeky pair of house martins building their nest under the eaves, everything is just as we left it three months ago. I opened up the windows to air the house a bit, and that's all it needed. The car started first time, too."

"That's good news! Have you seen anybody?"

"No, there's nobody in next door, and the village is quiet. So, did you bring me back a present from Australia?"

Oops! I hadn't.

"Yes," I said, thinking quickly, "but it's in the lost suitcase..."

"Never mind," he said, taking one hand off the steering wheel and patting mine, "being back in El Hoyo with you is the best present."

"Oh dear," I said, guilt painting my face red. "Actually, I didn't get you a present..."

"I know," he smiled, "but I still meant what I said. Do you want me to stop at Marcia's shop?"

"No, thank you. I'm too tired. I don't feel up to a long conversation now. Perhaps we'll pop down tomorrow and pick up our mail."

"Good idea. I think an early night is in order for you."

I yawned and agreed. Just now, all I could think of was curling up in bed.

The village square was empty, as were the streets, but that was normal for a week day. I noticed that the four ornamental trees, one in each corner, had buds about to burst into life. And who was that figure sitting on the bench in the far corner? I thought it was Geronimo, but he didn't look up.

Joe slowed the car down to a crawl as we passed Lola Ufarte's cottage and prepared to park outside our own. Out of the corner of my eye, I saw her front door close, but not before I glimpsed a face at the window. It wasn't Lola Ufarte, neither was it a child. The face belonged to a dark male, and I thought I recognised him.

"Joe, did you see the new priest just then? In Lola Ufarte's house?"

"No, I didn't. Honestly, Vicky, you've been in the village for thirty seconds and you're already imagining things. Now, come on, let's have a cup of tea and something to eat."

As I rested my cheek on the pillow that night, a host of unbidden thoughts crowded in.

How wonderful it was to be home, and in our familiar bed.

What time was it now in Sydney?

Had I really seen the young priest in Lola's house, or did I imagine that?

Why shouldn't there be an innocent reason for his visit, anyway?

But my main thought was, *I wonder what Joe wants to talk about? Had he noticed some serious repairs that needed doing?*

"Vicky, there's something quite important I want to discuss with you in the morning," he had said when I kissed him goodnight.

"Can't we discuss it now?"

"No. Get a good night's sleep. It will keep."

Normally, I would have badgered him to tell me immediately, but I was light-headed from tiredness and yearned for sleep.

As my eyes closed, I couldn't help puzzling over what it might be.

But I didn't ponder for long because I was asleep within seconds.

I doubt there are many rooms as dark or quiet as our cave bedroom. When I awoke the next morning, just for a moment, I had absolutely no idea where I was. I had grown accustomed to the early morning noises of the Sydney household. The raucous dawn chorus, including the Happy Birthday bird's song, had all become familiar to me. But here there was silence.

The bed was empty, so Joe must have already got up. I found him in the kitchen making coffee.

"Morning!"

"You certainly slept well! A full twelve hours! Do you feel better?"

"Thank you, yes. Now, what is the thing you wanted to discuss?"

Joe passed me my coffee and sat down at the kitchen table, opposite me. He reached for my hand and looked straight into my eyes.

My heart began beating a little faster as I read the signs. Whatever he was going to say now was serious.

"Vicky, this visit to the UK has been a bit of a wake up call."

"How do you mean?"

"My health. I have COPD, and, like I told you, there is no cure for that."

"I know, but we can keep it at bay with exercise and a good diet, and your meds, of course."

"Yes, but there's also my high blood pressure. I could have a stroke at any time."

"Not if you take your meds!"

"True, but now it seems that it's possible I may be also diagnosed with prostate cancer."

"No, I'm sure you don't have that!"

"Vicky, we are not getting any younger. We need to plan for the future."

"I don't understand. What do you mean?"

"We need to be realistic. We've lived in El Hoyo for eleven years now, apart from that year in the Middle East. I know it's hard," he took a deep breath, "but I think the time has come to leave."

I snatched my hand out of his.

"What? Leave El Hoyo? Why? Almería has a perfectly good hospital, if we ever needed it! Carmen next door says it's a fabulous hospital."

"I'm sure it is. But if I had a stroke, how long do you think it would take an ambulance to reach me up those winding roads?"

"You're not going to have a stroke!"

"Maybe not. Vicky, all I'm asking is that you think about it. I've thought about little else lately, and I think we should leave while we are in full possession of our faculties. Imagine if one of us became really ill, or died. How would the other one cope alone? We don't have family here."

"Don't be ridiculous, you sound as though we're about to crumble and die any second! We're only in our sixties."

Joe didn't answer. He knew he'd sown the evil seed of doubt, and that I would keep turning it over in my mind, wrestling with it, picking away at it.

I looked down at my hands, and saw they were trembling.

Outside the kitchen window, a song thrush landed on a branch of the grapevine. As always at this time of the year, the vine looked dead, but I knew the tight buds were developing and lush, green leaves would burst forth within the month. The bird opened its beak, tilted its head back and sang, a perfect silhouette against the blue March morning sky. How melodic and polite it sounded compared with the squawks of the parrots I had left behind in Sydney!

No, leaving our home and El Hoyo was unthinkable. I couldn't even bring myself to imagine life under English grey skies again. No, we were happy here in El Hoyo, where the sun could be relied upon and the blue sky stretched to the mountain tops.

"I don't want to move back to England."

"No. Not England. Australia."

I sat up straight. He had my full attention. I didn't even notice the thrush fly away.

"Pardon?"

"Australia. You see, that's the other thing. I know how much you miss Karly, Cam and Indy, you talk about nothing else. Wouldn't you like to be there permanently and watch Indy grow?"

"Of course, but..."

"Well, it's my wish that we go and set up home in Australia. I want to see you settled and happy, and I think now is the time to do it before my health gets any worse."

My heart thudded in my chest. I tried hard to absorb what Joe was saying but only felt rising panic. Joe reached for my hand again.

"I know it's a lot to take in, but I really believe it's what we ought to do."

"But..."

"Don't say another word about it now," said Joe. "Have a think. Come on, we should walk over to Marcia's shop and collect our mail."

I nodded dumbly, finished my coffee and we set off. It felt good to walk down our street hand in hand again after the time apart.

"I hope the airport doesn't phone while we're out," I remarked, in an effort to banish the thoughts that spun in my head.

"They'll leave a message," said Joe.

The square was deserted, but old Marcia was in her shop.

"Oh, you're back!" she exclaimed. "Did you enjoy your stay in Australia?"

"We did, thank you." We hadn't told her that Joe had gone to the UK. Joe didn't want anyone to know about his health worries. "We came to see you and collect the mail. How has the weather been this winter? And how are you?"

Marcia beamed at us, reached under the counter and pulled out a stack of letters.

"Just my knee playing me up a little, thank you. At my age I expect that. These letters are all yours. Just bills and stuff, I think." Nothing passed Marcia's scrutiny. "The weather has been very good. The nights are still cold, but my sons have made sure I have plenty of firewood for my stove. You know I usually stay down below with my sons until Easter, but this year I have returned early."

"Gosh, Easter is only a month away," I exclaimed. "How quickly this year is flying past already."

"Ah yes, the ladies in the village are deciding on the flowers that will decorate the church at Easter. Which reminds me, the new young priest, Father Samuel, has started a little Sunday school for the children. It is already very popular with the little ones. They play games, paint pictures, and Father Samuel gives them a little *bon bon* when they leave."

Clever Father Samuel, I thought. Knowing the kids in the village, I imagined only the *bon bon* bribe would draw them into extra schooling.

"Now more families are going to church, knowing their children are in good hands, learning things instead of fidgeting in the pews. Of course he had help with setting it up and running it every week," continued Marcia dryly.

"Oh? Who's helping him? Can I guess? Is it Lola Ufarte?"

"It is," said Marcia shortly. "And I'm not so sure that's a good thing."

She had a point, but perhaps religion would help keep Lola Ufarte on the straight and narrow. Somehow, I doubted it.

"And how is everybody else in the village?" I asked.

I saw Joe roll his eyes. He knew I was fishing for gossip. I was dying to know whether Geronimo and Valentina were together again, and Marcia didn't disappoint.

"Everybody is well," she said, "but Geronimo tries my patience." She tossed her head, sending a hair pin flying.

"Why? Is he back with Valentina?"

"No, he is not, silly boy. *Madre mía,* he just moons round the village with a long face. The good thing is that he has stopped drinking, but he will not approach Valentina again. I say to him, 'Go and talk to Valentina!' but he just shakes his head and walks off."

"Do you know how Valentina feels?"

"Yes, she comes to my shop every day with the mail. She pretends to be all cheerful and carefree, but I see her looking round for Geronimo."

"Perhaps *she* should approach Geronimo?"

"Bah! I suggested that, but she said if he was interested, he would make the effort and try to speak with her."

"Oh dear."

"I could knock their silly heads together," exclaimed Marcia, and another hairpin slid out of her silver hair onto the floor.

"Oh well," I said, "let's hope they get together soon."

"Well, are you satisfied now?" asked Joe as we walked back up the street.

"What do you mean?"

"Are you satisfied now you've had your gossip fix?"

"Oh, stop it. You know those two would be happy together. They just need to see sense, that's all."

"Hmm…" said Joe. "I wonder if the airport has tried to phone you?"

But they hadn't.

I phoned them, but was told my suitcase hadn't been found. Now I was worried. They advised me to email Iberia Airlines immediately, which I did.

I thought hard about what was in the case and suddenly remembered my camera with all those pictures I hadn't yet downloaded. There was my scruffy journal, packed with notes for my next book. There were toiletries, an alarm clock, the power cable for my computer, my black leather Filofax which I have had for twenty years and contains *everything*, and a little box of my most loved earrings and necklaces. When going on holiday, one takes one's favourite clothes. All mine, and my shoes, were in the suitcase, lost. The clothes I had bought in Australia were lost. It wasn't a pleasant feeling.

I couldn't manage without the basics, like underwear, a hairbrush, some toiletries and changes of clothing, so we drove down the mountain and went shopping. We also shopped for food, and by the evening we were both tired. I'd thrown together a pork casserole that required very little attention so I suggested we take a glass of wine up to the roof terrace and watch the sun go down.

The sun had already stained the sky orange, and the shadows under the crags of the mountains had deepened. Although beautiful, the sun would take all its warmth with it, and as it slipped into the sea, we would go back into the house.

From our high vantage point, we could see the village was virtually deserted. A curl of smoke drifted from Marcia's chimney, and also our own, as Joe had lit the kitchen fire. I caught a glimpse of Felicity, hunting in the long grass by the cemetery. But the streets of El Hoyo were empty apart from Geronimo, who trudged along in the direction of his own house. Easily identified by his Real Madrid scarf, his head was bowed and his hands were pushed deep into his pockets. He walked as though he had the cares of the world upon his shoulders. His three dogs trotted in front of him, oblivious, keen to go home to supper and bed. He opened his front door, let them in and disappeared inside, closing the door firmly behind him.

In the distance, a deer barked, then silence fell. I peered over the wall, where the house martins' new nest was being made. No activity.

"I miss the chickens, don't you?" I said suddenly.

In the old days, we'd have heard the girls preparing for bed, bickering about who was going to perch where, and finally settling down.

"I do, but..."

And there it was again, the elephant in the room.

PORK AND TOMATO STEW
MAGRA CON TOMATE

Hailing from Murcia, this stew-like dish is fantastic served with chunks of crusty bread and plenty of wine.

Ingredients (serves 2)

A couple of pork chops, boned and cut into small pieces, or diced pork

1 tin of chopped tomatoes

2 medium roasted red peppers, finely diced... or about 3 or 4 gorgeous *pimenton piquillos*

1 medium green pepper, finely diced

1 medium onion - the sweeter the better - finely diced

4 to 6 garlic cloves, finely chopped or in wafer thin slices

1 tablespoon or two of smoked paprika

Couple of hearty glugs of olive oil

Splash of wine (red or white)

Salt and pepper for seasoning

Method

Put the oil in the pan and bring up to a medium high heat.

Season and brown the diced pork.

Set the pork aside, but leave as much of the oil in the pan as possible.

Throw in the onion, and both types of pepper.

Sweat them gently until almost translucent and cooked through.

Add the garlic, stir well and cook for a couple more minutes.

Add the chopped tomatoes.

Sprinkle in the paprika, return the pork, and season.

Turn the heat down low so it cooks really slowly. Cover and continue for about 30 or more minutes, adding a little water if needed.

Serve hot.

17

LETTERS

The subject I had been carefully avoiding all day had reared its ugly head. I'd tried hard to stay busy and keep it at bay but I knew I had to confront it at some point. The thought of leaving El Hoyo was unbearable, almost too painful to even consider.

The sun was steadily dipping down and I began to feel chilly. My wine tasted bitter.

"I know what you're thinking," I said. I felt terribly sad. "You're thinking that if we're moving, we shouldn't get any more chickens."

"Yes. Have you thought any more about what I said?" Joe asked gently.

I sighed, unwilling to have this conversation. If we talked about the possibility of leaving, that would make it more real, wouldn't it?

"Yes," I said reluctantly. "I have thought very hard about it. I don't want us to leave, not yet. And I don't think there's any rush. Besides, it's the worst time to sell. We won't get much for this house because of the European economic crisis. Houses are selling for peanuts here and Australia is really expensive."

"Vicky, my health is going to deteriorate."

"But I can look after you here!"

It was Joe's turn to sigh.

"Don't you want to be near the family, and watch Indy grow?"

He had me there.

"Yes, but…"

"And we both love Australia."

"Yes."

"And I want you to respect my wish to see you settled and happy, near the family, so if anything happens to me, I'll know you'll be okay."

He had played his trump card, and we both knew it.

We lapsed into silence in the twilight. The sun had almost disappeared from view. Despite a few remaining streaks of dark orange in the sky, the village was bathed in deep shadow.

"Let's wait for your results," I said quietly. "If you are diagnosed with prostate cancer, and of course you won't be, we'll put the house on the market and move to Australia."

The sun vanished. The temperature dropped.

I shivered, whether at the thought of what I'd just said, or because of the cold, I'm not sure.

"Okay," said Joe. "We'll wait for the results."

I opened the email from Iberia, and read it through, my heart sinking.

We apologise for any inconvenience we may have caused you due to the baggage-related incident that occurred on flight IB8592 of March 2nd 2015.

Customer care is a fundamental goal for us and it is essential for us to consider each case individually in order to handle it correctly and to determine if it gives entitlement to compensation under the terms of the legislation in force.

To help us look into your case and reach a solution, please send the documentation listed below to Apartado de Correos 36.299, 28080 Madrid.

- Original of the PIR - Property Irregularity Report - which is the reference of the claim you made at the airport.

- Name(s) and surname(s).

- The number of your National Identity Document, Passport or Resident's Card.

- Contact telephone, e-mail and a full address, including the street, the number of the house or flat, the postcode and any other information which may help to locate the address.

Original of the check-in labels and boarding passes.

- Original receipts for the expenses in which you incurred for the purchase of essential items.

- An Inventory of the Contents and an approximation as to the value both of the contents and the suitcase (including any pertinent receipts if at all possible).

We thank you in advance for sending us this information, which will help us to deal with your claim.

Hmm… This was going to take time.

Have you ever tried remembering everything that you packed in a suitcase several days ago? And could you recall how much you paid for each item? It took me all day to gather the information they wanted. Still, if they were going to compensate me, it had to be done. After all, accidents do happen.

I posted the letter to Madrid. A week went by, and I had no response.

Later that month, I was having a coffee with Carmen, next door. It was a Thursday, not a day that Paco and Carmen usually spent in the village.

"Paco was owed a day from work," she explained. "You know what he's like, he'd much rather be up here than down below. We have not seen much of you since you came back from Australia," she said, pouring coffee into two glasses. "Is everything well with you and Joe?"

I patted Yukky's soft head and looked into the plump face of the lovely lady who had always made us so welcome. Family photos smiled down at us from the whitewashed walls. I could smell coffee, and cinnamon. The domed quail cages with their noisy occupants were missing from the wall, so I guessed Paco was out shooting. I always felt extremely sorry for the poor females, confined to tiny cages and used as decoys to lure out males. In spring, no male quail could resist the females' clacking call and Paco rarely returned home empty-handed.

"Have they found your suitcase yet?" asked Carmen.

"No, no sign of it so far."

"*Madre mía*, what a nuisance!" She peered at me closely. "Is anything else worrying you?"

So I told her about Joe's health. She already knew about his high blood pressure but the COPD was news to her, as was the possibility of prostate cancer.

"*¡Madre mía!*" Her hand clapped over her mouth in shock. "That is terrible news. What will you do? It is at times like this you need your family around you."

I hadn't breathed a word about our possible move, and her reaction rocked me. Was Joe right? Was I being unrealistic in wanting to stay in Spain, so far from family?

A face appeared at the door.

"Ah! Valentina! *¿Qué tal?*" said Carmen, getting up. "How are things? Come and have coffee with us."

I'd been so absorbed in my own thoughts I hadn't even heard the postlady's moped buzz up the street.

"I would love to, Carmen, but I'm late for my round already. Here, I have a letter for you." She suddenly noticed me and reached back into her sack. "And one for you, too."

"Thank you," we chorused as she handed over the mail.

"You can spare five minutes," insisted Carmen. "Look, I have made *polvorones de canele.*"

But even cinnamon shortbread wouldn't detain Valentina. With a cheery wave, she was gone.

"It is a pity she did not stay awhile," remarked Carmen. "I wanted to ask her why Geronimo is moping round El Hoyo with a face like a dog who has dropped its bone down a well."

I couldn't help smiling at that image.

"From what Marcia says, I think if Geronimo and Valentina just sat down together and talked, they would resolve their differences easily," I observed.

"Yes, but he is too shy and proud, and she is too stubborn," agreed Carmen.

"I must go," I said. "Thank you for the coffee and *polvorones*."

I popped back next door and looked at the envelope in my hand. I was expecting it to be from Iberia about my lost luggage, but it wasn't. It was an official-looking letter from the UK, addressed to Joe.

"Joe, this is for you," I said, and stood while he tore open the envelope.

He frowned as he pulled out the letter and began reading.

"It's from the hospital. Not good news, I'm afraid."

"Oh no!"

"It seems I *do* have prostate cancer."

"Oh no!"

I sat down quickly. I was terribly shocked. I had convinced myself that the tests would show that he was clear of any cancer.

"So what happens now?"

"They've made an appointment for me for the 2nd of April. I have to see the specialist prostate nurse."

"But that's less than two weeks away!"

"I guess they need to start treatment as fast as possible in these cases."

Joe's calmness impressed me. I glanced up at the kitchen calendar.

"That's Easter week! April the 2nd is the Thursday before Easter. We'd better book flights immediately."

"Yes, we must, but there's no point in you coming, too. Besides, you may be really busy while I'm away."

"Why?"

"Come on, Vicky. We agreed. If I was diagnosed with cancer, we would put the house on the market."

Shocked by the bad news, I had forgotten the bargain we had made. I gaped at him and the blood drained from my face. That letter in his hand had changed our lives.

"Mum, are you serious? You are going to come and live in Australia *permanently*?"

"Yes."

"It's not a joke?" Karly squeaked. "You haven't been drinking?"

"No! Of course not!"

"That's *amazing* news! I can't take it in! I can't wait to tell Cam and Indy!"

"Obviously we have to sell the house, and apply for Australian visas. It's going to take some time."

"I know, but it's just the best news! I wish the prostate cancer thing hadn't happened, of course, but I'm so glad you are both going to be here. How do you feel about leaving Spain?"

"Terribly sad, but it's the right thing to do. I know that. And being near you is going to be fabulous."

"Kurt?"

"Yes, this is I."

"It's Vicky here. How are you?"

"I am vell."

Kurt was the German estate agent who had sold us our house in 2004. Now, eleven years later, we were going full circle and talking to him about selling it.

"Kurt," I took a deep breath, "we have decided to sell the house. Can you help us?"

"Of course, yes," he said, but I heard the surprise in his voice. "I vas always thinking that you stay in El Hoyo."

"We thought so, too, Kurt. But things have changed a little. We love the house and we love living in El Hoyo, but now we've decided it's time to leave."

I explained the situation to him and he listened carefully.

"I understand," he said. "I vill help you get the best price, but you have chosen a bad time. Nobody has any money and property prices are at the bottom rock."

"I know," I said. "It can't be helped."

"Okay. I vill come and take some measurement and photograph. There are many things ve must do."

Telling my friend and neighbour, Carmen, and also Marcia at the shop, that we were selling our house and leaving El Hoyo was a task I dreaded. What I hadn't taken into account was the enormous value Spanish people place on family, which made my job much easier.

"¡Madre mía!" said Carmen. "Prostate cancer is very common, and I believe they can treat it if it is caught quickly. But as I said to you before, it is at times like this that you need your family around you. We will miss you, but I hope you sell the house quickly, even though it is a bad time to sell."

"Of course you must go," said Marcia. "Your family will give you strength. I will tell all the villagers that your house is for sale. Sometimes buyers come as a result of word of mouth. Somebody may have relatives who would like a house in El Hoyo."

That hurdle overcome, I could now concentrate on the house itself.

I didn't allow myself to think much about Joe's diagnosis. Instead, I threw myself into preparing to put our beloved home on the market.

I decided to tackle the massive tasks ahead in my usual way. Lists.

Starting from the front door, I conducted a walk-through with my notebook in hand, trying to imagine I was a prospective buyer and seeing everything for the first time.

Our window boxes, crammed with pink geraniums, looked glorious, but a couple of pots, one either side of the front door, wouldn't go amiss. The front door itself could probably benefit from another coat of varnish, and the porch had a cobweb or two that needed whisking away. High above my head, the pair of house martins chittered at me.

"Don't worry," I said to them. "I won't disturb you. You are welcome here, it's just spiders that I'm evicting."

I continued inside, and my list grew alarmingly. I would need to buy white paint, filler, tile grout, a new handle for the bathroom door, some window cleaner, a new broom, and many bits and pieces.

I never grew accustomed to the empty chicken coop. Filled with ghosts of chickens we had loved and lost, it now served as a reminder of our uncertain future. I found myself saving all our vegetable scraps as I had always done, then remembering we had no hens. Now, the highly-fertilised empty run had sprouted vigorous weeds. Another job for me. I certainly wasn't going to be bored while Joe was away, and neither would I have much time for brooding.

CINNAMON COOKIES
POLVERONES

These taste very similar to shortbread, and although common in Spain at Christmas time, they are well worth making all year round.

Ingredients

FOR THE DOUGH

1 cup of butter

½ cup of icing sugar (confectioners' sugar)

½ teaspoon ground cinnamon

¼ teaspoon salt

1 teaspoon vanilla extract

1½ cups bread flour

FOR THE COATING

1 cup of icing sugar (confectioners' sugar)

1 teaspoon ground cinnamon

Method

Preheat oven to 180°C (350°F).

Cream together icing sugar and butter. Stir in the vanilla.

Combine flour, salt, and cinnamon in a separate bowl. Mix into the butter/sugar mixture to form a stiff dough.

In a third bowl, combine sugar and cinnamon. Shape dough into 1 inch balls and roll in cinnamon mixture.

Bake for 15 to 20 minutes, until lightly browned.

Cool cookies on wire racks.

18

APPOINTMENTS

We had just one weekend together before Joe returned to the UK, and it was a busy one. Kurt visited, and took a great many photos and measurements.

"Zis is a good house," he said, which he always did when he visited.

"We'll miss it," I said.

"And do you think how much you vant to ask in price?"

"We've discussed that," said Joe, and named a sum.

Kurt looked concerned. He drew a property newspaper out from under his arm and spread it on the table.

"Five years before, yes, that price exactly," he said. "But now it is more different. Look at this house, it has eight bedrooms, a swimming pool and field with many orange trees. It is more cheaper."

We read the description with mounting dismay.

"And this one. Five bedrooms, double garage, footpath to the beach. It is more cheaper."

"This house has a private cinema and grandmother apartment. It is more cheaper."

"Yes, yes," Joe cut in. "I can see we were being too optimistic. How much would you suggest?"

The figure Kurt quoted caused us both to gasp.

"Really?" exclaimed Joe.

"But that's about what we paid for it eleven years ago, when it was a ruin!" I whispered. "You know how much work we've done on this house..."

Kurt looked unhappy.

"I am sorry," he said. "It is the Crisis." He pronounced it the Spanish way, sounding like 'creases'. "Please to think around it and tell me on the phone. I understand if you vant to exchange your minds."

We looked at him, speechless.

"Thank you," we said, but without much enthusiasm.

"What a shock!" I said, when Kurt had left.

"What terrible luck," said Joe bitterly. "I knew we'd have to take a hit, but a hit this size? It's hard to believe Spanish property prices have dropped so low. It's going to make buying a property in Australia very difficult. Their property market is soaring."

It was all very depressing.

"I don't suppose we have much choice, really," I said. "We have to go, I know that."

"I wish it hadn't come to this. It's all my fault," said Joe.

"No! Let's concentrate on getting you better. Don't worry about the house, I'll sort all that. I'll phone Kurt and tell him we still want to go ahead."

Spring was in full swing. Sparrows twittered from dawn to dusk, nest-building and preparing to bring the next sparrow generation into the world. A pair of eagles had chosen a crag in our valley to set up home, and could be seen soaring overhead, silhouetted against the cloudless sky. Our house martins' new nest, neatly tucked under the eaves was an architectural wonder, perfectly domed and secure from Felicity and the village cats.

In April, the sun is kind and it is a pleasure to be outside, absorbing the rays without feeling as if one has stepped into a furnace. Joe and I sat on the roof terrace, savouring our coffees and enjoying the wonderful warmth and scents of spring.

If we looked down onto our own garden, we could clearly see the grapevine's bulging buds, some of which had already burst to reveal fresh green leaves that would grow to the size of my hand. Beyond was the cemetery with its large, ornate gate. Turn around, and the village rooftops came into view, most below us, but a few higher on the mountain slope.

It was Sunday, and at this time of day, the village was unusually quiet. Earlier, Geronimo had rung the church bells, a solemn summons for the village faithful. Most of the population heeded the call to prayer and headed to church. From our vantage point, we watched them troop past below us.

Lola Ufarte, carrying her little girl, hurried past. Our other neighbours, Federico and Roberto, passed by, marching in step. Their adopted daughter, Emilia, looked a picture in her pink dress with matching shoes. Next came the Ufarte family, except for the grandmother, who preferred to doze in her armchair in the street beside their front door.

"Hurry, boys," called their mother, Maribel. "Father Samuel told me he has some new games for you."

Her sons' expressions and rolling eyes said it all.

Who cares! We'd rather play football in the square.

Carmen popped out of her cottage next to ours. Like everybody else, she wore her Sunday best. Today a lacy shawl was draped over her shoulders and her feet were squeezed into shiny, heeled shoes that clacked as she walked up the street.

"No sign of Paco," remarked Joe.

"No, he always gets out of going to church if he can. I expect he's got some urgent quail business to see to."

"I didn't see the twins, or little Pollito, did you?"

Before I could answer, the Ufarte door slammed again and light footsteps ran up the street.

"You must not hide away, Pollito!" said Twin #1.

"You've made us late!" said Twin #2.

Pollito's chubby hands were firmly in his big sisters' grasp. There was no escape. The twins hurried along, almost dragging their little brother off his feet. Unseen, Joe and I smiled down at the scene.

"If you are late, Father Samuel may not have any *bon bons* left."

That seemed to do the trick, and Pollito's feet scampered a little faster.

The village was quiet except for the sounds of nature and a distant tractor labouring high above us on the opposite mountain slope.

An hour passed, and the church bells began to ring again, more joyously this time. I saw the first villagers begin to emerge. Instead of hurrying, as they had earlier, they now sauntered along in knots, deep in conversation. I knew Carmen would take a good ten minutes to get home, even though I could already see her heading up our street.

The Ufarte boys barrelled out as though escaping from a prison, nearly knocking over old Marcia. They headed towards the square and another never-ending game of football.

The twins appeared, Pollito between them. Pollito was clutching a large, rather crumpled sheet of paper. As they drew closer, we could hear their conversation.

"Did you have fun today, Pollito?"

"Yes."

"And did Father Samuel give you a *bon bon*?"

"Yes, and *tía* Lola gave me another. I had two!"

"Lucky boy!"

"And did you do painting?"

"Yes." Pollito waved the big sheet of paper. "Father Samuel told us to paint a picture of God."

"But nobody knows what He looks like!" teased one of his big sisters.

"They will when they see my picture!" announced the little boy as they disappeared into their house.

"I shall miss all this, while I'm away," said Joe, smiling.

"Well, I don't believe you'll be stuck in the UK for long. I wonder what the treatment is?"

"I don't know, but I guess we'll soon find out."

While I remained in Spain, busying myself with the house sale, Joe was in the UK. He had already been assigned two specialist prostate nurses, Debbie and Angela, who had rooms in the Acute Services Division of the hospital. Joe's first appointment was with Debbie, a very business-like Scots lady.

"Now, Mr Twead…"

"Please call me Joe."

"Thank you, Joe. would you mind if Beth here sits in with us? She is training to be a prostate nurse."

"Not at all." Joe smiled at Beth who was young enough to be our granddaughter.

"Right, Joe, how familiar are you with the prostate?"

"Er, not very, though I did Google it."

"That's an excellent start, it'll make our job easier. What did you find out?"

"Um…"

Joe hesitated, a little unwilling to regurgitate the rather intimate facts that he had gleaned about the prostate in front of the two ladies.

"It's a gland about the size of a walnut," he offered.

"Quite right!" approved Nurse Debbie. "The prostate produces prostate fluid, part of the seminal fluid that nourishes and transports sperm. It sits below the bladder, near the rectum."

"Yes," said Joe, nodding.

"Sometimes abnormal cells develop in the prostate," continued Nurse Debbie. "These cells can multiply uncontrollably and spread around the body."

Joe listened carefully, trying not to look alarmed.

"But in most cases, prostate cancer is slow-growing and, if treated in time, will not be allowed to spread or become life-threatening."

"So what will my treatment be?"

"Your precise treatment depends on an MRI scan."

"I've heard of an MRI," Joe said.

"Beth, tell Joe what MRI stands for."

"Magnetic Resonance Imaging," said young Beth smoothly. "It provides us with a clear picture of the internal organs."

"Exactly. The MRI should reveal how much of your prostate has been affected. You will also be sent for a CAT scan of the surrounding bones just in case the cancer has already spread to them."

"What's that?"

"Och, it's Computerised Axial Tomography but we need not concern ourselves with that. Basically it's the same as the MRI but uses X-rays."

"Oh."

"Normally, the treatment begins with hormone injections which are administered every three months."

"Hormone injections?"

"Yes. I know my gentlemen clients find that strange, but the reason is very simple. Testosterone is the main carrier of the disease, and the hormone treatment will reduce your body's supply of testosterone."

"Really?"

"Och, aye."

"Will I grow breasts?"

"In unusual cases, some gentlemen may notice a small increase in breast tissue."

Joe looked horrified, and another question sprang into his mind.

"Um, does the reduction in testosterone affect one's, er, you know..."

Young Beth stared out of the window, sparing Joe's embarrassment.

"Intimate relations? I'm afraid it might, Joe. But we can suggest aids to help you through it."

"Aids?" Joe's mind was doing somersaults.

"Well...you know..."

"I'm really sorry, Nurse, but I don't know."

"Well, vacuum pumps for example."

"Vacuum pumps? *Vacuum* pumps? I'm not going to use a blasted vacuum pump! Austen Powers might need one but I most certainly do not!"

Young Beth giggled. Even Nurse Debbie was smiling.

"Let's move on, Mr Twead. These hormone injections can continue forever, if necessary, or for the next two years, depending on how you respond. There is a weekly discussion group here at the hospital. It's for prostate patients who will describe their own experiences during treatment. They also talk freely about any side effects like a reduced libido. You, of course, are welcome to attend."

Joe thanked her, knowing that he was unlikely to take her up on the offer as he was anxious to return to Spain.

"Do you have any other questions?"

"I wondered how many patients you look after, Nurse."

"Och, I have about six hundred gentlemen patients. Angela, the other prostate nurse, has the same number."

"And they all have prostate cancer?"

"Yes."

"Good grief! Do many patients die from it?"

Debbie paused as she considered Joe's rather crass question. When she looked up she was not smiling.

"I like to think that my gentlemen are all doing very well."

"I understand and I apologise if you think me rude. I just want to know what my chances are."

"No apology necessary. Your chances are very good. In fact I would say they are excellent. Most of my gentlemen simply shake off the news of their cancer and get on with their lives. I have to admit though, that a tiny handful can't handle the news. They become depressed, and are convinced their days are numbered. Gentlemen like these sometimes simply give up. Please don't be one of them, Joe, because, as I said, your chances are very good."

"Not to worry, Nurse, I intend living life to the full! I won't let this nonsense concern me at all."

"Aye, well, I'm pleased to hear that. Now, I'm going to prepare your first injection. You can have the injection in your stomach or in your buttock. You choose."

"Buttock please."

"Good. Then I will make a note that it is your right buttock. In three months time I will send for you to have another injection in your left buttock. Then three months after that, we'll swap buttocks again. Here is a booklet that keeps a record of the injections."

Debbie pulled Joe's trousers down to reveal his right buttock and, with Beth observing, injected him. Then she handed him a small white booklet with columns for the dates and comments. The first injection was already recorded, with 'right buttock' written neatly in the comments column. Joe looked worried.

"Debbie, I live in Spain and will have to return for the next injection."

"Not to worry," said Debbie, "I will give you the next injection to take with you to Spain. All you need do is ask the local doctor to administer it. I have quite a few gentlemen who are doing the same thing. I will also give you a letter explaining the injection so you won't have any trouble at the airport."

Joe couldn't thank her enough for all she had done and for her consideration regarding the subsequent injection.

"My pleasure," she said, "but you must have two scans done before you return to Spain. These are vital. They will show how far the cancer has spread."

CANADIAN CUSTARD
HUEVOS MOLES

This dessert is a great option if you have guests coming because it can be made well in advance and left to chill in the fridge until needed.

Ingredients (per person)

3 egg yolks, whisked until creamy

3 tablespoons of sugar

3 tablespoons of water

CHOOSE FROM THE FOLLOWING TOPPINGS

Grated chocolate, white, milk or dark

Chocolate powder

Cinnamon

Hundreds and thousands

A few raspberries or strawberries

Method

Put the water and sugar into a heatproof bowl over a saucepan of water and heat quite vigorously.

Once a caramel, or syrup is formed, and all the sugar is dissolved, gently add the whisked eggs.

Keep stirring for about five minutes but turn the heat down to medium/low.

When it all thickens (couple of minutes) pour into individual containers.

Chill for at least an hour.

Sprinkle with your chosen topping.

19

A STRESSFUL COUPLE OF WEEKS

The telephone rang. I was painting, so I carefully climbed down the ladder and reached it just before the automated voice kicked in. I knew it would either be Kurt wanting to talk about the house sale, or Joe phoning from the UK. It was Joe and his familiar voice boomed in my ear.

"Are you managing okay?"

"Of course I am! I've been painting like crazy, I dread to think how many gallons of white paint I've got through. Kurt phoned, he's bringing some people to see the house this weekend."

"Gosh, already?"

"Yep, I've got so much to do! But never mind the house, what happens next with you?"

"Nurse Debbie said the specialists would decide which treatment I need. It'll probably be radiotherapy."

"Radiotherapy? Is that like chemotherapy?"

"No, not at all."

"What happens?"

"They use a powerful X-ray beam to kill the cancerous cells. It's all quite painless, or so I'm told."

"That's good."

"Nurse Debbie said they'd need to prepare me first. She said in the old days, her 'gentlemen' would have been castrated!"

"What?"

"I know, but she was quick to reassure me that doesn't happen nowadays. They put gold 'seeds' or 'fiducial markers' into your prostate. Gold because it doesn't react with what's inside your prostate. They're about the size of a grain of rice. They act as markers for the X-ray beam to be directed accurately on the affected area. The gold will also be easy to spot when scanned and used to line up the beam."

"Gosh, I had no idea!"

"Me neither. Nurse Debbie said I'd get a letter telling me when I'll have the markers implanted."

"How long does the radiotherapy take?"

"The sessions last for either four-week or eight-week periods. When the specialists have had a look at my MRI and CAT scans, they'll decide which I should have."

"Well, I'm very pleased that you are getting sorted. What about your COPD? How is your breathing?"

"Not too bad. It's been drilled into me again how important daily exercise is and to eat properly, so I'm doing my best. I have inhalers, and they help a bit. It's still pretty cold here though, I can't wait to come home to Spain. Have you heard any more about your lost luggage?"

"Nope, not a word, so I phoned Iberia. Honestly, it makes me furious just to talk about it. I phone them every day, and get passed from pillar to post, then have to repeat the whole story again. They say they'll look into it and phone me back, but they never do. I got so angry about it all, I started Tweeting them. They didn't like that but what else can I do to get their attention? One person said that I was now entitled to full compensation because twenty-one days has passed and they still haven't found it."

"That's good!"

"I'll believe it when I see it. I'm sure they are trying to fob me off. They say things like they need to see my passport again, or the list of what I've lost. They've asked for my bank details three times! I'm so sick of it, and I really miss my camera and all my favourite clothes and stuff."

The next day was busy. I wasn't intending to paint the whole stairwell, but the one wall I had already freshened up made the remainder look shabby, so I just carried on. Annoyingly, there was a small, high section that I couldn't quite reach.

As luck would have it, Geronimo happened to pass our front door, so I jumped at the opportunity.

"Geronimo!" I called out of the window, paintbrush in hand. "*¿Qué tal?*"

"*Malo,*" he replied. Bad.

I wasn't concerned because this was his stock response.

"Geronimo, if you are not in a hurry, could you possibly do me a favour? Would you mind painting a little section of wall I can't reach above the stairs? I'd be so grateful."

Geronimo was a man of few words, unless the subject was Real Madrid or football.

"*No hay problema,*" he said, taking the paint brush out of my hand. "No problem. Show me."

"Thank you!" I walked ahead and pointed up at the section that needed painting. "Can I get you a drink at all?"

In the past, Geronimo would have happily accepted a beer, or brandy, but now his reply delighted me.

"*Café solo,*" he said. Black coffee.

I went into the kitchen to make the coffee and was just returning with it when somebody knocked on the front door.

"I'll just put your coffee down here, Geronimo," I said, and hurried away to answer the door.

It was our postlady.

"Good morning, Valentina, *qué tal?*"

"Good, thank you! Marcia said you were at home. I have a letter for you that needs signing for." She passed me a large brown envelope. "Would you mind signing here, please? And then printing your name. And your NIE number in the box."

In Spain every foreign resident was given an NIE, or tax identification number, and by now I knew mine by heart. I signed.

I suddenly remembered who was behind me in my house, and my sneaky match-making tendencies slipped into overdrive.

"Would you like to come in for a coffee, Valentina?" I asked casually. "I've just made some."

"Thank you, but I must go," she replied, smiling. "Another time, perhaps."

Disappointed, I watched her sail off down the street on her yellow moped. I returned to Geronimo but he was nowhere to be seen. The section of wall, however, had been painted and the brush rested neatly on the old newspapers I had provided. The coffee, still steaming, was untouched.

In the kitchen, the back door hung open. Geronimo must have heard who was at the door and had executed a quick, silent getaway. My plan to throw them together had been foiled.

"For goodness sake!" I muttered to myself, exasperated.

I turned my attention to the envelope in my hand. It was stamped with the word *Iberia* which made my heart race. It could only mean one thing.

Oh! I thought. *I think this may be the compensation cheque…*

I tore it open but my elation was short-lived. Yes, it was a compensation cheque, but the sum was precisely 96.24 euros (approximately £80, or $105 US dollars). This did not even *begin* to cover the loss of my rather nice Fuji digital camera, my clothes, and the other items in my suitcase.

Disgusted, I wrote a furious letter of complaint back, returning the cheque.

"You weren't tempted to cash the cheque then?" asked Joe when we spoke on the phone that evening.

"Nope. Why should they get away with it? I'm going to carry on being a nuisance until they give me what they owe me."

"Are you ready for the first viewers this weekend?"

"No, but I will be."

It was the Easter long weekend, but I never saw the villagers arriving. This year I didn't see the village ladies carrying armfuls of flowers to decorate the church. Neither did I hear the church bells ringing to celebrate Easter. One of Marcia's sons brought me a plate of aromatic rice pudding but, apart from that, I refused to be interrupted from my painting and tidying duties. Marcia's *arroz con leche* was delicious, as always, still warm, sprinkled with cinnamon, and scented with lemon and vanilla.

On Easter Sunday, in the afternoon, the house and garden was ready. I felt they had never looked better. Inside, the house was decluttered, scrubbed and freshly painted, the shutters thrown open to let in the sweet mountain air. Outside, the grapevine was bursting with new leaves, and pink geraniums bloomed in pots.

The first viewers arrived, escorted by Kurt. A large English family, so large that they arrived in three cars, stampeded past me into the house. I felt quite overwhelmed.

"I'll leave you to show them around," I said to Kurt, who was bringing up the rear. "I think I'll just stay out of the way."

I hid myself away on a shady seat in the garden, away from the main activity. I couldn't work out who belonged to who, as there were at least three generations, including children of all ages. I couldn't even begin to imagine them all living in our house. Although I was out of sight, the windows were open and snatches of conversation reached me.

"Have you seen how thick these walls are?"

"Nice kitchen, but the dining room only seats eight."

"Have you counted the bedrooms?"

"Yes, three so far. Not enough."

"You can see the sea from the roof terrace."

"Mum! The beach is miles away!"

No, the signs were not good. I didn't think we'd be getting any offer from this family, and I was right.

"It's a lovely house," said one of the ladies as they were leaving, "but we really need five bedrooms. And we wanted to be able to walk to the beach. I don't think it will suit us at all."

I agreed with her, and wondered whether they had even read the particulars before the viewing.

When they left, I felt quite exhausted, and deflated. We needed to sell the house. Was there somebody out there who would fall in love with our house and El Hoyo?

The next day, Monday, brought a surprise. At Easter time, Spanish public holidays begin on Thursday, and Easter Monday is a normal working day. Our phone rang, and a Spanish voice spoke.

"Señora Twead? This is Iberia calling from Almería airport. We have found your suitcase."

"You have? That's wonderful! Where was it?"

"I believe it has been to India, but it was found at Heathrow."

"Fantastic news! When will you deliver it?"

"Oh no, señora, you must come to the airport and collect it."

"But I was told you would deliver it to my house as soon as it was found!"

"No, you must come and collect it yourself. Please bring identification and a copy of the Property Irregularity Report, the claim you made at the airport."

I was too excited to get the suitcase back to argue. It was late afternoon, so, to avoid the evening rush hour, I waited until the next day to drive the forty minutes to the airport.

Parking was easy, but collecting the suitcase was harder. I was told to stand in the checking-in queue which, of course, took ages. When I finally reached the front, the hostess held out her hand.

"Passport, please," she said, bored.

"No, I'm not travelling today."

This piqued her interest. Her plucked eyebrows arched in surprise.

"You are not flying today?"

"No. I was told to speak to you. I've come to collect my suitcase which has been found."

"Your suitcase?"

"Yes." It was hard to stay patient.

"Lost property? Then you are in the wrong place. I will phone a member of staff to meet you." Crimson manicured fingernails clattered on the keyboard, and she spoke rapidly into her mouthpiece.

I waited.

"Please stand aside, my colleague is on her way."

I obediently stood back and waited. And waited.

"Have I been forgotten?" I asked Crimson Fingernails after fifteen minutes had elapsed.

"Oh no, my colleague is on her way."

I reflected that it was a good thing Joe was not with me.

Half an hour went by before a uniformed lady appeared. She examined my passport and Property Irregularity Report, then I was taken to a small room off the big hall where the luggage carousels turned. The lady unlocked the door, and there was my suitcase.

"Is that yours?" she asked.

"Yes!" I said, relieved.

"I will call customs to check it," she said and spoke into her walkie-talkie.

More time passed, and eventually two customs officers arrived.

"Do you have anything to declare?" one of them asked, as he lifted my case onto a counter and unzipped it.

"No," I replied.

Nothing to declare? Huh! I nobly resisting the temptation to declare my fury at having my case lost for thirty-five days, the letters, the emails, the endless, fruitless phone calls and tweets, the lack of compensation, being told to collect the case myself, and finally being kept waiting so long today.

He swung the lid back and I caught a glimpse of the contents. Although rather muddled and disordered, my possessions looked familiar.

"You can go," he said, losing interest, and continued the conversation he was having with his colleague.

Without another word, I zipped up the case and wheeled it out to the car. I didn't know it at the time, but I was making a big mistake.

EASTER TREATS
TORRIJAS

Spanish folklore says that these sweet treats were made by nuns centuries ago, and they're certainly a great way to use up day old bread.

Tip: If you don't have any stale bread, lightly toast or microwave so that it doesn't disintegrate during the dipping.

Ingredients

Half a dozen slices of stale bread

100 mls (3.5 fl oz) of milk

1 egg

Vegetable or sunflower oil for frying (not olive oil as it is too strong)

A couple of drops of vanilla extract (not essential)

Sugar for coating

Method

Mix the egg and milk together in a large bowl.

Add the vanilla extract.

Gently heat the vegetable oil in a large flat pan.

Quickly dip each slice of bread into the egg/milk mixture, flipping once so that both sides are covered.

Transfer immediately to the frying pan and cook until golden brown on both sides.

Once cooked, keep warm in a low oven whilst you cook the rest.

Arrange on a plate and sprinkle with sugar, cinnamon, a drizzle of honey... or whatever else takes your imagination.

20

WORRIES

I couldn't wait to open my suitcase. In Australia, Karly had teased me about the size of my knickers next to hers on the washing line. Of course hers were tiny wisps of nothingness.

I knew she would be asleep, but I sent her a text message.

"I'm delighted to announce a touching reunion with my big bloomers."

But my glee was short lived. Alarm bells should have rung when the customs officer had opened my case at the airport and I'd glimpsed my possessions.

I'm a neat packer. I fold everything carefully. I pay great attention to what should be carefully wrapped in towels, or padded out with soft clothing for protection. The contents of my case were all jumbled up, and definitely not how I'd packed them.

And the reason?

My suitcase had been ransacked. My camera, hard drive, and some other bits and pieces had been stolen. Once again, I sighed with relief that I had kept my laptop with me in my hand luggage.

"Bad news," I texted Karly. *"Camera and stuff stolen from suitcase."*

Karly must have woken up, because the reply came straight back.

"Bet they didn't steal your knickers."

She was right, of course.

I was grateful, too, that they hadn't stolen my journal and book notes, either. Nor my Filofax. So it could have been worse.

I phoned Iberia, and after being kept holding the line for fifteen minutes, I told them my news.

"Did you report your loss to the airport police and make a statement?"

No! Of course I hadn't. I hadn't even realised that items had been stolen at the time, and making a list of what was missing wouldn't be an easy task. The case had been missing for thirty-five days, and I needed time to compare its contents with the list I had already made. Yet again, I was told to write to the Madrid office.

I washed all my clothes, dried them, then took them to the charity clothes bin. There was nothing wrong with the clothes, but I couldn't bear the thought of dirty thieving hands rifling through my belongings.

"Did you give your bloomers to charity?" asked Karly.

"Excuse me, they are *not* 'bloomers', they are just sensible knickers. And yes, I did."

"Good. That way you can at least feel good that some poor homeless person has found shelter in your bloomers. Tents are so useful, aren't they?"

In the UK, Joe opened a letter from the Acute Services Division of the local hospital. Nurse Debbie instructed him to report for a CAT scan of his bones.

It was a worrying time. If the cancer had been discovered too late, and had spread to his bones, then Joe's prospects would be extremely bleak.

"Remove your clothes and put on this gown," said a nurse.

Joe did as commanded and was shown into another room. This one had a narrow flat table that would slide through a donut-shaped machine which, Joe presumed, recorded the images.

"Now, Mr Twead, just hop up onto the bed," said the nurse.

Joe's hopping days were over, but he hoisted himself up and lay on the table obediently.

"Now, don't move," instructed the nurse.

Don't worry, thought Joe, *I'm too scared of falling off this wretched table.*

Twenty-five minutes later it was all over. A series of clicks and buzzes was all that broke up the monotony of having to lie still for a prolonged period of time.

"It was no problem," Joe confided later. "It's the MRI I'm a bit nervous about. I've heard it's not so easy."

"You'll be fine," I said.

I worked like a beaver keeping the house as tidy and fresh as possible at all times. I never knew when Kurt might phone to bring viewers. And at the weekends, villagers often knocked on the door to view the house. It was always women, and often in groups of three or four.

"We have family who may be interested," they would say, not quite meeting my eye.

Off they would march, from room to room, opening cupboards and peering into drawers. The ladies had probably seen the house eleven years ago, when Alfonso had owned it, and it didn't have a kitchen, let alone bathrooms.

"*¡Guapo!*" they exclaimed. "It looks good!"

I could tell that some things left them rather bemused. For instance, the rather ornate, though now empty, chicken coop with its water feature and mirror. And the sun loungers on the roof terrace were eyed doubtfully. No Spanish person ever lies in the sun by choice.

I am almost sure that none of these viewers *really* had family with a genuine interest in buying our house. I think the visits were pure curiosity but I had to tolerate them, just in case. As Kurt said, we only needed one buyer.

Then one of the ladies would ask about the price of the house. When I told them, there was a unanimous intake of breath and they would roll their eyes at each other. In whispered tones, the younger ones would convert the sum to *pesetas* for the benefit of the older ones, even though Spain had embraced the euro in 2002, thirteen years before. More gasps and eye-rolling.

"Honestly," I said to Joe, "you'd think we were asking a ridiculous price. It's about the same as what we paid all those years ago, when it was a ruin. Do you think we're asking too much?"

"No," said Joe, "don't worry, it will happen. Kurt knows what he's doing. We just have to be patient."

I tried to take my mind off it all with my writing, but there was a lot to worry about. Had Joe's prostate cancer already spread? What about his breathing, how quickly would that deteriorate? Would we ever sell the house? What about Australian visas? Could we afford a house in Australia?

I did some research on the Internet and discovered a depressing fact, one that I had already guessed. Houses in the Sydney area would be well beyond our financial reach.

"They are like London house prices," I told Joe on the phone. "Crazy prices, unless we opt for a tiny flat in a grotty area. They call them 'units'."

"How tiny?"

"Well, one bedroom, no outdoor space... Garage in a complex, that sort of thing."

Silence. I'm sure we were both thinking the same thing. We were remembering what we were giving up. We lived in a spacious home with three good bedrooms, two bathrooms, an enchanting walled garden, roof terraces and a 360 degree view of the mountains.

"I think I may have thought of a couple of options," I said. "I'll run them past you, and you can have a think. Then we can discuss them properly when you come home."

"Go on."

"Well, we could move further afield. The Central Coast is about an hour and a half north of Sydney, and property prices are much cheaper."

"That's quite a long way away from the family."

"I know, but the roads are good."

"Okay, and the other option?"

"Um, we could probably afford to move into a retirement village."

"Really? What are they like?"

"Well, they vary, but some have bungalows with gardens. They are much cheaper to buy, and the village provides loads of amenities like a pool, dining rooms, gym, outings, library, gardeners, visiting doctors, and stuff like that."

I could almost hear Joe thinking.

"Outings? Gardeners? What's the average age of people in a retirement village?" he asked.

"Well, I don't know. Probably quite a bit older than us…"

"Vicky, I don't think we're ready for a wrinkly-ville yet."

"I know, but we might be surprised. It could be worth checking out."

"Let's get the house sold first, and I have the MRI appointment, too. The results of that could change everything."

On the day of the MRI, Joe was again asked to don a hospital gown.

"Are you claustrophobic by any chance?" asked the nurse, who had probably read Joe's body language.

"Actually, yes."

"Don't worry, we are just in the next room. Nothing will go wrong, so do try to relax and don't move. You will be in the scanner for about thirty minutes and you will hear a lot of loud noises. Don't be alarmed, they're perfectly normal."

She was strapping Joe to the table ensuring he could not move. Joe eyed the huge, donut-shaped machine which would envelope him entirely.

"Now, what music do you like?"

"Music?"

"Yes. We play music through these headphones."

She showed them to Joe and he realised that they would also serve as ear protectors.

"What music did you choose?" I asked. "Can I guess?"

"Go on then."

"Something classical… No, wait, the Beatles!"

"Yup."

"Did the Beatles help?"

"Yes. You can't imagine how loud it was in that machine. Nothing could have prepared me for that cacophony of screeches and groans. It was almost unbearable being strapped down. Seriously, I thought it would never end. But I forced myself to close my eyes and listen to the Beatles, song after song, and that saved me."

"Great! Now what?"

"Well, that's pretty much it. I have an appointment with the respiratory nurse, and I need to know the results of the MRI, then I can come home."

My heart soared.

"I vill come tomorrow at two o'clock," said Kurt. "A man from England vants to see your house."

At two o'clock, I opened the door to Kurt and a middle-aged man wearing a baseball cap at a jaunty angle.

"This is Barry," said Kurt.

I shook hands and introduced myself, then left Kurt to provide the guided tour. I couldn't help overhearing snippets of conversation and they didn't fill me with hope.

"Good house, Kurt, but it's much too big for me."

"It vill be good to have space if your family stay."

"That's why I've come to Spain, to get away from my family!"

"Oh, but you said you vanted a bigger place than you haf now."

"Yes, that's true. But my place in London is unusually small."

"Ah, it is an apartment? Like a grandmother apartment?"

"No, it's a houseboat on the river Thames."

When I bade them goodbye, I already knew that Barry the Boat would not be buying our house.

The next viewer was a single lady, English again.

I was clearing out a cupboard in the workshop and was surrounded by various tools, oily rags and pieces of pipe. When one lives in a remote village, where the nearest proper stores are half an hour away, one tends to keep odd bits and pieces in case they come in useful someday. The telephone rang in the house. I ran to answer it and got there just in time.

"Today I cannot be at your house," said Kurt. "Anastasia is coming up the mountain now. Please show her your house."

"No problem, Kurt."

Would this be the one?

I put the phone down and zoomed round the house, lightning-fast, making sure it was tidy and ready for viewing. In the workshop, I threw the stuff back into the cupboard. I washed up a few bits in the kitchen, wiped the bench tops and was just opening some windows when I heard her arrive.

Yikes! No time to change my clothes.

A red, open top sports car drew up and parked outside the front door. Luckily it was a weekday, or that might have caused a problem. Our street was one of the main arteries of the village, and only one vehicle wide, with no room to pass. Paco would not have been able to drive his tractor past, and this lady's thoughtless parking would have blocked off the bread, fish or vegetable vans, had they arrived. The car was a beauty, with gleaming paintwork and cream leather upholstery.

I peeped out of the window and watched the lady get out of her car. In true model style, her legs came first, then her body followed. I was transfixed by her shoes, which were bright red with heels like skewers. Bleached blonde hair was teased into waves that rippled over her shoulders, and she wore a red dress that clung to her curves. Almost her entire face was shielded by oversized dark glasses. The lady was dressed for a cocktail party on the deck of a glitzy yacht in Marbella, not a property viewing in a remote mountain village.

I opened the door and stood on the doorstep wearing what I hoped was a welcoming smile, painfully aware of the dirty stains on my T-shirt.

I greeted her and shook her manicured hand.

"You must be Anastasia," I said. "I'm Vicky."

"Pleased to meet you," she replied, though her expression didn't match the sentiment. "Will my car be safe here?"

"Oh yes, of course," I said confidently. "Perfectly safe."

AUBERGINE (EGGPLANT) WITH HONEY
BERENJENA CON MIEL

A really easy recipe, so easy that, as they say in Spain, *"No es moco de pavo"* which directly translates as "It's not turkey snot". Yes, you read that correctly... Bleugh!

Ingredients

One eggplant, or aubergine, or whatever you want to call it

Couple of tablespoons of honey for drizzling

Couple of spoonfuls of flour for coating

Plenty of olive oil for frying

Method

Slice the aubergine really thinly.

Pop the slices into a bowl of water and leave it for half an hour. Soaking before cooking takes some of the bitterness out.

Drain well and toss in the flour, ensuring a good coating.

Deep fry in batches. When they are golden brown and floating, they are ready. You can keep them warm in a low oven while you fry the rest.

Drain on paper towels and arrange on a plate or in a bowl.

Drizzle with honey, or *miel de caña* which is molasses.

Serve immediately.

21

VIEWINGS

Anastasia hesitated for just a moment before pointing her car keys at the car and pressing a button. The headlights flashed briefly and the car beeped to signify it was locked.

"The car is new," she said. "I only picked it up yesterday."

"It's a lovely car," I said. "Do come in and I'll show you the house."

I began the tour in the living room, pointing out the wood-burning stove and the alcove that had been a bread oven years ago. She didn't seem particularly impressed.

"Tell me about the village," she said.

"Well, it's very quiet," I said. "Of course it's much busier at the weekends, and in the summer months."

"What shops do you have?"

"Um, we don't really have any, except for Marcia's shop in the square."

"What does she sell?"

For the life of me, I couldn't think of anything Marcia sold except sweets for the children, and cigarettes and beer for the adults. And then only enough to half fill one shelf in her shop.

"Oh, this and that."

"There's no supermarket?"

"No. There are vans that come into the village most days. There's a bread van, a fish van, a fruit and vegetable van. There's even one that sells peaches in the summer. And oranges in the winter."

Anastasia's high heels clacked on the floor tiles.

"You buy your produce from vans that deliver?"

"Yes," I replied. "It's all locally grown and very fresh."

"I like to hold parties. What would I do if I ran out of martini, or nibbles, or something?"

"I'm afraid you'd have to drive down the mountain. We tend to be quite organised and stock up on supplies to avoid running out of stuff."

Anastasia arched her eyebrows.

"Restaurants?"

I shook my head.

"Bars?"

"Yes! We have a brand new bar in the square."

I omitted to mention that it was only frequented by very old men playing dominoes except on special occasions, like the annual *fiesta*.

I showed her the dining room, and the kitchen, then led her to the main bedroom.

"It's a cave," I said proudly. "It stays beautifully cool in summer and it's warm in winter."

I flicked a switch and a hundred tiny white fairy lights twinkled in the ceiling. I loved this room.

"No windows at all?"

"No," I said firmly. "No windows at all. It's a cave."

I took her upstairs and showed her the other bedrooms and the little kitchenette, used by visitors to make drinks and snacks when they stayed. Anastasia didn't comment.

"And every room up here has wonderful views of the mountains," I enthused, although I was rapidly losing the will to live.

I threw open the doors to the roof terraces.

"Up here," I babbled, "there is a wonderful view of the whole village, and the sea in the distance."

Anastasia clacked over to the wall and looked in the direction I was pointing.

"And over there is the church, and those gates are the entrance to the village cemetery…"

Out of the corner of my eye I saw the pair of house martins flit away from their nest under the eaves, probably startled by my energetic arm-waving. Each dropped a deposit as it flew, and I knew without a shadow of a doubt that the shiny red car below had just been bombed.

Luckily, Anastasia had been looking in another direction and hadn't noticed her car being targeted. She looked down and along the street. I followed her gaze and saw a black shape walking towards us, hugging the shadows. I recognised him immediately. It was Black Balls, as Joe insisted on calling him. The huge, extremely well-endowed, jet black, battle-scarred tom cat that ruled the village.

"What's that?" asked Anastasia, pointing a polished, ruby fingernail.

"Oh, that's just Blackie," I said. "He's, er, a local cat."

"Who does it belong to?"

"Well, nobody, really."

"You mean it's a *feral* cat?"

"Um, yes, I suppose so."

Below us, Black Balls continued padding along with purpose. He was carrying something, and as he got closer, I could see what it was. A whole fish, rotting and falling apart, was clenched between his teeth. Heaven only knows where he had found it, perhaps it had been thrown from the fish van at some time.

I knew Black Balls would be looking for somewhere private to enjoy his feast, and my heart sank. He was probably going to eat it under Anastasia's car. Sure enough, looking up and down the street to check that no cat, dog or human was going to interrupt him, he began to approach the shiny, red car. I held my breath, feeling Anastasia tense beside me.

"That *creature* is heading for my car!"

Oh dear. She'd noticed.

"And it's carrying something revolting in its mouth!"

"I expect he's looking for somewhere quiet to eat it," I said.

"I don't want that disgusting brute under my car," exclaimed Anastasia, whipping off her sunglasses to see better.

Black Balls didn't go under the car.

He did much worse.

He jumped up onto the bonnet, probably intending to use the car as a step to jumping up onto the opposite roof.

"Oy!" shouted Anastasia, leaning over the wall.

Black Balls froze.

"Get off my car!"

Black Balls spun his head round to see where the shouting was coming from, then saw us above. Quick as a flash, he leapt over the windscreen and into the car, landing on the cream leather upholstery, rotting fish still firmly clamped between his teeth. The sudden activity didn't do his meal any good, and I was dismayed to see bits of rotting flesh falling off the fish. I lost sight of him but I knew he would be crouched in the darkness of the foot well.

"Good grief!" screeched Anastasia. "It's in my car!"

She whipped round and ran back inside as fast as her stilettos would allow. Down the stairs she flew, through the dining room and living room, and burst out of the front door. I followed her.

"Get out of my car, you brute!" she shouted.

Black Balls didn't hang around. He probably thought this crazy human was after his fish. Out he scrambled and legged it up the street to safety, Anastasia waving her fist after him.

I stood on the doorstep, uncertain what to say, but I might as well have been invisible. Anastasia had reached the end of her tether.

"I've had enough of this God forsaken place," she muttered, unlocking the car and getting in.

Without a backward glance, she roared off up the street.

But not before I spotted twin white splats on the car's shiny paintwork.

As I had suspected, our house martins had scored direct hits.

I met Joe at the airport on a cloudless day already showing signs of the heat that summer would inevitably bring.

We hugged for a long time.

"I'm so pleased to be home," he said, at last. "I'm looking forward to a nice relaxing time."

"Oh dear, I'm afraid we have viewers tomorrow."

"Never mind, as long as they aren't as bad as that awful Anastasia woman you told me about."

"Most of them are really nice, she was a bit, um, unusual."

"Did Kurt say anything about these ones?"

"Just that they're a German couple."

Fritz and Helga were delightful. They both spoke almost flawless English and had wonderful manners. Helga declared that they'd already fallen in love with El Hoyo as they descended into the valley, and that our home was perfect.

They loved the cave room, the big kitchen and the wood-burning stoves. They admired the walled garden and the chicken area. They adored the roof terraces and the stunning views. They enthused over the big garage and the workshop. But something didn't feel quite right to me. The way they kept looking at each other, as though communicating silently about something, puzzled me.

"You haf a beautiful haus," said Fritz. "Ve like to live here very much."

Helga, at his side, nodded.

"The village it is perfect, too. Ve can understand how you haf been so happy here."

Joe and I waited. To be honest, I could sense a 'but' coming, and sure enough, it appeared. And it was a big one.

"But you haf no space for a horse."

We stared at them.

"A horse?" Kurt asked.

"Yes. We dream to keep horses. Already ve haf one horse ve vill take from Germany."

"Yes," said Helga, her eyes shining. "Our Gunther is an eight-year-old Hanoverian gelding."

"Goodness," I said.

"I think there is no stable here? No place for a horse?"

"No," said Kurt.

"No," agreed Joe.

"Chickens, yes," I said. "But horses? No."

I was sorry to see Fritz and Helga leave. They genuinely liked the village and our house, and I would have been quite happy handing the keys over to them.

But there was nowhere to keep a horse.

Not even a small one.

"I did not expect that," said Kurt, after they'd driven away. "But I haf two more viewings up my arm."

"Oh, that's good!"

"Yes, both they vill come on Thursday. In the morning, a twosome from Germany, and in the afternoon, a twosome from England."

"Right, we'll keep our fingers crossed."

"Yes. It only takes one."

It was strange, but as soon as Kurt mentioned the English couple, a tingly feeling swept over me. I'm a very down-to-earth person. I never read my horoscope and am a little sceptical about astrology and spiritual matters. I've never seen a ghost, nor had genuine premonitions. But I suddenly *knew* that we would sell our house to the English couple who were coming to see the house on Thursday.

That Sunday, Joe and I sat on our roof terrace watching the activity in the village. The cobalt sky stretched away in all directions, unbroken by cloud. The house martins flitted to and fro, doubtless feeding their babies.

"I wonder how many eggs hatched?" I said, leaning over the wall a little.

The nest was placed so that I couldn't see in, and I didn't try very hard because I didn't want to disturb the parent birds.

To my right was the church. Mass had just finished and the villagers were leaving the church in dribs and drabs. Carmen was in deep discussion with another village lady, and Marcia hobbled back to her shop. As always, nobody ever looked up at the roof tops or they would have seen us. It was as though we were invisible.

Little Pollito Ufarte was also heading home under the watchful eyes of his big sisters. He ran ahead, clutching his latest creation.

"Pollito!" called a twin. "Wait! Show us what you have made in Sunday School today!"

The little boy stopped right below us, and held up his treasure for them to see. From above, it looked like two cardboard tubes, toilet paper roll holders, stuck together with sticky tape.

"What are they?" asked one of his big sisters when she reached him.

"¡Prismáticos!" he declared. "Binoculars!"

"Oh! Of course they are!"

"What a clever boy you are, Pollito!"

Pollito beamed and pressed his binoculars to his eyes, scanning the mountainside. Then he peered at our front door through the cardboard rolls, and finally at his own feet.

"Look!" he squeaked, pointing down. "Look what I have found!"

His sisters bent to look, then pulled him away quickly.

"Pollito! Do not touch it!"

"Why not? I want to look! It is a tiny bird."

Unseen, I peered over the wall and spotted the tiny body of a fledgeling lying in the street, directly below our house martins' nest. *How sad*, I thought, *one of the babies must have fallen out.*

"Yes, it is a poor baby bird," said Twin #1.

"It has fallen out of a nest perhaps," said Twin #2.

"It is asleep?"

"No, Pollito, it has died."

"It will not wake up in a minute?"

"No, it has gone to heaven to be with Jesus."

"Does Jesus not like little birds?"

"Of course He does! Why?"

"Then why did He throw it back down?"

"Oh, Pollito!"

Smiling, the twins gathered up their little brother and bore him off down the street leaving Joe and I chuckling above.

"It's hard to believe that we may not be here to watch that little chap grow up," I mused.

"But you'll be able to watch Indy. That'll be even better."

It was a heady notion.

"We have a busy time ahead of us next week," I said. "Two viewings scheduled already, and we need to go to the medical centre and get your next injection done. I forgot to tell you, I had an email from my sister this morning. She's kindly translated your letter from the UK hospital, into Spanish. I'll print it out and we can take it with us to the medical centre in case the doctor doesn't understand English."

My phone rang, and I picked it up.

"It is I, Kurt."

"Hello Kurt, how are you?"

"I am vell. The Germans vill not come on Thursday. They haf discovered another house."

"Oh, okay," I said, but Kurt had already hung up.

"That was Kurt. The German couple cancelled."

"Oh dear, does that blow your theory about receiving an offer for the house on Thursday?"

"No, not at all. I'm positive the English couple will want it."

"Well, don't be too disappointed if they don't turn up, or don't like the house."

"I won't."

PRAWN BITES
MONTADITOS DE GAMBAS

These *montaditos de gambas* are tasty, healthy, and easy to make. They are ideal for a quick lunch, as *tapas,* or as a starter for your dinner guests.

Ingredients

8 slices of bread, toasted or fresh

½ kilo (1lb) of raw prawns, shells and veins removed

1 or 2 garlic cloves, chopped really finely, or crushed

1 chilli, chopped very finely (optional)

½ teaspoon of paprika

Small bunch of spring onions, very finely sliced, including green parts

Olive oil for frying

Method

Cut each slice of bread in half

Pour a good splash of olive oil into a very hot frying pan.

Throw in all ingredients, except the paprika and bread, and fry for a couple of minutes until the prawns turn pink, stirring well.

Spoon the cooked mixture over your slices of bread.

Sprinkle the paprika over the top.

Serve immediately.

22

IT ONLY TAKES ONE

I'm not sure why I persevered with phoning, emailing and tweeting Iberia Airlines. I could have spent the time more profitably by sticking pins in my feet for half an hour a day, but I guess I couldn't drop it because the injustice smarted.

It was clear to me that airport staff, most likely at Heathrow, had stolen my camera, external computer hard drive and other stuff, and I felt I deserved compensation. I'd trusted my belongings to the airline and they had betrayed my trust.

With hindsight, I should have simply accepted the insultingly small compensation cheque they sent me, and forgotten all about the incident instead of stressing about it. But I carried on phoning, emailing and tweeting. I rarely received a reply, and when I did, I had to repeat the whole sorry saga from the beginning.

"Yes, you are definitely due full compensation," they would say. "We'll phone you back."

But they never did.

Other issues also preoccupied me, like Joe's next hormone injection. The timing had to be exactly right, three months from the last one.

When we first moved to El Hoyo, the doctor visited the village once a week and consultations were conducted in a villager's living room or kitchen, often Marcia's. I clearly remembered the time when Joe had allowed Marcia to give him a routine injection more than ten years before. Joe had expected to be injected in his arm, and insisted that her family need not vacate the kitchen. All Marcia's family members stayed and, to his horror, watched as Marcia pulled down one side of his shorts and injected him in the buttock.

But time had marched on and brought progress with it. Our village shared a brand new town hall and modern surgery that had been built in a neighbouring village.

And time hadn't stood still in El Hoyo either. When the council built the new bar, they included a consulting room for the doctor's once weekly visit. There was even a free delivery service to El Hoyo for filled prescriptions. These arrived on the fish van.

We could have seen the doctor in El Hoyo, but we didn't want to wait for his weekly village visit as the hormone injection had to be administered on a particular day. So we decided to go to the surgery in the neighbouring village.

In we marched, armed with the syringe and the explanatory letter. To our surprise, the waiting room was empty, although the doctor's door was slightly ajar.

"It's quiet today," observed Joe. "Shall I knock on the door?"

"Yes," I said. "We're in luck! There's no queue."

Joe tapped on the door.

"Come in," called a female voice.

"It must be the new lady doctor, or the nurse," I whispered, and followed Joe in.

A nurse stood with her back to us, doing something at the filing cabinet.

"Good morning," said Joe brightly, in his best Spanish. "I have a letter that explains everything. If you could please just inject my left buttock, *señora*, I'd be most grateful."

He put the injection on the doctor's desk and, pulling down his shorts, helpfully bared his snowy left *nalga* (buttock) in her direction.

The lady turned, and her eyes widened as her gaze settled on Joe's exposed pale posterior.

"*¡Madre mía!*" she exclaimed, one hand flying up to clutch the gold crucifix round her neck.

A duster hung limply from her other hand.

I would say that it was probably at that point that both Joe and I noticed what she was wearing. It was a uniform, yes, but not a nurse's uniform. It was an overall.

Joe yanked his shorts back up.

"You're not a nurse, are you?" he asked.

But we both already knew the answer.

The cleaner shook her head, her eyes still wide.

"The surgery is closed today," she said. "Come back tomorrow."

We backed out of the surgery, apologising profusely.

"Do you know, when she turned round, I thought I recognised her!" I said later. "I think she's Carmen's cousin. I know she has a cleaning job at the town hall."

"Well, why didn't you say something?"

"I wasn't sure, and you already had your pants down by then."

Joe doesn't blush easily, but I think he did that day.

We returned the next morning and the doctor read the letter my sister had translated. The injection was administered without mishap.

"Well, that's another thing you can cross off your list," said Joe. "Mission accomplished."

"You can scoff at my lists as much as you like."

Without lists, I am lost. And I was pretty excited about the next big item on my list; the viewing.

"I honestly think we might sell the house today," I said to Joe again as we waited for the 'English twosome' to arrive, "but I almost *don't* want it to happen. If I had a fairy godmother, I'd ask her if we could definitely sell it today, and that the buyers wouldn't want to move in until after the summer."

"Hardly likely!"

"I know, but I'd so love to have one last summer here in El Hoyo. I want to taste our grapes one last time, and I'd love to see Sofía get married. I just want to hang on to every last moment."

High on the mountain, we saw Kurt's car begin to descend the hairpin bends into the valley, closely followed by an unfamiliar car.

"That's them," Joe said.

I jumped up to check around the house, probably for the tenth time that day. When the knock came at the door, I counted to five before opening it. I didn't want them to know I'd been waiting right behind the door.

"Good afternoon," said Kurt. "Here are Alison and Steve to examine your house."

I maintain that you can tell a lot from first impressions. Alison was smiling and friendly, and Steve's handshake was warm. I liked them both on sight. I guessed they were about ten or twelve years younger than us and I recognised the expression on Alison's face. It was the same enraptured expression that I had worn when we first set foot in El Hoyo so many years before.

"The village is beautiful," breathed Alison. "Almost magical! All those wildflowers on the slopes, and the ancient mine. I love this place already."

"She's the airy-fairy one," said Steve, laughing, nodding to his wife and pretending to roll his eyes. "She's an artist, and we're looking for somewhere quiet to live."

"Here you vill discover quiet," said Kurt.

Joe and I nodded.

"Oh gosh, don't tell me that's a bread oven over there!" exclaimed Alison. "And look at the thickness of these walls!"

"We'll let Kurt show you everything," I said. "Joe and I will be here if you need us. I'll pour out some lemonade and take it into the garden for you when you've finished your tour."

I'd never offered any of the other viewers refreshments.

"Well," I hissed at Joe, "what do you think?"

"Nice couple, but way too early to say if they'll buy it."

"They will," I said confidently.

The tour took a long time. While Alison soaked in the views from the roof terrace, and explored every room, Steve fired sensible questions at Kurt. Eventually the party returned and joined us under the vine.

"Oh look! The grapes are already forming!" said Alison looking up in delight. "And we would definitely keep chickens!"

"Well, the coop is all set up and ready to go," I said, pouring iced lemonade into glasses. "All you need to do is pop in some chickens and you'll have fresh eggs every day, just like we had."

Alison leaned forward, and her eyes were shining.

"This is like a dream," she said. "We definitely want to buy your house."

Just for a second, everything went quiet.

Then all heads turned to Steve. He was grinning.

"Oh, I'm just here for the ride," he joked. "If the boss says she wants it, then that's that. Happy wife, happy life, that's what I always say."

Suddenly everybody was talking at once, laughing and shaking hands. It was wonderfully informal, not a bit like any house sale I'd ever made before.

"I just love it!" said Alison, her hands clasped under her chin. "I love everything about it."

My heart soared knowing that our beloved home would be in good hands, cared for and enjoyed by its new owners just as we'd done in the past.

"Oh, there's just one thing we haven't mentioned," said Steve, looking concerned. "I do hope it's not going to make a difference."

Kurt, Joe and I looked at him. *Not a fly in the ointment already?* We waited.

"The thing is, we haven't sold our house in England yet. We've only just put it on the market and these things take time. It's a nice house in a nice area, and there's no reason why it shouldn't sell quickly."

My mind was racing, trying to absorb this latest information.

Steve must have seen my expression.

"Of course we'll make an official firm offer for this house tomorrow," he added quickly, "and we'll get the Spanish solicitor to draw up everything. And if you accept, we'll pay the deposit. We definitely want to buy this house. There's no question of that."

"Oh yes! We definitely want to live here!" said Alison.

"But I doubt we can actually finalise and move in until early

September," continued Steve. "We'll need the summer to sort out our affairs."

My mouth dropped open. This was unbelievable! This was what I had hardly dared to dream. We'd not only sold the house, so *that* worry was lifted from our shoulders, but we were also being handed one last summer here in El Hoyo!

I couldn't speak.

Joe and I exchanged glances. I knew he was reading my mind.

Steve and Alison were watching us, and I suddenly realised they were misreading our signals. Both looked extremely worried.

"September would be *perfect* for us," I said, smiling, and saw Alison, Steve and Kurt relax. "In fact, it couldn't be better."

"We're going back to England in a couple of days, but I'll be returning next month to help my sister who is moving into a house in Almería," said Alison. "Would it be okay if I pop back? I know I'll have a lot of questions and I'd love to show my sister the house and village."

"Of course! Make a list of questions and we'll do our best to answer them."

"You and your lists," said Joe, but he was smiling.

We waved our visitors goodbye and watched their cars climb the road out of the valley. It had been an important, life-changing day.

I'll never forget that evening on the roof terrace. It was a perfect setting, and as the shadows deepened and the sun dipped behind the mountain, we sipped Paco's homemade wine and breathed in the scented air. Bats flitted around the church tower against an orange, fiery backdrop.

"I still can't believe it," I repeated for the millionth time. "A whole summer! Oodles of time to sort out the Australian visa and to pack."

"Yes," said Joe.

I knew he was just as delighted as I was, but he is much better at controlling his enthusiasm. Me? I felt my cup was running over, and my head was spinning. And it wasn't Paco's wine that was making my head spin, it was joy.

"Plenty of time to go to the enchanted pool as often as we like, and the beach," I said.

"Yes."

A thought struck me.

"And we'll be here in the village for Sofía and Alejandro's wedding!"

"Well, that'll be quite an experience."

I agreed. We sat in silence, each lost in our own thoughts. I was recalling when we first arrived in the village, back in 2004, eleven years ago. We'd met our neighbours, Paco and Carmen, and they'd told us about their children. Their youngest, Little Paco had been nine years old. He was nearly twenty now. And they had despaired of their beautiful daughter, Sofía, ever marrying.

I recalled that day, and the memory was still fresh.

"Pah!" Paco had yelled, thumping his fist on the table as he fumed over his wayward daughter. "She should be married by now! But always there is something wrong with every boy she meets."

"*Claro,*" Carmen had nodded sadly, "that's true."

"The boy is too thin, or too fat, or wears the wrong clothes... No boy is good enough! Many times she meets a very nice boy, but never does she want him for a husband!"

It took a long time, but ten years later, Sofía had finally found The One. This summer she would marry Alejandro, the local millionaire's grandson.

And everybody was delighted.

FRUITY ICE
GRANIZADO

When the temperatures hit 40 degrees celsius in Spain, this easy *granizado* recipe makes the heat easier to handle.

Ingredients

5 lemons

2 oranges

500g (18oz) of white sugar

1.5 litres (3 pints) of water

Method

Grate the peel from the oranges and lemons, avoiding the bitter pith.Put the peel in a saucepan.

Get as much juice as you can from the fruit and add to the pan.

Add the sugar and 500ml (1 pint) of the water to the pan.

Bring it to a rolling boil until the liquid has reduced by half.

Set aside to cool for 5-10 mins.

Pour into a large, fairly shallow, freezer-proof container and top up with the remaining water.

Stir and place in the freezer.

Freeze for 3-4 hours but take it out and stir with a fork every ¾ of an hour or so. When it resembles a slush, it is ready to serve.

23

PREPARATIONS AND JANE

The subject of Sofía and Alejandro's wedding was a red-hot talking point in El Hoyo that summer. Carmen, as the bride's mother, could think about little else, and confided in me often.

"Can you believe it?" she said, all her double chins jiggling. She looked up from sewing her daughter's wedding dress. "Sofía and Alejandro, they could have their wedding anywhere! The family of Alejandro has told them to choose any venue in Andalucía. They could get married in the biggest church, and have their reception in a luxury hotel."

"Wow!"

"They could hold their reception on a boat, or even in a castle. But where have they chosen?" Carmen stared at me, her lips pressed together, waiting for me to reply.

I knew the answer, but I wasn't going to pour water on her bonfire.

"I don't know. Where have they chosen?"

"They have chosen here! El Hoyo!" Her chins fairly danced with glee.

"No! Really?"

"Yes, Sofía has all the latest gadgets and modern things, but really she is a traditional, home-loving soul at heart."

"I think that's wonderful!"

To me, it seemed absolutely right that the pair should marry in the village, even if money was no object, and I was very much looking forward to comparing the event with an English wedding.

"But the church is so small! Not all our guests will fit in," Carmen exclaimed.

I could certainly believe that. Spanish families are very big.

"Oh dear, what will you do?" I asked.

"Well, some people will have to stand outside."

"Never mind, I'm sure it'll all be just perfect. We'd like to give the *novios* (bridal pair) a gift," I said. "Do they have a wedding list?"

Carmen looked confused for a second, then jumped up.

"Ah! You mean a number! I will write it down for you on a piece of paper."

She scribbled something, and passed the paper to me. I glanced at it, but said nothing. Later, when I showed the paper to Joe, we realised what it was. It was Sofía and Alejandro's bank details. We were a little surprised, but when we talked to others, we were informed that this is a typical Spanish wedding practice. Guests are given the bride and groom's bank details so that they can make a direct deposit into their bank account.

"That seems a bit clinical," said Joe, "but I guess it saves the happy couple from unwrapping twenty salt and pepper sets as gifts."

That last summer evaporated faster than any I could remember. Now that our house was sold, *everything* needed sorting. Packing, visa, flights… I began to generate enough lists to paper a wall and I tossed and turned in bed every night before falling asleep, exhausted.

I searched online for shipping companies that would take our possessions to Australia. I spent hours costing it, and finally came to a conclusion.

"Joe, I think we should leave all our furniture and stuff here."

"Really? Are you sure?"

"Yes. All our furniture is good and solid, but it's twenty years old, or more. I don't think it will travel well, and it will be hugely expensive. And we'd have to store it until we found somewhere to live. It'll cost about the same to buy everything new in Australia."

"Heavens! What should we do? Sell it here?"

"I don't really know who would buy it in Spain. I was thinking we should just leave it with the house."

"Well, Alison and her sister are coming on Friday, we can check with them."

And that was another of my many worries. What if Alison and Steve didn't like our house as much after a second viewing? What if they changed their minds and pulled out? They hadn't paid a deposit and everything was sealed with a mere handshake.

But I needn't have worried. Alison happily toured the house with her sister in tow.

"Just look at the view," she enthused to her sister. "I can't believe I'm going to wake up to this every morning."

The sun was high in the sky and the shadows on the craggy mountains were crisp and deep. In the distance, the ocean glimmered, just a shade paler than the sky.

"Is everything as good as you remembered it?" I asked.

"Better," she replied, "even better. I just can't wait! We fly back to England tomorrow and I'll get the deposit sent out to you immediately. I don't want you selling the house to anybody else!"

"Thank you. The deposit would secure the house for you. I've been thinking about the furniture," I said, changing the subject. "It's going to be really expensive to ship it out to Australia. All the beds, the dining set, the three piece suite, chests of drawers, coffee tables… We were wondering whether we could leave them here?"

To my astonishment, Alison clapped her hands.

"Perfect!" she cried. "I love all this solid wood furniture, and it fits so well here. The people who are buying our house want our furniture so it couldn't be better! It will save us bringing our furniture from England, too, and the house will be ready to move into immediately."

"So that's two things less for you to worry about," said Joe that evening, as we sat on the roof terrace watching the sun go down. "They didn't change their minds about buying the house, and we don't have to worry about packing up the furniture."

"Yes, it all went like clockwork, didn't it? The next thing on my list is to book the flights to Sydney for September."

"Ah."

Joe sighed and looked at me.

"What?" I couldn't read the expression in his eyes.

"Vicky..."

"Yes? What?"

"I've been putting off saying this, but I've been doing a lot of thinking. My next hormone injection is due in September, and it looks as though I'll probably need radiotherapy treatment."

"Yes, but..."

"Please. Just listen."

Joe must have known that his treatment had been another of my worries, and I was glad it was now out in the open. We needed to talk. I waited.

"Both the injection and the radiotherapy are routine and will be done in the UK without any fuss. They have all my medical history and I'm already booked in for it. If I go straight to Australia in September, I'll have to enter their medical system and start from scratch. And that's if they'll even agree to treat me. The Australian health system is nothing like the British National Health Service."

This was much worse than I had imagined. I felt shaky. My mouth was dry and my head spun.

"Yes, but..."

"My COPD is slowly getting worse, as we knew it would. You must have noticed how breathless I get climbing the stairs to the roof terrace now."

"What are you saying?" I asked at last. "Are you not coming with me to Australia?"

"No, I'm saying I can't come with you *this September*."

"But..."

"I'm saying that I need to go back to the UK for treatment. I'm saying you should go alone, and I'll join you just as soon as I can. Go and stay with Karly, Cam and Indy and find the perfect home for us. You know you love looking at houses, and I trust you utterly to find something that will suit us."

"Alone?"

"You won't be alone. You'll have Karly and Cam."

"But house-hunting, and…"

I stopped. He was right. There really wasn't any choice. Of course he'd much prefer not to be ill, and not to need treatment and to come with me, but that wasn't possible. Complaining about it wouldn't help either of us.

"Come here," he said, reaching for me.

He pulled me close and we sat like that for a long time until the sun slipped behind the mountains.

With a heavy heart, I typed in the details.

One passenger.

Departure 7th September, 2015.

Arrival 9th September, 2015.

No return ticket required.

It felt so final.

I have to admit to shedding a few tears as I booked my flight to Australia. There were so many things to assimilate. We were leaving Spain and all our friends. We'd never experience another *fiesta*, and the coming wedding would be our last village event. The fact that Joe wouldn't be sitting beside me on the plane, sharing the sadness, and the excitement of beginning a new chapter, made it even worse.

Joe and I had discussed our travel arrangements. For me, it was easy. All I needed to do was board a flight from Almería airport to Sydney, where Karly and Cam would pick me up.

For Joe, it would be tougher. He didn't want to be without a car in the UK, and decided that he would drive. The plan was that he would drop me off at the airport, then continue up through Spain to Bilbao, where he would board a ferry and cross to England.

Our car was going to be tested. It was an elderly vehicle and had never given us any trouble, but was this marathon journey asking too much of it?

"The other thing that worries me," said Joe, "is that you usually do the navigating for me. What if I get lost and miss the ferry?"

So we decided to invest in a Sat Nav, the sort that fixes to the dashboard. Joe loves gadgets and was in his element. He opened the box and started fiddling right away.

"I've chosen Jane," he said.

"Jane?"

"Yes, the voice on my new Sat Nav. I'd rather have Jane telling me what to do than George."

"I think we'd better test it, don't you?"

"Good idea, let's use it the next time we drive to the Enchanted Pool."

It was a sensible plan.

We climbed into the car and Joe, manual in hand, tapped in our destination, then Start.

Nothing happened.

He tried again, to no avail.

"Oh, that's just typical!" said Joe. "I've been sold a mute."

"Have you turned the volume on?"

"Oh. Righty-ho. It's on now."

"Turn back where possible," said Jane.

"Steady on, old girl, we haven't got out of the garage yet," said Joe.

"Turn back where possible," said Jane.

"Gosh, she's feisty, isn't she?"

I rolled my eyes. I would sit back and allow this embryo relationship between Joe and Jane to develop. After all, they would soon be spending many hours together.

Once we had reversed out of the garage, Jane got into her stride and directed us correctly out of the valley and onto the main road. All was well.

"She's doing fine, isn't she?" commented Joe. "And doesn't she have a deliciously posh voice? I think we're going to get on nicely together."

I didn't reply. I was going to reserve judgement. I would wait to see how Jane and Joe coped with the simple journey ahead.

SPICY MINCED PORK
PICADILLO

This recipe is very simple, but to create the best taste, it does need plenty of time to marinade and soak up those flavours.

Ingredients (serves 2)

250g (9oz) pork mince

3 or 4 cloves of garlic, unpeeled but lightly crushed

¼ to ½ teaspoon of hot or smoky paprika

½ to 1 teaspoon of sweet paprika

Salt and pepper

Olive oil for frying

Method

Drizzle olive oil into a frying pan and add the garlic cloves.

Fry over a medium heat until the garlic skins are crispy.

Peel the garlic and then mash it with a pinch of salt.

Mix the garlic with the mince and add the two types of paprika.

Keep stirring and mixing until well blended.

Put into a bowl, cover and refrigerate for at least 8 hours.

Remove the bowl from the fridge about half an hour before you are ready to cook, so that it rises to room temperature.

Drizzle olive oil into a large frying pan and add the mince, stirring until it's cooked.

Serve with rice, and add two fried eggs on the top (optional).

24

SMALL CAR, BIG LORRY

We had driven so often to the Enchanted Pool that the route was as familiar to us as the layout of our house. We just needed to follow the only tarred road over the mountains, then down the other side to join a motorway for a short distance, and finally to turn into the village.

Easy.

So we were both a little taken aback when Jane, the Sat Nav lady, spoke again.

"In one hundred and fifty metres," she said, "turn right."

Joe was negotiating a particularly tight hairpin bend at the time.

"What is she talking about?" I asked. "There's no right turn here!"

"Yes, there is!" said Joe, swinging the wheel right, and turning the car down a track I had never noticed before.

"This isn't the way!" I protested.

"Well, perhaps it is! Perhaps it's a shortcut we never knew about. We ought to give Jane a chance. After all, she has GPS on her side. She's receiving signals from satellites orbiting the earth, you know."

Joe's confidence in Jane was definitely not shared by me, and his passion for shortcuts was a personal dread of mine. I don't believe any 'shortcut' he ever took actually shortened our journey. On the contrary, it often doubled it, or worse, got us hopelessly lost.

The track was boulder-strewn and didn't look as though anybody or anything had ventured down it for years.

"Joe! Seriously! This isn't a shortcut!"

The car was bumping along so violently that we were being thrown about. To one side was impenetrable undergrowth, and on the other side was a steep drop down the mountainside. To my horror, the path almost petered out altogether, continuing as a mere goat track.

"Joe! Stop! This is ridiculous."

"Turn back where possible," said Jane.

"Now you're both ganging up on me," said Joe, applying the brakes, but I wasn't amused.

"How on earth are we going to get back to the road?"

"Turn back where possible," said Jane.

"We can't turn here, there isn't space," I said, peering at the thicket on one side and the drop on the other.

"Then we'll have to reverse," said Joe, scratching himself. "If you get out, you can direct me."

"Turn back where possible," said Jane.

"Oh, be quiet!" I said crossly, getting out of the car. "It was you who got us into this mess in the first place."

I didn't enjoy directing Joe back to the road. I was convinced he would drive off the edge of the cliff, but we finally made it to safety. By the time I climbed back into the car, I was hot and bothered, and looking forward to my swim even more than usual.

As we drove down the mountain, we realised that Jane had a foible. Hairpin bends confused her.

"That's women for you," observed Joe. "I've never understood how they think. I don't mind. Now that I'm aware of her little flaw, I'll be more careful."

We eventually reached the outskirts of the village.

"Cross the roundabout and take the third exit," said Jane.

To my annoyance, Joe ignored her and sailed all the way round the roundabout.

"Route recalculation," said Jane, then repeated herself. "Cross the roundabout and take the third exit."

"What did you do that for?" I asked. "Why did you drive all the way round again?"

"Oh, I just love hearing her say 'cross'. She sounds like royalty, she pronounces it *crawss*."

I shook my head. Those two deserved each other.

I now began to pack in earnest and needed to donate our superfluous belongings to anybody who wanted them. I was horrified at how much we had accumulated over the years.

Charity shops were not common in our part of Spain, but charity bins were lined up on the pavement on the street outside the Enchanted Pool. They would make the job of clearing the house much easier for me.

Unworn shoes, unwanted clothes, towels, sheets, blankets and all manner of surplus items were pushed into the bins. The economic crisis had hit Spain hard and I hoped that the items would be of use to someone.

Joe did his best to help, but the slightest exertion made him breathless.

"I wish I didn't feel so useless," he said many times.

"You're not!" I protested. "Your help is invaluable."

And it was true. He had now taken over almost all the cooking and shopping duties, leaving me free to sort the house, pack and write. As long as he could be left alone to do things at his own pace, he could cope.

The next big date in my diary was the day the international removals company would arrive.

I had chosen a company that offered a packing service. Then, all I needed to do was choose which of our possessions we wanted to ship to Australia, for the men to pack.

I gave over the dining room for this, carefully stacking our belongings in piles. I also had to make an inventory of everything, another time-consuming task.

I thought long and hard about each item before including it in the

To Be Shipped pile, but some decisions were hard. We all have our favourite kitchen items, but most are replaceable. I tried to be strong, but I confess my special bottle opener, a few beloved pans, some bowls and favourite glasses found themselves on the To Be Shipped pile. Of course there were clothes, the portrait of Great Aunt Elsa, and other precious personal belongings that had to be included, too.

Just to be safe, Joe scanned all our photograph albums, which took several days, particularly as he kept calling me over to look at old photos that reminded us of past adventures and brought back memories of places and people we had forgotten.

As the day of the removal men's arrival neared, I began to worry.

"Will they find us?" I asked Joe.

"Of course they will! They'll use Sat Nav."

"Well, I hope their system is more reliable than Jane or they may drive off the side of a mountain. I wonder how big the truck will be?"

"Not very big. They know we don't have much to ship. And we did warn them that our streets are narrow."

"I hope they understand our Spanish."

"Oh, Vicky, stop worrying. It will all be fine."

But it didn't stop me consulting Google Translate at length, checking how to say "the corners are very tight" and "if the truck is too wide, you won't be able to get out of the cab."

On the day of their arrival, the telephone rang, making me jump.

"Hello, is that Mrs Twead?" asked a polite English voice.

"It is."

"This is Craig, from LetUsMoveIt. We're at the bottom of the mountain. We estimate we'll be with you in twenty to thirty minutes."

"Oh good, thank you!"

I turned to Joe.

"They're English!" I said. "They're coming up the mountain now."

"There you see? What did I tell you? Nothing to worry about. It is an English company after all."

"I know, but I fully expected the drivers to be Spanish."

"Let's take a coffee up to the roof terrace and watch them drive into the valley."

"Great idea."

We were sitting up there, surveying the village and watching the road, when the telephone rang again.

"Hello, Mrs Twead, sorry we're a little late, but we hadn't factored in all the tight hairpin bends. We're still about fifteen minutes away."

"Oh, that's perfectly okay. Um, our street is very narrow and the corners are tight. Will that be a problem? How big is your truck?"

"Could you get a London bus into your street?"

My jaw dropped. A London bus? No way would a vehicle that size negotiate our street.

"No, I don't think so," I said weakly.

"Well, not to worry, I'll phone you again when we reach El Hoyo."

The phone went dead.

"It's the size of a London bus!" I said to Joe. "I told you it was going to be a problem!"

Eventually a huge, white vehicle crested the mountain and turned down the winding road into our valley.

"It's a monster!" I squeaked. "That's never going to get into our street."

In silence, we watched it descend. Neither of us spoke.

"I think I've had an idea!" said Joe suddenly.

The lorry was approaching the little stone bridge that spanned the gully at the entrance to the village. It stopped. Before Joe could explain his idea, the phone rang again.

"Craig here."

"Hello Craig, we can see you. We're on our roof terrace."

"Right. We don't want to risk crossing the bridge, it doesn't look that strong."

"Yes, I understand… What are we going to do?"

Joe grabbed the phone from me and took charge.

"Craig? We can see it's impossible for you to drive into the village. Even if you managed to get up our street, you'd never be able to reverse out again in a thing that size. If you'd like to wait there, we'll come and collect you in our car. There isn't much to pack and we can use the car to ferry it back to the truck."

I didn't hear Craig's reply, but Joe looked satisfied.

"We're going to pick them up," he said to me.

And that's exactly what we did. We drove past the square, over the little bridge and drew up alongside the lorry. Two men climbed out of the cab, one bald, the other with long hair pulled back into a pony-tail. We all shook hands and stood talking for a moment. Then the men opened the back doors and lifted out piles of flat folded cardboard boxes and rolls of bubble-wrap and brown paper.

We were in business.

Almost.

With hindsight, I shouldn't have accompanied Joe. There wasn't enough space in our small car for two removal men, one driver, one nosy woman and all those boxes and rolls of bubble-wrap.

"No problem!" I said, always keen to add steps to my daily quota. "I'll walk back."

But the men wouldn't hear of it. Tony was slightly smaller than Craig, and he generously volunteered to lie down in the boot of the car on top of the bubble-wrap rolls, with the boot lid wide open. He lay on his back with one leg in the air, preventing the boot from slamming shut.

"It's not too bad," he said. "The bubble-wrap's quite comfy."

I didn't envy him the ride, even though it wasn't far. It was a typically hot day, and perspiration was already running off Joe's bald head.

"Drive slowly," I said, sitting alongside Joe as he started the engine. "We don't want to bounce Tony out."

"In one hundred metres, turn right," announced Jane.

"Oh, be quiet, Jane, not now," muttered Joe, switching her off.

We drove at a snail's pace over the bridge and round the square. Pancho, the mayor, was chatting with Geronimo and Marcia on the shop's doorstep. All three looked up, when they saw our car approaching. Normally we would have stopped for a chat.

"I can't stop now," Joe said to me, "not with Tony in the boot."

Without increasing or decreasing his speed, we crawled past the mayor, Geronimo and Marcia whose eyes followed us in astonishment.

"Just smile and wave," said Joe, setting the example.

Obediently, I raised my hand to wave as did Craig behind me. The car was travelling at walking pace, and I felt like royalty must feel on a tour, waving to the crowds.

Clearly puzzled, Pancho, Geronimo and Marcia waved back politely.

"Friendly lot," commented Craig.

I found it deeply embarrassing to creep past without stopping or explaining why we were driving so slowly. In my side mirror, I could see Marcia, Geronimo and the mayor gaping after us, then their jaws drop and hands stop in mid-wave as they caught sight of Tony lying in the boot with one leg in the air, propping open the lid.

It seemed like forever before we reached home.

"I'm terribly sorry about the uncomfortable journey," I said to Tony, handing him an ice-cold drink.

"Oh, it wasn't too bad," he said. "Actually, it reminded me of the time when we were in the Swiss alps, and we opened a trunk and found a body…"

I stared at him, eyes wide.

"Come on," interrupted Craig, clearly the senior of the two. "No time to waste, we have to be in Malaga later today."

"I'll tell you later," said Tony, and began to wrap Great Aunt Elsa in bubble wrap before pushing her into a box.

Joe and I left them to work in peace, but I couldn't help wondering about the body in the Swiss alps. I'm a writer. I treasure such stories. They are exactly the sort of tales that inspire my fiction series.

Later, I took the pair another drink, intending to raise the subject again. Tony was beavering away on his own, Craig having left the room briefly.

"Gosh, you're doing well!" I said, striking up a conversation. "I'm sorry there's not much space for you to work in. This house is really quirky."

"Oh, there's plenty of space," said Tony. "You should see some places we've had to work in. Once, we were in a *château* near Paris, and the owner, who was a French Count or something, showed us into his library. We thought we'd be packing books, but he reached for a hidden lever, and a whole wall moved. There was a secret passage behind it! Well, we were a bit surprised but he led the way and to our amazement..."

"Tony! I told you, we don't have time to chatter," said Craig, coming back into the room. "You are paid to pack, not yak."

"Sorry, boss," muttered Tony.

"I'm so sorry," I said, "it was my fault."

I joined Joe outside under the vine, feeling frustrated.

"What's the matter with you?" he asked.

"I know they've got a job to do, but Tony has these brilliant stories, and I want to hear the end of them. But Craig won't let him talk."

"Is that all?"

"Well, it's driving me crazy. He started telling me about a body in a trunk in the Swiss alps, then about a secret passage in a French castle. I want to hear what happened!"

"Patience is a virtue," said Joe.

He could be infuriatingly smug at times.

SPICED CHICKEN KEBABS
PINCHITOS MORUNOS DE POLLO

These are wonderful served with pitta bread and yoghurt sauce. Simply stir together a teaspoon of chopped mint, one small tub of natural yoghurt, and a squirt of lemon juice.

Ingredients (serves 2)

One large chicken breast, cleaned & cut into chunks

2 tbsp *pinchitos* spice mix (see below)

1 tbsp olive oil

SPICE MIX:

1 tsp sea salt

1 tsp ground fenugreek

1 tsp ground cumin

1 tsp cayenne pepper

1 tsp ground coriander

¼ tsp cinnamon

1 tsp sweet smoked paprika

1 tsp ground black pepper

1 tsp dried oregano

1 bay leaf

1 tsp garlic granules

½ tsp dried yellow mustard

1 tsp turmeric powder

A pinch of ground Spanish saffron

1 tsp ground ginger

Method

Mix 2 tbs of the spice mixture with olive oil to achieve a paste.

Add the chicken chunks, mix well to coat & set aside to marinade (preferably overnight).

Thread pieces chicken onto skewers & grill over BBQ or griddle pan.

25

SPELLBINDING STORIES

Yes, patience is a virtue, but I was rather short of it that day. I was determined to hear the end of those delicious stories. Who was the body in the trunk? And what was down that secret passage in the French *château*?

I tried once more.

"Just popping in to make sure everything is okay," I said casually.

"Tony and me are nearly done here," said Craig. "Just packing up the last of the breakables. These are nice. Are they heirlooms?"

They were carefully wrapping up Great Aunt Elsa's little glass vanity boxes and their silver lids.

"Hey, Craig," said Tony, "do you remember that former Miss World we packed for last year? These little boxes remind me of her stuff."

"Ah yes," said Craig. "She was going to emigrate to America, wasn't she? But she never got there. Sad story, that was. We couldn't quite believe it. And all because of those heirlooms."

"What happened?" I asked. "And what about the body in the trunk? And the secret passage?" I was trying hard not to sound like a petulant child but probably not succeeding.

"Oh, they are all good stories," said Craig, "but we can't hang around. Tell you what, we've finished now, and we've just got to ferry the boxes to our truck. After that, I'll do the paperwork with your husband, and Tony can tell you those stories."

I was delighted.

Joe handed over the car keys. The men loaded our little car and set off on the first of three trips to the lorry.

"There, you see!" said Joe. "I told you to be patient. All good things come to those who wait."

This comment should have infuriated me as Joe is the least patient person on earth, but I ignored him. Soon I would hear the end of the stories.

At last the job was done. Craig, holding a sheaf of papers, followed Joe into the kitchen, leaving me with Tony.

"I love a good story," I said. "Do sit down and have a rest. I've been dying to hear what happened to the beauty queen! Do tell!"

"Ah," said Tony, warming up. "That was an amazing tale, that was." He perched on the arm of the couch. "We didn't hear the whole story until it hit the international news headlines, but what happened was..."

Bang! Bang! Bang!

Somebody was knocking on our door. I couldn't believe it.

I was tempted not to answer it, but the caller knocked again, harder. I sighed. Tony raised his eyebrows.

"Vicky!" shouted Joe from the kitchen. "Are you going to answer that?"

"Excuse me, Tony," I said, and quickly made my way to the front door.

On the doorstep stood Geronimo.

"I was wondering if you needed any help with taking your boxes to the lorry," he asked.

"Hello, Geronimo, thank you very much, but no. That's really kind of you, but the men have just finished."

Geronimo nodded and turned away down the street. I hurried back to Tony.

"I'm so sorry about that. You were saying?"

Before Tony could utter another word, somebody else knocked on the door.

"Vicky! Door!" yelled Joe from the kitchen.

"I know!" I said crossly.

This time the mayor was standing on the doorstep.

"Pancho," I said, my heart dropping.

"Beaky, how are you?"

"Good, thank you. Very busy, I'm afraid..."

Like a true politician, Pancho possessed skin as thick as rhino hide. He stepped forward, preparing to enter, even though I hadn't invited him in. I blocked the doorway, preparing to close the door, desperate to return to Tony and his story.

"Ah! Beaky!" said Pancho, stopping short but by no means put off. "There is something I'd like to discuss with you."

"I'm sorry, Pancho, not now. I must go."

"Beaky, there is always time for a chat with good friends. You are looking a little tired."

"No! I'm fine! I..."

"Perhaps I could persuade Joe to let me whisk you away for a little while?"

"I'm afraid we're much too busy," I said. "I'm sorry, Pancho, I don't have time to talk right now."

"I understand, I understand," said the mayor, winking at me theatrically. "Perhaps we could arrange a time later? It is not too late for a final English lesson. I could collect you and take you somewhere quiet where nobody will disturb us..."

"Pancho, I have to go," I said hurriedly.

I'm ashamed to admit that I shut the door in his face.

Tony had been watching the interchange.

"I don't know about *my* stories, but I bet you have some to tell yourself, living here in this village," he said, laughing.

"Um, yes, you're quite right. Honestly, if anybody else knocks on the door, I'm not answering it. Please tell me about the beauty queen."

To my utter despair, before he could begin again, Craig and Joe returned, shaking hands. I was beginning to believe it was already written in the stars that I was destined never to hear Tony's stories.

"Well, we'll be on our way, then," said Craig to me. "All the papers have been signed and the company will make contact at your address in Australia. Come on, Tony, Mr Twead has kindly offered to give us a lift back to the lorry. We need to head off right now if we're going to reach Malaga today."

"I'll ride with you," I said quickly, sensing a final lifeline. "I mean ride to your lorry, of course, not Malaga! Then Tony can quickly finish telling me his story in the car."

They all nodded. Then, just as we were walking out of the house, the phone rang.

"You'd better get that, Vicky," said Joe. "It's bound to be for you. I'll take Craig and Tony to their lorry."

With a cheery wave, the removal men left, taking their juicy stories with them for ever.

The telephone call was a wrong number.

The holiday month of August was drawing to a close. In September, families would leave El Hoyo to return to the cities and the children would go back to school. But first, preparations were underway for the wedding of Sofía and Alejandro Junior. I needed a haircut and ventured down the mountain to Maria's salon in the city. It would cross another thing off my To Do list.

Maria had looked after my hair for years, and I was disappointed to discover that her salon was closed for the day.

Where to go? I didn't want to waste the trip and recalled another hair salon down a side street nearby. Sure enough, it was exactly where I remembered. The windows looked a little dirty, but when I tried the door, it opened. A distant bell clanged somewhere, deep from within.

The place was deserted and as my eyes adjusted to the light, I saw the corpses of long-dead flies on the counter. There was dust on the black vinyl salon chairs and the posters on the wall were tattered and faded. I should have walked out right then, but I dithered.

"*Buenos días,*" whispered a voice at my elbow, making me jump. "Can I help you?"

The owner of the voice must have been ducked behind the counter which was why I hadn't noticed her.

"Oh, I didn't see you there," I said, "You gave me a fright! I'd just like a shampoo and trim, please."

The lady was probably in her late sixties, and her own hair was not a good advertisement for the salon. It was much greyer than mine, shoulder-length and stringy. It wasn't styled in any way, hanging limply, a slave to gravity. She was wearing a shapeless black shift and black lace-up shoes, which I didn't find unusual. Ladies in Spain don black and wear it for evermore when a close member of their family passes away.

"Please sit down," she whispered, brushing off a dusty chair with her hand.

I decided it wasn't her fault that she was missing her front teeth.

She took a towel from a shelf and wrapped it around my shoulders.

"Excuse me, we have no water at present," she said. "I will get some."

She disappeared through a door at the back of the salon.

No water? A hair salon with no water? I had never heard of such a thing. But in rural areas of Spain it was common to lose electricity for days, so why not water? She returned with a two-litre bottle of water.

"Lean back," she breathed, and I rested obediently back on the sink, aware that my throat was very exposed. I tried not to think of the story of Sweeney Todd. I couldn't help smiling at my own silly thoughts.

Thank goodness it was summer, because the cool water was quite refreshing. The wash, rinse, and conditioning process took a long time because my elderly stylist frequently shuffled off to collect more water. Silently, she worked away. The head massage she gave me, digging her bony fingers into my skull, was surprisingly invigorating. I tried not to focus on the large cracks in the ceiling.

At last it was over and she led me to another dusty chair. Next she rummaged in drawers for scissors.

"I will follow the cut you already have," she said.

I nodded, but she had already started.

The mirror was as dusty as the chairs but I watched her reflection as she worked. Beginning slowly, she appeared to gather in confidence and was soon snipping away quite merrily. Snippets of my hair drifted to the floor.

Next came the hairdryer which blew out a puff of white dust when it was first switched on. My hair is very fine and dries extremely quickly, so it didn't take long.

"It is finished," she said, standing back.

I examined myself in the dusty mirror, turning my head from side to side. She held up another mirror so I could inspect the back.

"It looks good," I said. "Thank you very much."

The lady beamed, revealing her gums.

"What do I owe you?"

"*Nada,*" she said, shaking her head. "Nothing."

"What? But I must pay you!"

"No, I do not want to be paid."

"But I'm very pleased with my hair."

"No. No money. *Es un regalo.*" It is a gift.

I couldn't believe my ears. I argued but she was adamant; she would accept no money.

"Well, I'll just leave this on the counter," I said, laying down some notes. "Please put it in a charity box if you don't want it."

I stopped off for a quick chat with Carmen on the way home. Her little house was cool, a welcome retreat from the sun. She admired my hair.

"Did you go to Maria, as usual?" she asked.

"No, Maria's shop was closed. I went to that other little salon nearby."

"What other little salon?"

"It's just down the next side street."

"Which street, Calle Jaén?"

"Yes, I think so."

"You must be mistaken. There is only Studio A in that street, and the young lady who owns that shut the shop at least a year ago. She and her mother used to live in the apartment above the salon. I don't know if they still do."

"That's it! I remember now, it *was* Studio A."

"No, it can't be. That shop was repossessed by the bank and put up for sale. It was a very sad story. The old lady had mental problems, I believe, and her daughter could not cope with caring for her and running the salon."

"Are you sure?"

"Yes! I passed it only the other day and it was all shut up tight. It is empty, and definitely for sale."

This was impossible. And yet...

I told her about the dusty shop, the lack of water, and how the old lady refused to be paid. She listened, spellbound.

We stared at each other.

"*¡Madre mía!*" Carmen said at last.

"So who did my hair? It can't have been the deranged mother, surely?"

"Who else could it have been?"

Joe and I drove down Calle Jaén soon after, just out of interest. The salon looked just as dusty as when I'd seen it before, but now it had a big *Se Vende* sign stuck on the window. I jumped out of the car and tried the door handle. The door was firmly locked.

That week was a busy one. Workmen arrived in vans and started to transform the village into a venue fit for the wedding of a millionaire's grandson.

The *fiesta* stage was erected in the square, and the shade trees were decorated with thousands of tiny white fairy lights woven through the branches. Wide white ribbon and giant bows were draped around the trunks of the trees. Lanterns hung from cables strung between posts. El Hoyo was almost ready for the biggest village wedding in its history.

PORK AND CHICKPEA SOUP
PUCHERO

Being stew, this recipe works well with any meat. Add paprika or a pinch of crushed chillies for extra heat.

Ingredients (serves 4)

A stew pack of veg, or 3 carrots, 1 suede or turnip, and large onion

2 large potatoes

Half a white cabbage - sliced thickly

A good bunch of fresh, roughly chopped spinach

One litre (2 pints) of your favourite stock

500g (16oz) of chickpeas (from a jar is best)

500g (16oz) of diced pork

One large chicken breast, diced

A good glug of olive oil (not extra virgin)

3 or 4 peeled and crushed garlic cloves

Method

Peel and dice all vegetables, except the spinach. Dice the same size so they cook evenly.

In a large saucepan, pour a good glug of olive oil and heat gently. Throw in the meat and cook slowly until it starts to brown.

Remove from the pan with a slotted spoon and add more oil.

Add all the vegetables except the spinach and cook gently for about 5 minutes.

Return the meat and mix well.

Add the garlic and mix well.

Rinse and drain the chickpeas before adding.

Add the stock and spinach.

Boil for 5 mins, then cover and simmer until the meat is tender.

Add salt and black pepper to taste.

Serve hot with fresh bread.

26

TWO BECOME ONE

On the morning of the wedding, activity in the village escalated. Workmen arrived and set up tables in the square. These were dressed with white tablecloths, carefully pinned to prevent them from being blown away by the wind. Then white chairs were arranged round each one. The stage was draped in white fabric, adorned with flounces and bows that swept the ground.

A truck filled with flowers drew up. A crew of ladies placed giant silver vases in all corners and another crew filled these with white flowers before disappearing into the church with armfuls of the same.

"*¡Madre mía!*" said Marcia, whose windows and shop door overlooked the square. "It looks like a fairy town!"

But she didn't mind, and I noticed she'd placed a big vase of white chrysanthemums on her windowsill and another on the shop counter.

The older Ufarte boys arrived to play football in the square and turned away, disgusted. Their pitch had been commandeered by the wedding preparations. In contrast, their sisters, the twins, watched enraptured as the square was transformed into a frothy white wonderland.

Joe and I watched from the roof terrace. Spanish weddings often take place in the evening, and during that afternoon, unfamiliar cars began to wend their way down into the valley. Sometimes the lowering sun caught the windscreen of a car as it descended, causing a bright flash of light.

"So much to do, so much to do," I heard Carmen exclaim above the babble of voices pouring out of our neighbour's house.

"Pah!" shouted Paco. "At last our daughter has found a husband! We will open my wine. It is the best in the village. No, it is the best in Andalucía, and today is a good day to drink it!"

Much cheering and hilarity ensued. Paco and Carmen's little house was bursting at the seams with friends and family and I could imagine the chaos within. It would be a miracle if they all made it to the ceremony on time.

As the sun began to sink, cars squeezed into every available parking space around the square and in the village. I looked at my watch.

"Joe, are you ready?"

"Yes, I suppose so."

It's never easy to separate Joe from his beloved shorts, but today I had insisted. I thought he looked very dashing in the clothes I had laid out for him.

People began to emerge from their houses to make their way towards the church. Some were strangers, and others, dressed in their finery were almost unrecognisable. The ladies' high heels clacked and the gentlemen's polished leather shoes gleamed. Everyone wore smiles and a buzz of anticipation filled the air.

We waited a little while longer. We'd already decided not to try to find a seat in the church because we felt that others had more right than we did. Some guests were very elderly and needed to sit. Others were closely related, or old friends of the bridal party, and deserved priority. If Carmen's prediction was right, not everyone would fit in the church.

By the time we reached the entrance, a small crowd had already gathered outside. The church doors had been thrown open, and I peeped inside.

I gasped. A thousand white candles flickered and every niche and sill boasted a vase of white flowers. White silken bows hung from the end of each wooden pew. The air was heavy with the scent of flowers, incense, candles and anticipation.

The congregation waited, men perspiring in their suits, the ladies looking like birds of paradise. Some chatted quietly, others waved merrily to recognised friends.

"Look out," hissed Joe, elbowing me in the ribs, "they're here!"

I jumped away from the doorway. Approaching us was young Alejandro, the bridegroom, walking beside his mother. In Spain, the groom's mother escorts her son to the altar.

Alejandro looked splendid in his pale grey tailored suit, complete with white rosebud pinned to his lapel. His mother looked equally wonderful, and I was delighted to see she was wearing a traditional black *mantilla*, the lacy veil supported on a high comb. Arm in arm, completely in step, they walked into the church and up the aisle, heading for the front where the rest of the family was already seated.

The congregation nudged each other and turned their heads to watch Alejandro's entrance. I recognised many of the faces. Marcia sat at the end of a pew, next to her sons and their families. Valentina, our postlady, sat nearby though I couldn't see Geronimo. All the Ufartes were already there, the boys looking bored and fiddling with hymn books. Little Pollito sat on one of the twins' lap.

In the front, Carmen, the bride's mother, was dressed in purple and sat with her sons. Also in the front, but on the other side of the aisle, was Alejandro's family. The dying sun's rays shone through the stained glass windows, painting coloured splashes on the stone floor.

It was getting harder to see into the interior of the church because latecomers were still arriving and squeezing into spaces reserved by friends and relatives. Now there were people standing at the back of the church, behind the pews. Outside, the crowd was also growing, and individuals jostled for position to view the coming ceremony.

Everybody shuffled their feet, waiting for the bride to arrive.

"Pah!" shouted a familiar voice. "Stand aside! Make way for the bride!"

And suddenly, there they were. The bride and her father.

A gasp arose from the crowd, and I'm sure I gasped along with everyone else. All brides are beautiful, but Sofía could have stepped out of the pages of a book of fairytales. Leaning on Paco's arm, she swept along, her white satin gown swishing. All the tiny seed pearls her mother had sewn onto the bodice and hem gleamed as the sun caught them. I knew they'd look magical in the candlelight of the church, and remembered Carmen sewing each one onto her daughter's dress with love. Sofía's expression behind her lacy veil seemed serene, but I was sure I caught her eyes glittering with excitement. Understandable. She had waited a long time for the right man, and this was no ordinary village wedding.

Paco looked splendid in his suit. Carmen told me that he had refused to go to the outfitter for a fitting.

"Pah! What do I know about wedding suits?" he had said. "I have work to do! I do not have time to stand around being measured by a fancy man with limp wrists!"

"But you are the father of the bride…"

"Pah! And you are my wife! You can measure me, and you can pick the suit."

And Carmen had done exactly that, and had chosen well. The suit fitted perfectly. Paco's polished shoes shone, as did the oil in his hair. It was rare to see Paco without his flat cap. It was all so perfect, and I felt tears pricking my eyes.

The bride and her father passed into the church and the organist went into overdrive. The low hum from the congregation stopped abruptly as they feasted their eyes on Sofía. I can only imagine what her future husband, Alejandro, felt when he looked at her. I don't believe I've ever seen a more beautiful bride.

The crowd at the doors prevented me from seeing inside but I didn't mind. I was content to wait outside.

"They're packed in like sardines," I whispered to Joe as we heard Father Rodrigo begin the service. "You'd need a shoehorn to get any more in."

But I was wrong.

Something pushed past me, heading for the open church doors.

Before anybody could react and try to stop them, Bianca and Yukky had squeezed through the forest of legs and barged into the church. Bianca may have been a very old dog with only three legs, but nothing was going to stop her following Yukky inside.

Outside, those who had noticed the canine gatecrashers were either chuckling or standing with open mouths, unsure what to do.

"Bianca and Yukky know the whole family is inside," I said to Joe, trying not to laugh. "They don't want to be left out!"

A wave of laughter burst from inside the church as the congregation saw the latest arrivals. I imagined the dogs were heading up the aisle to the altar. Father Rodrigo's voice faltered and stopped. Voices buzzed.

"Pah!" shouted a familiar voice. "Let them stay! They are God's creatures and part of the family, too. Father Rodrigo, please continue!"

Father Rodrigo must have agreed with Paco because, after the briefest of pauses, he took up his chant again and the congregation fell silent.

The remainder of the service was uneventful. At one point, we heard the chink of coins.

"*Las arras matrimoniales*," murmured people around us.

I knew about this custom. Alejandro would be pouring thirteen gold coins into Sofía's open hands to represent the groom's promise to provide for his wife. Some say that the thirteen coins symbolise Jesus and the Twelve Apostles. Others maintain that each coin represents a month of the year, with one extra for the poor. Either way, I thought the custom was charming.

The shadows lengthened and the men around us, Joe included, began to steal glances at their watches. I sensed that the wedding service was drawing to a close. Joe nudged me and pointed up. I shaded my eyes and caught sight of Geronimo in the church tower high above us, clambering up the rickety ladder to the bell.

The sky was turning orange when the organ music inside the church swung into a thumping, joyous, triumphant melody. Now we heard the murmur of voices, and then the congregation spilled out to join us, chattering like children let out into the playground after lessons. Paco and Carmen grinned like Cheshire cats. Alejandro's father clapped Paco on the back.

"Now, Paco, we really are brothers!" he announced.

"Pah!" bellowed Paco. "We have always been brothers!"

Everyone in the village knew the pair had been friends since childhood. They embraced and everybody smiled.

We all stood waiting for the happy couple to emerge. The church tower and Geronimo were silhouetted by the setting sun. Soon the street lamps would flicker on. I looked around and found we were standing next to Marcia.

"Here," she said, thrusting a paper cone filled with rice into my hand. "To throw over Sofía and Alejandro."

We didn't have to wait long. The smiling newlyweds appeared, hand in hand, pausing in the church doorway. Right behind them, to the crowd's amusement, came Bianca and Yukky. Everyone applauded, and in the tower above us, Geronimo began striking the church bell with a hammer, sending the bell rocking and peals that echoed around the valley. Terrified pigeons burst out of the tower, no doubt disturbed from their roost. It was a noisy affair, made even more raucous by the fire-crackers the older Ufarte boys were letting off.

The crowd parted, and the laughing couple stepped forward to begin their walk through the cheering, rice-throwing well-wishers. The Ufarte twins, and some of the older girls, threw white flower petals that were soon crushed underfoot. The couple passed through and made their way towards the square where the celebrations would continue.

It took a while to reach the square as nobody was in any hurry, and many people were taking photos. As we arrived, waiters offered us drinks and exquisite little *tapas* and we joined the milling throng, chatting with Marcia and her family.

"How are your packing arrangements going?" asked one of Marcia's sons.

"Good, thank you," I replied. "Although I can't believe how fast the time is going."

"Are you excited?"

"Yes, very. But terribly sad about leaving El Hoyo."

I looked at Joe and he nodded.

Being surrounded by the villagers, it was brought home to me just how much we would miss this life. I was determined to enjoy the evening as much as possible, to commit it to memory, a treasure to take out later and enjoy.

Sipping my drink and nibbling at paper-thin slices of *jamón*, I had time to look around.

On the stage, a lady in a flowing gown plucked at a harp providing background music. The tables set out in the square were too numerous to count. They varied in size, but each was adorned with a centre-piece of white roses. The silverware gleamed, the glasses sparkled and white rose petals were scattered across the tablecloths.

"Will there be a seating plan?" I had asked Carmen before.

"No. Apart from the top table, everybody can sit wherever they like," Carmen answered.

The top table was situated directly below the stage, laid for six, and the chairs were a little more ornate and grand than those at the other tables. I knew that this table was reserved for the bride and groom, and their respective parents. In Spain, traditionally, there are no bridesmaids, no best man and no speeches.

"Come and sit with us," called Marcia. "We've taken this table, and there is plenty of space. Come, sit beside Valentina."

It was nice to see Valentina in her party wear instead of the familiar fluorescent orange jacket she wore on her post round. Her off-the-shoulder sky-blue dress suited her perfectly and set off her dark, wavy hair which tumbled down her back. She looked stunning. I cast my eyes around and spotted Geronimo, right on the other side of the square. He was sharing a table with the mayor and his family, Father Rodrigo and young Father Samuel. A waiter was pouring Geronimo a drink from a jug. It was water. Geronimo looked up, but not at me. It was Valentina he focused on. If she was aware of Geronimo's eyes boring into her, she didn't show it.

Gradually, the guests seated themselves, and the waiters brought platters of seafood.

"I don't think I can eat much," I said to Joe. "I probably had too many *tapas*."

On the table adjacent to us, the Ufartes were enjoying their seafood. I was happy to see that Lola was one of their party, and her little daughter was seated in a high-chair, alongside Pollito and her other cousins. I really hoped that Lola would behave herself tonight, which would perhaps allow Valentina and Geronimo to find each other again.

Joe was watching me. Unfortunately, he can read me like a book.

"Mind your own business," he mouthed.

NUNS' SIGHS
SUSPIROS DE NOVICIA

If you'd like to tone down the sweetness of these, sprinkle them with a little cinnamon or grated dark chocolate instead of sugar or icing sugar.

Ingredients

½ pint of milk

1 tablespoon of sugar

Pinch of cinnamon

Day old bread

2 eggs, whisked in a separate bowl

Hot olive oil to fry

Honey (or syrup) to serve

Method

Cut off any really firm crusts from the bread.

Pour the milk into a bowl, and add the sugar and cinnamon.

Now add the bread, pressing down to submerge / soak.

After a minute, take the bread out and wring the milk out.

Form into balls or egg shapes and dip in the beaten egg.

Fry gently.

Once brown, drain and drizzle with honey or sugar.

27

TRADITIONS

"Not another course!" I protested as a waiter hovered at my elbow.

But while one waiter topped up all our glasses, another was clearing the seafood platters, and a third was bringing dishes laden with meat.

"Leave some space for the dessert, too," advised Marcia's son.

"*Viva la novia,*" somebody shouted. *Long live the bride.*

We all raised our glasses.

The wine had been flowing without check, and some of the younger guests were getting quite rowdy. Calls of *Viva la novia* were occurring regularly, and now these chants were being interspersed by another.

Sofía blushed and waved the comment away, the brand-new wedding ring sparkling on her finger. Alejandro, too, shook his head. But now the chant was taken up by all the young men guests.

"*¡Que se besen! ¡Que se besen!*"

Marcia's son leaned over to me.

"Don't worry, it's traditional," he said. "This always happens at weddings."

"*¡Que se besen! ¡Que se besen!*" clamoured the guests. *Kiss each other!*

The newlyweds, fully aware that they wouldn't be left in peace until they obeyed, finally obliged, to much applause. Unfortunately for them, the chant was repeated many times.

The sun had long ago excused itself from the party, but the moon hung in the sky. The four lamp posts, the lanterns, the fairy lights and countless candles lit the scene.

While the desserts were being served, another Spanish wedding tradition surfaced. One of Alejandro's friends marched over to the top table with a pair of scissors in his hand. To our astonishment, he seized Alejandro's beautiful silver silk tie and sliced it off.

Joe and I were horrified and looked at Marcia's son for enlightenment.

"He will cut it into pieces, then auction the pieces," he explained. "This is a common practice, especially here in Almería. The pieces of tie will bring luck to the purchasers."

There is nothing hurried about a Spanish wedding, and the meal hadn't yet finished. After the dessert came liqueurs. The bride stood, and carrying a basket, began to circulate round the square, stopping to chat at every table. She seemed to be handing things out, and accepting envelopes.

"Marcia, what is Sofía doing?"

"Ah, another tradition. She is giving out small *detalles*, wedding favours. And the envelopes are gifts of money from the guests to the bridal pair."

While Sofía handed out beautiful, delicate fans to the ladies and fat cigars to the gentlemen, something else was happening on the stage. The harpist had taken herself off and Geronimo was clearing the stage, leaving three high stools. I stole a glance at Valentina, and caught her watching him from under her eyelashes as she sipped from her glass.

Aha, I thought, *so those embers are still smouldering.*

"Where did the Ufartes go?" asked Joe.

I looked round. I hadn't seen them leave. Only the old grandmother remained at the table, with the youngest children. Lola's little girl was on her lap.

The mystery was soon solved. Papa Ufarte and two other men, who I recognised to be Ufarte cousins, climbed onto the stage, carrying guitars. The wedding guests burst into a spontaneous round of applause; we knew what was coming. The men claimed the stools and sat.

Then Mama Ufarte, the twins, Lola and several female cousins appeared. They climbed the steps and took their positions on the stage. I was mesmerised. Each lady was dressed in exquisite flamenco costume. All the dresses were identical in style, with the traditional polka dot design, but sported different colours. Tight-fitting, scooped low both front and back, and with the feminine frills and flounces, the dresses were unashamedly seductive.

Each dancer stood poised, proud and tall, with arched back and raised arms, staring haughtily into the distance. Each flirtatious hand held an open fan, the same colour as the dancer's dress. I think if a hairpin had slipped out of Marcia's hair at that point, we would have heard it. Nobody spoke and the air was electric with anticipation.

Papa Ufarte glanced at his two cousins, giving them a silent signal. Simultaneously, their fingers began to move over the guitar strings, slowly at first, but gathering speed.

The dancers remained motionless, arms curved above their arrogant, tilted heads. Their faces were impassive, detached, showing no expression. Then, as though absorbing the guitars' notes, their feet began to tap. The music speeded up and the passion could be contained no longer. The dancers sprang into life, whirling and stamping, undulating their hips and tossing their hair. The hypnotic gypsy music had taken hold.

I watched the performance, spellbound. What a privilege to be sitting here on a sultry summer night, surrounded by Spanish friends. How lucky we were to witness the passionate, provocative, whirling of polka dots that is unique to flamenco, in this authentic setting. What an honour to hear the Spanish guitar, hand claps, and rhythmic stamping of the performers' feet on a stage under the stars.

The Ufartes were magnificent and I knew I would never forget that night.

At the end of the performance, the Ufarte ladies left the stage, flushed and breathless from the exertion. The audience clapped until their hands were sore.

The twins headed back to their table, passing us.

"*Tía* Veeky! Did you see us dance?"

"I did! You were fabulous!"

"Thank you! *Abuela*, did you see us dance?"

"Yes, I was very proud of you," said their grandmother.

"Pollito, did you see us dance?"

Pollito said nothing but smiled at his sisters with adoration. They gathered him up and kissed his dark head.

"Will you play the guitar with Papa when you are a big boy?"

Pollito nodded, and I felt sad that we would never see that day.

Now the stage was being cleared and Geronimo was helping to set up equipment for the band who would play until dawn, or until the guests could dance no more. Drums, guitars, keyboards, and amplifiers were put into place and microphones were positioned and tested, *uno, dos, tres.*

The band members took their places, ready to begin.

"*¡Un momento!*" roared a voice. "Wait one moment!"

All heads turned to the top table where Paco was now standing. He had been wearing the same broad grin all evening, and it hadn't deserted him yet.

"*¡Un momento!*" he shouted again as he mounted the stairs on the side of the stage.

The band relaxed and rested their instruments, waiting for Paco to join them. In one hand he held a glass of wine and he grabbed the central microphone with the other. The whole square burst into a round of applause. Some wags began heckling.

"Sing us a song, Paco!"

"Are you going to dance us a flamenco?"

"*¡Madre mía!* Can a man not say a word at the wedding of his only daughter?" he roared, laughing.

It occurred to me that he didn't really need the microphone as his voice naturally boomed round the valley.

"Pah! I'm not a man of words," he said, "but I just wanted to thank all of you, on behalf of my family and Alejandro's, for coming to Sofía and Alejandro Junior's wedding today. I know some of you have travelled a long way to be here to see my daughter and Alejandro's son get married."

Another round of applause.

"They took their time, but they got there in the end!"

The guests cheered, and Carmen beamed.

"Now, will you please raise your glasses," Paco raised his own to the crowd, "to the happy couple!"

"*¡Salud!*" the guests yelled. "*Felicitaciones!*"

"*¡Arriba, abajo, al centro y adentro!*" shouted the young man who had sliced up Alejandro's tie. "Up, down, towards the center, and down the hatch."

Everybody laughed and followed the young man's example.

"One more thing," roared Paco. "In 2004, the English moved to El Hoyo, into the house next door to us." He pointed to our table and all heads swung round. "Joe and Veeky have been our neighbours for more than eleven years. Very soon they leave for a new life in Australia. Please raise your glasses and wish them well."

"*¡Los ingleses!*" chanted the crowd.

I couldn't have been more surprised and felt myself flushing scarlet. Joe squeezed my hand and we smiled at all our well-wishers. I was trying very hard to hold back tears.

"And now the party *really* begins!" bellowed Paco, replacing the microphone. "Music! Sofía, Alejandro, take the floor!"

As the band struck up a waltz, the bride and groom danced alone, gazing into each other's eyes. They fitted together like the last two pieces of a jigsaw, and I prayed their marriage would be long and happy.

The balmy night, heavy with the scent of jasmine, lent itself to romance and I hoped Valentina and Geronimo would help themselves to a share of it. At that moment they were on opposite sides of the square, but who knew what the night might bring? Little Paco and his girlfriend were on the dance floor, wrapped in each other's arms. At a quiet table sat Lola Ufarte and the young priest, deep in conversation, both looking serious.

We stayed until past two o'clock, but finally surrendered. We knew the party would continue until the sun rose over the mountains, but were unable to keep up with the diehard revellers.

We walked home in silence, hand in hand.

"It was a lovely night, wasn't it?" I murmured as we laid our heads on our cool pillows. "A perfect wedding. And I hope Geronimo and Valentina come to their senses."

But Joe was already asleep.

In my dream, I was wearing a wedding dress and carrying a bouquet of white jasmine. We were checking in at the airport and Joe was hauling the big red suitcase.

"We're not taking that," I said. "It will only get lost or stolen. Leave it here, we don't need it."

"You *must* take the suitcase," said the airport official, stamping our passports.

Stamp! He then stamped a pile of papers.

Stamp! Stamp! Stamp!

"Vicky, wake up!"

Joe was shaking my shoulder. Somebody was hammering on our front door and shouting. I sat up, rubbed my eyes and looked at my watch. Half past eight.

"Joe?"

But Joe was already heading for the front door. I pulled on some clothes and went to join him just as he was closing the door.

"Whatever's the matter?" I asked. "Who was that?"

"It was one of the Ufarte cousins. He said little Pollito is missing. They woke up this morning and found his bed empty. Come on, the whole village is looking for him."

FIGS WITH HONEY AND CINNAMON
HIGOS CON MIEL Y CANELA

Although the recipe suggests the figs should be served hot, apparently they can also be chilled and eaten safely within a couple of days.

Ingredients (per person)

2-4 figs, dependent on size

1-2 tablespoons of honey

A pinch or two of cinnamon

A dollop of *creme fraiche*, ice cream or pouring cream

Method

Halve or quarter the figs, and place them, cut side up, in an ovenproof dish. If you can find one that they fit snugly into, even better.

Drizzle honey all over the figs and sprinkle the cinnamon.

Bake in a medium oven (about 180C / 350F) for around 20 minutes until the honey is only just melted.

Serve hot with a dollop of *creme fraiche*, ice cream or cream.

28

THE SEARCH

The news of Pollito's disappearance chilled me to the bone. Outside, I could hear feet pounding up and down the street and voices rang out.

"Pollito! Pollito!"

"I'll look in our garden, in the chicken coop and on the roof terraces first," I said. "You never know, he could have got in somehow."

"Good idea."

"Pollito!" I called, as I searched, "Pollito!"

No reply.

"You stay here," I said to Joe when I rejoined him. "I'm going out to help look in the village. I don't want you exhausting yourself."

I ran out into the street. There were so many places where a small child could hide. Many of the cottages were deserted or falling down. Perhaps he'd been chasing kittens into a ruin and a wall had fallen on him? Had he tumbled into the gully that ran under the bridge at the entrance of the village? Had he wandered into the woods? Everyone knew that he was an adventurous soul and loved to explore.

So many possibilities, each one too terrifying to consider.

Outside their house, the Ufarte twins were sobbing, their arms around each other. The streets were full of people as most of the wedding guests had stayed in the village overnight. Some still wore their party finery, and I guessed the party hadn't wound up long ago. Some wore hastily pulled on clothes, and I even saw a few in bathrobes. They all may have been very differently attired, but everybody's expression was the same.

Profound concern.

The church bell began to clang. Yesterday it had pealed, joyous and triumphant, announcing the marriage of Sofía and Alejandro. Today, it was a clamour for help. Up in the bell tower, Geronimo struck the bell with his hammer, slowly and repeatedly.

"Everybody go to the square!" somebody shouted. "Go to the square!"

Oh good, I thought, *somebody has taken charge,* and we all hurried in the direction of the square.

Although the tables had been cleared, there was still plenty of evidence of the party. Cigarette ends and bottle tops littered the ground and white paper napkins clogged the gutters. But nobody was thinking of the clearing up job now.

On the stage stood Pancho, the mayor. I joined the growing number of people who had already gathered there waiting for him to speak. He held up his hand, hushing us into silence. Although he was not a tall man, his presence commanded the audience.

"You will know by now that Pollito Ufarte is missing."

Everybody nodded.

"The police have been called, but there is a lot we can do before they arrive. Pollito has been known to wander off many times, but has always been found not long after," said Pancho. "But today he has been missing for two hours already."

Somebody sobbed, and we averted our eyes, hanging onto Pancho's words.

"That's much too long," somebody whispered.

"There is probably a very simple explanation for Pollito's disappearance, but we must look for him, nevertheless."

"*Sí, sí,*" agreed the crowd.

"This is what I think we must do. First we must all check our own houses. Look under the beds, in closets, look everywhere. Check your cars, garages and outhouses. Look in the dog kennels, cellars, wood stores, everywhere. You know what children are like. The little fellow could be curled up asleep somewhere for all we know."

More nodding.

"Members of the Ufarte family, please go home. The police will need to speak with you. Father Rodrigo and Father Samuel, please search every corner of the church and tower."

The Ufartes and clergy left.

Pancho drew himself up to his full height and addressed the crowd again. He held his head high, his hook nose silhouetted against the blue, cloudless sky.

That day I forgave him all his bad behaviour. I forgave him for pursuing me endlessly, for pestering me for so-called English lessons. Today he was the perfect mayor, totally in command, and ready to lead his community. Today he had earned my respect.

"I am going to divide everybody else here into four groups," he announced. "I will appoint a leader for each group. Then I shall divide El Hoyo into four areas, and each party will be responsible for one of those areas. This will make our search more efficient and stop us wasting time searching an area that has already been searched."

Pancho held up his arm and metaphorically sliced the crowd into four, gesturing them to bunch together in their groups. I found myself in a group with Valentina, some villagers I knew only slightly, and some guests I remembered from last night.

"Alejandro!" called the mayor.

"Yes, Pancho!" replied the groom's father.

"Alejandro, please take charge of your group. Search the village from here, and work north. Check the cemetery and the olive groves beyond."

Alejandro beckoned to his group and they followed.

"Paco, take charge of your group, and work east. Check all the buildings, the gully and the woods."

"Pah!" shouted Paco, thumping his fist so hard on a table that an ashtray jumped. "If Pollito is to be found, we'll find him!"

"Manolo," said Pancho, pointing at Marcia's son. "Please take charge of your group. Work your way to the west. Start from the square, like the others. Check all the buildings. Then your group will need to climb the mountain, search the shrine and all the crags and outcrops."

Manolo, a quiet, intelligent, and sensible man, led his team away. Only my group remained. Geronimo had returned from ringing the bell and stood watching and listening.

"Ah, there you are, Geronimo," said Pancho. "I want you to take this group. Search the south part of the village. There are plenty of derelict buildings where a little chap could get into trouble. Search along the mule track to the old lead mine."

Not for the first time that day, my heart went cold. Surely Pollito would never have made his way to the disused mine?

Valentina gripped my arm, the same thought must have struck her. Our eyes met.

"We must find him!" she whispered, and I nodded.

"How many of you have already searched your own houses?" asked Geronimo.

Most of us raised our hands.

"Good. Those of you who haven't done so already, search your own property. Do that first, then come and find us. Everybody else, we will fan out, starting from here."

Geronimo had an air of authority that I'd never seen him display before. Under his direction, the search began in earnest. We spread out, determined to check our areas thoroughly.

"Pollito!" we called and I could hear his name being called by search parties all over the village.

There were several tumbledown cottages in our area, and we scoured every one. Then we walked abreast, in a line, stumbling over the boulder-strewn waste ground beyond the last cottages at the edge of the village.

Nothing.

Now there was nowhere to go but the narrow mule track that hugged the mountain slope, leading us towards the disused mine. On one side, the ground fell away steeply. On the other, the mountain rose, craggy and unwelcoming, even with the summer sun beating down.

It occurred to me that the rough path we were treading must have been well-worn in the days when the mine was being worked. Miners' boots must have tramped along it, as must the hooves of pack-mules, ferrying food and equipment to and from the village and hauling the lead that had been extracted.

Much of the old mine's infrastructure still exists. The steep steps built into the mountainside remain, as do the tracks of the little railway that carried the rock out into the sunshine.

There are open tunnels, either side of the steps, although the entrances are either entirely or partially blocked by fallen rocks. The mine is home to colonies of bats. But what sent shudders down my spine was the memory of the deep ventilation shafts, still open, unguarded and treacherous.

Geronimo led the way along the winding track to the mine. We followed, our eyes sweeping the ground and bushes for clues, but finding none. The sun beat down. Our feet crunched on the rocks and summer-dried vegetation. Nobody spoke.

When we reached the foot of the steps, Geronimo stopped and turned.

"Quiet," he said.

Then he cupped his hands to his mouth and shouted. A breeze stirred his long hair, and his voice echoed round the valley.

"Pollito! Pollito! Are you there?"

The whole search party had frozen like statues. I strained my ears. Nothing but the breeze stirring leaves, and the distant calling of villagers.

And yet...

I wasn't positive, but I thought I had heard something... In fact I wondered if my mind was playing tricks on me, because I was so desperate to hear an answer.

I glanced at Valentina, knowing her ears were a lot younger and keener than mine. She returned my look, and her eyes told me she had heard something, too.

"Call again," said Valentina.

Geronimo took a deep breath.

"Po-lli-to! Po-lli-to! Are you there?"

And there it was again. Louder this time. A kind of snuffling sound.

Most of us heard it this time. We gaped at each other. Could it be Pollito? Or had we disturbed a wild animal, perhaps? Ibex and wild boar were common in the mountains.

"There is definitely something in the mine," said Geronimo, speaking for us all.

"How do we get in?" somebody asked.

"It is a very dangerous place," said Geronimo. "I know it well because I used to play here as a boy. There are many openings and tunnels where a child could crawl, and shafts that any child could fall down."

We stared at him in horror.

"Come, we will climb the steps," he said. "The main ventilation shaft is at the top. Take care, because the steps are old and crumbling. At the top, we will call again. There is no time to lose."

He set off, his feet hardly touching the steps. Valentina and a couple of younger folk followed close behind, while the rest of us made our way as fast as we could manage. Nature was reclaiming the steps. Weeds sprouted and whole sections were missing.

At the top of the steps, the others were already gathered around the old ventilation shaft. Geronimo was lying on his stomach, trying to peer down into the darkness.

"That looks deep," someone said.

"Surely Pollito would not come here?"

"What a dangerous place!"

"Quiet, everyone," Geronimo barked over his shoulder.

Everyone fell silent.

"Pollito, are you there?"

Then we all heard it. Down in the depths of the mountain, a snuffle, then a whimper.

"Pollito?"

"I want my mama!" sobbed the little boy and his voice echoed off the stone walls.

"Pollito!" we all shouted. "Pollito!"

"Quiet!" hissed Geronimo. "Pollito, we are coming to get you and take you to your mama. Are you hurt?"

"My foot hurts, and I do not like the dark!"

"Stay still. Do not move! Did you fall down the hole, Pollito?"

"Yes!" Renewed wails.

With his bare hands, Geronimo pulled at the brambles that partially obscured the shaft. I saw blood as the cruel thorns ripped into him.

"Is that any better, Pollito? Is it lighter now? Can you see?"

"Yes, a bit. I want my mama!"

"Wait, Pollito, I'm going to climb down and get you."

"No!" breathed Valentina by my side. Her face was ashen.

Geronimo rolled over and sat up.

"Emmanuel, Felipe, Juan Pablo! Run back to the village as fast as you can! Go to the Ufartes' house, tell Maribel and Juan Ufarte that we have found Pollito. Tell the search parties. Hurry!"

The three youths scrambled down the steps, intent on their errand. Geronimo turned back to the hole.

"Your mama and papa are coming, Pollito," he called. "I am going to climb down and help you."

"No!" said Valentina, probably louder than she had intended.

Geronimo looked at her directly for the first time.

"I must," he said gravely.

"It's so dangerous," I said. "The police will be here very soon. They'll know what to do. Perhaps you should wait..."

Geronimo shook his head once, his long hair flying out.

"I want to go home!" wailed Pollito's voice, sailing up from below, then subsided into hiccuping sobs.

"When we were boys, we used to climb down this shaft using a rusty old ladder," said Geronimo, pulling away at more of the undergrowth at the lip of the shaft. "Ah, here it is, just like I remembered."

The metal ladder he had revealed was bolted into the rock, another relic of the mining era. He grabbed it and gave it a tug. A little shower of small dislodged stones cascaded into the hole. However, the ladder held. Geronimo got into position and tested the top rung with one foot, putting more and more weight on it until he was satisfied.

"Pollito! Did you see some stones fall down?"

"Yes!"

"Pollito, you must cover your head and keep out of the way. I'm coming down the ladder and some more stones may fall. Can you do that?"

"Yes."

"*Bravo!* You are a brave boy. I'm coming down now."

TOAST WITH SALTED CHOCOLATE
TOSTADA CON CHOCOLATE Y SAL

If you have a sweet tooth, you'll enjoy this Spanish recipe for *tostada*. Of course children love it, and it's perfect for adult late night snacks.

Ingredients (per person)

A couple of slices of toasted bread per person

Chocolate (as much as you like, your choice of type)

Olive oil

A pinch or two of chunky sea salt

Method

Fill a saucepan a third full of water and bring to a very gentle boil. Place a heatproof container on top and break the chocolate into pieces. Heat it gently, stirring occasionally.

Alternatively, carefully melt the chocolate in a microwave.

Drizzle a little olive oil over the toast.

Once the chocolate is melted, spread on the toast.

Sprinkle with a pinch or two of the chunky sea salt.

Serve warm.

29

THE HOLE

"That ladder is so old, it may not hold you," somebody said.

"I am accustomed to old ladders," smiled Geronimo. "Don't forget how many times I have climbed the church tower!"

Slowly, he descended, testing each rung as he went. Like a professional climber, he moved just one limb at a time. I noticed that he always maintained three points of contact with the ladder, either two feet and a hand or two hands and a foot. More and more of his body disappeared, until the hole swallowed him completely.

"Pollito, can you see me coming down to you? Are you okay?" echoed his voice.

Pollito didn't answer but the heartiness of his bawls reassured us all that there was not much wrong with him.

I have no idea how deep the shaft bored into the mountain, but it seemed like an age before we heard Geronimo reach and make physical contact with the little boy.

"It is okay now," he said so softly that Valentina and I had almost to lean into the shaft to hear his voice. "I've got you. You are safe. Mama and Papa are coming, they have been very worried about you."

Pollito howled, but the urgency had gone.

"Soon you will be home, and your sisters will make you toast with chocolate."

The howls subsided.

"You were very clever to stay here on this big ledge."

Sniff.

"Show me your foot. Where does it hurt?"

Silence.

"There, when I rub it, does it feel better?"

"Yes."

"Can you walk on it?"

"Yes."

"Good. I think you just bumped it when you fell."

Sniff.

"Now, Pollito, I need you to be really brave again. Do you think you can be really brave for me?"

No answer, but I guessed Pollito was nodding.

"I'm going to pick you up and I want you to put your arms round my neck, and your legs round my waist, and hold tight."

Pause.

"Like this?"

"*Sí, exactamente.* Exactly like that."

"Like a monkey?"

"*Exactamente,* just like a monkey."

Pause.

"Now, you must keep holding tight, because I need both hands to climb the ladder. Do you think you can do that?"

"Yes."

"Good boy."

"Will my mama be waiting for me?"

"Yes, she knows you are safe and will be waiting for you."

"And Papa? And my sisters?"

"All of them. Now, are you ready?"

"Yes, I'm ready."

"*¡Hola!*" Geronimo called up the shaft. "Can you hear me?"

"We can hear you clearly!"

"Tell the Ufartes that Pollito is not hurt at all. We are coming up now!"

Everybody was smiling at the good news, but I'm sure we were all thinking the same thing. Would the ancient ladder hold?

"Be careful, Geronimo! Hold tight, Pollito!"

"Look!" said somebody, pointing in the direction of the village.

The messengers, Emmanuel, Felipe and Juan Pablo, had carried out their task efficiently. The whole village had heard the news that little Pollito had been found.

Like a giant, colourful crocodile, all the villagers and their guests were hurrying along the mule track. Dogs bounded alongside, delighted at the unexpected adventure. The sun shone down, and tiny white puffs of cloud scudded across the cobalt sky. The scene must have resembled a Sunday village picnic.

At the head of the crocodile was the Ufarte family, the boys scampering ahead, the twins right behind their parents. Then came the familiar figures of the mayor, Paco, Alejandro and Manolo followed by the rest of the village. Every generation was represented, from tiny babies to old Father Rodrigo and Marcia, hobbling along, bringing up the rear.

"Pollito!" Valentina called down the shaft. "We can see your mama and papa! They are coming! Everybody in the village is coming to see you."

Slowly, the distant figures grew larger and larger until they reached the bottom of the crumbling flight of steps.

"How is Pollito?" called Juan Ufarte.

"He's fine!" we all replied. "Geronimo is bringing him up the shaft."

Papa Ufarte began scrambling up the steps, followed by his wife and the twins, helping each other. Those who were sufficiently able-bodied, followed. Soon a crowd had gathered around the shaft, looking down into the blackness, such a contrast to the bright sunshine above ground.

"Pollito! We are here!"

"Mama? Papa?"

Pollito's voice sounded very close.

"Stand back!" said Papa Ufarte. "They are coming!"

We all held our breaths. Slowly, the top of Geronimo's head appeared, his hair dusty and soaked in sweat. Then came Pollito's face, tear-stained and filthy. The ladder had held.

The whole gathering burst into a spontaneous round of applause, and I doubt there was a dry eye amongst us. Below us, those who had waited at the foot of the steps caught the applause and joined in. I saw Father Rodrigo make the sign of the cross.

A dozen hands reached out to pluck Pollito from the shaft, then help the hero, Geronimo, out of the hole and onto solid ground. Geronimo's hands were bloodied and stained orange with rust. He looked exhausted.

Mama Ufarte swooped, enveloping her little son and smothering him in her embrace.

"Pollito! How could you worry us so!" she cried, but her voice lacked any anger and tears of relief rained on his head.

"Pollito! Pollito!" cried the twins, and joined the embrace.

Now no part of Pollito was visible as the Ufartes hugged him and each other.

Papa Ufarte turned to Geronimo.

"My friend," he said, "I will be forever in your debt."

"Think nothing of it, anybody in the village would have done the same thing."

"No, not many of us would be brave enough to climb down into that evil hole with nothing to trust but God and a rusty ladder. I will never forget what you have done today."

Far away on the other side of the valley, three police cars, their blue lights flashing, crested the mountain and descended their winding way into the valley.

"Well, they are a bit late," somebody remarked, voicing all our thoughts.

But it didn't matter, Pollito was safe. Papa Ufarte took his son and began their descent down the mountainside to join the waiting people below. We followed behind, all delighted with this story's happy ending.

"Thank the Lord," said Father Rodrigo, making another sign of the cross. "Jesus was watching over you today, Pollito."

Men clapped Papa Ufarte on the back and ruffled Pollito's hair. Women stroked Pollito's dirty cheek and smiled at him.

"*¡Madre mía!*" they said. "What a fright you gave us, Pollito."

"We are so happy you are safe."

"Keep away from the mine, Pollito."

The mayor held up his arm, and we all fell silent.

"I will organise workmen to fence off the mine," he announced. "It is a dangerous place and our children must not be allowed near it."

"Pah!" said Paco. "As soon as possible! This cannot happen again! Who will help me build a fence?"

"*¡Sí, sí!*" said Papa Ufarte, nodding vigorously.

"I will!" called Manolo.

"And I!" said Alejandro.

"And I!" volunteered another dozen voices.

"Good, we will begin work tomorrow."

"*Bravo!*"

Everybody clapped, and we turned and began the trek back to the village. The sun smiled down on the procession, and the mood was light.

It suddenly occurred to me that I hadn't seen Geronimo come down the mountain. And where was Valentina?

I stopped and looked back along the track, then raised my eyes. There on the mountainside, at the top of the steps stood a figure. I shaded my eyes from the glare of the sun to see more clearly.

No, I was wrong. It wasn't one figure. It was two.

Geronimo's arms were wrapped around Valentina, and her head was resting on his shoulder. Neither moved.

It had taken a little lost chicken to bring them together.

Like water from a dripping tap, our time in the village had trickled away. September had arrived, and the evenings were cooler. Dew-spangled spider webs decorated the grass in the early mornings, a sure sign of autumn. Our house martin babies had grown up and flown away. Soon the swallows and other migrating birds would leave, heading south for warmer climes.

And so would we.

Next year, the birds would be back, but we wouldn't. We'd be on the other side of the planet.

It was difficult to believe.

Karly phoned me from Australia.

"Everything is ready for you here, can't wait! Indy keeps telling people, 'My Nanny's coming to my house.' She even told the parcel delivery man."

"Haha!"

"And we had friends to stay last weekend, and she said, "Why are you sleeping in Nanny's bed?" Made us laugh."

"I'm so sorry I wasn't there for Indy's birthday."

"Never mind, you are going to be there for all her next ones."

"Can't wait to see you all."

"How long before you leave now?"

"Five days, fourteen hours, twenty minutes and five seconds."

"Haha!"

Now only a handful of days remained and almost every item on my To Do list had been crossed off.

Iberia Airlines, in spite of all my efforts, sent me another cheque for exactly the same amount they had sent before: 96.24 euros. It was doubly insulting now than when they had sent it the first time because of all their empty promises, and the time I had wasted on phoning and writing to them. I was in the process of closing my Spanish bank account so I decided that enough was enough. I cashed the cheque and put the matter to bed.

My Australian visa had been granted. I'd had to undergo a police check, both British and Spanish, which hadn't been easy. Not because of any criminal record, I hasten to add, but because of the red tape involved.

I also had to fly to Madrid for a health check at one of Australia's approved clinics. To my relief, I was pronounced fit and well.

Finally, I had paid the massive sum that the Australian visa office demanded which entitled me to permanent residency.

And so the deed was done.

Later, when Joe was ready, we would apply for his visa.

The major tasks had been accomplished, including taking the car to a garage to have a roof rack fitted. There were many items that we didn't want to throw away, so Joe decided to take them back to Britain to give to friends and family.

Whatever tasks we still needed to do, we made it a rule to visit the Enchanted Pool daily. The water, warmed by natural springs, was still very pleasant, despite the onset of autumn and the cooler nights. The children had just begun a new term at school, and in a few days, the Enchanted Pool's gates would be locked.

Then the pool would be drained, and over the winter months, it would be abandoned. Rain would fill it. The wind would add leaves and debris. Winter storms would throw in broken branches, and by next spring, the neglected pool would look very unattractive. The water would be sludgy and dark green, with litter floating on the filthy surface. We'd seen this happen year after year.

But in May, the council workmen would arrive. They would set to work and restore the Enchanted Pool to its former pristine condition. Once more the water would sparkle in the sunlight, and the railings and building would boast fresh coats of paint. The sun loungers would be set out under the shade trees, and the Enchanted Pool would be ready to welcome its first visitors in June.

But the English couple from El Hoyo would not swim there again.

Our last journey to the Enchanted Pool was a poignant one. I drank in the scenery on the journey, trying to commit to memory every crag and silhouette of the dramatic views. We passed the row of olive trees that grew close to the roadside, and I recalled the herd of wild goats we had once seen feasting in the branches.

"I hope we see some ibex today," I said. "We haven't seen any for a while, and it would make our last day very special."

We passed the Mustard House and I marvelled yet again that the owner of this house had been permitted to paint his dwelling such an unpleasant colour, when Andalucía is famed for its whitewashed villages.

We drove through the deep, steep-sided ravine that we had named Vulture Gulch after the young vulture that we saw falling off the crags high above and into our path, more than ten years before.

Such memories.

"I hope all the regulars are at the pool today," I said. "I want to remember them all."

FRIED CHICKEN LIVERS
HÍGADOS DE POLLO

Ingredients

200-250g (8oz) of chicken livers, washed, trimmed and drained

A few spoons of any flour for coating

1 egg

Dribble of milk

½ teaspoon of paprika

Salt and pepper to taste

Plenty of oil for deep frying

Method

Set out 2 shallow bowls.

Bowl #1: Mix the flour, paprika, salt and pepper and mix well.

Bowl #2: Lightly beat the egg and add just a dribble of milk, stir well.

Dip the chicken livers in the egg mix, then in the flour mix.

Deep fry for 4-6 minutes until golden brown. Test by cutting into a piece to check it is cooked through. Pink is good, red is not.

Serve immediately with fresh bread and maybe a squeeze of lemon juice.

30

SEPTEMBER

My wish was partially granted. Alberto, the least attentive and laziest lifeguard in the history of Spain, perhaps Europe, was sitting under a tree rippling his muscles and playing games on his phone. He had the grace to look up when we arrived, but just waved us through. Clearly the task of snipping off the small pieces on our *abonos*, or season tickets, was simply too much effort for him.

There was nobody in the pool apart from the elderly couple who always stood in the shallow end, leaning on the side and chattering. I wondered whether they ever ran out of things to talk about, but it was charming that they enjoyed each other's company so much.

Joe and I left our belongings on a couple of loungers, and entered the water. Golden autumn leaves floated on the surface of the water but I knew they would be ignored by Alberto, so I navigated my way around them.

I was happy to see a few of the beautiful Red Darter dragonflies that always swooped near the water's surface. These scarlet-bodied creatures loved to settle on the edges of the pool, allowing us to examine their exquisite gossamer wings at close quarters before they darted away. Now they were not in such abundance as they had been, when their mating dances had added to the enchantment of the pool.

The Metronome arrived, and placed her towel on the sun lounger next to ours.

"Can you believe it?" hissed Joe as usual. "Probably twenty others to choose from, all round the pool, and she has to plonk herself right next to us."

For once, I didn't mind. And when she began to swim her widths that rudely interfered with our lengths, I didn't mind that either. I wanted to remember everything just as it always had been, however irritating.

But the next event panned out rather differently than it normally did.

I checked my watch. Two o'clock, and right on time, the old Spanish man appeared, dragged along by his two overweight labradors. When they reached the entrance to the Enchanted Pool, the two dogs strained and pulled, as they always did.

"No, you can't go in there!" said the man loudly. "Come on!"

But instead of continuing their walk, the dogs strained harder, and, to my amazement, broke free.

"Come here!" yelled the man.

But the labradors were having none of it. Still tied together by their double leash, they pounded along the path to the pool and launched themselves into the deep end.

"¡Madre mía!" squeaked the Metronome and for the first time in living memory, was forced to swerve and change her path to avoid a collision with the oncoming dogs as they paddled towards her.

Labradors are water dogs, and this pair amply demonstrated that fact. Tied loosely together, they looked like a double act as they swam the entire length of the pool, side by side. Ignoring Joe and me, they paddled past us and headed for the shallow end where the elderly couple were standing watching, mouths open.

"Hugo! Horacio! Come here!" yelled the old man.

And where was the custodian of the pool? Asleep in the shade, his mouth slightly open, his mobile phone still in his hand.

Having reached the shallow end, Hugo and Horacio ran up the wide steps and out of the water.

"Here, boys!" called the old man.

The labradors, panting, shook themselves then raced back to their master.

A few drops must have reached the slumbering Alberto, because he opened his eyes in surprise. He held out his hand, testing for rain drops and checked the clear blue sky for stray rain clouds. He glanced at the pool, and nothing seemed amiss. The Metronome was swimming her widths, Joe and I were swimming our lengths and the elderly couple were standing in the shallow end.

By the time he looked over his shoulder, the dogs had been secured and were already pulling their master out of sight up the road. I imagine Alberto never found out who or what woke him that day.

"I reckon the Loch Ness Monster herself could take a dip in this pool and Alberto wouldn't notice," said Joe.

I agreed with him. But I'd enjoyed the interlude, and filed this last visit to the Enchanted Pool away in my Spanish memory archive. Sadly, we didn't spot any ibex that day, but Hugo and Horacio made up for that.

On the evening of Sunday, 6th September, our car was packed and ready for the journey the next morning. The house was spotless, the roof terraces and patios were swept, and the garden was weed free. Our grapes were ripe and had never looked or tasted better.

But we wouldn't be there to eat them.

None of our goodbyes were easy. We'd made so many friends during our time in the village and each farewell was painful.

"Come back to the village and visit us someday," said Paco. "Pah! We'll always be here in El Hoyo!"

We nodded, but I think we all knew in our hearts that we might never see each other again.

"And there'll always be a bottle of my wine for you. You know my wine is the best in Andalucía, and I think this year's harvest is going to be the best yet! Here, take this bottle. You should have a drink on your last night."

It sounded so final. My eyes misted.

"You are doing the right thing," said Carmen, as we hugged for the last time, and I was glad she understood.

We were leaving very early in the morning, so we'd already said our goodbyes to Marcia. We'd kept it brief and as light as possible. Years ago, I'd taken a rather nice photo of the village in spring, with poppies nodding in the breeze. We'd had it framed and presented it to Marcia, who loved it.

"I shall put this up in the shop," she declared, "and it will always remind me of you. And I have a little snippet of village information for you to take away with you. It's not general knowledge yet, but I think you would like to hear it."

"Oh!" I said, grateful for any distractions. "What is it?"

"It concerns the young priest."

"Father Samuel?"

"Yes. He has requested, and been granted, laicisation."

"What's that?"

"It means he has been relieved of his priestly duties. From now on, he will be treated as a layman. He has asked Lola Ufarte to marry him, and she has accepted."

Joe and I stared at her.

"Well, I sincerely hope that young lady makes him a good wife," said Joe drily.

"¡Madre mía!" I said, absorbing the news.

"Listen to you!" exclaimed Marcia. "Sounding so Spanish just as you are leaving!"

We hugged for the last time as her black cat looked on haughtily.

It was almost dark as we stood on the roof terrace looking out over the village. The remaining hours in the village were ebbing away and our last moments together were precious.

We watched Paco and Carmen's ancient Range Rover climb out of the valley, crest the mountain and disappear from view over the other side. They would return to the village next weekend but Joe and I would not be there to greet them. For a long time, neither of us said a word.

We'd watched our last Spanish sunset and the street lights were flickering into life. High above us, a crescent moon hung. Joe topped up my glass with Paco's wine, the rich, ruby-red wine sparkling as he poured.

"Did you know this summer has been the hottest on record in this part of Spain?" he asked.

"Has it?"

"Yes, and we were here for the coldest winter on record."

"How could I forget! When we were snowed in, remember? And we didn't have a kitchen."

"Or anything, really. No proper bathroom."

"And we'd just bought our first chickens. You had to dig them out of the snowdrift in the morning."

"And last year was supposed to be the driest winter."

"And we were here for the wettest winter. It rained for weeks and weeks, all over Christmas, and it didn't stop until February, if I remember correctly."

"And the roof leaked."

"And we had a row of saucepans and buckets set out to catch the drips."

We fell into silence again.

So many memories.

"Look," said Joe, suddenly. "Who's that?"

On the far side of the village, a couple were walking hand in hand. As they approached a street light, there was no mistaking the Real Madrid scarf, or the long hair. Geronimo and Valentina were taking a moonlight stroll.

"Well," announced Joe, "I think your matchmaking work is done. There are no more unhappy couples for you to meddle with. It must be time to move on."

"Don't be ridiculous," I said, but I was smiling.

"I only hope you've got it out of your system now. Otherwise, look out, Australia!"

I don't think either of us slept much that night, and the sun was barely peeping over the mountains when we locked the front door and posted the keys into Paco's mailbox. The village was still asleep, wooden shutters closed tightly. Pearl droplets hung from spiderwebs in the bushes that lined the road out of the valley. We'd nearly reached the top when I saw a movement.

"Joe! Stop!"

On a crag, silhouetted against the pink dawn sky was a small herd of ibex, their curved horns held high. For a good thirty seconds they paused, allowing us to admire them before they melted away amongst the boulders.

"Oh! What luck to see them!" I said. "It's like they were saying their farewells."

Joe didn't reply but I sensed he felt the same.

At the airport, we ordered coffee at the characterless cafeteria. I felt quite numb, almost light-headed, and it wasn't because of my restless night.

"We shouldn't string this out," said Joe. "We both have very long journeys in front of us."

It was agony.

Leaving Spain. Leaving our friends. Heading in different directions to opposite ends of the planet, for who knew how long?

"This is just terrible," I whispered.

Joe squeezed my hand.

"It won't be for long, I promise. The radiotherapy will be easy, and I'll be with you in Australia before you know it. Enjoy being with Karly, Indy and Cam. Keep busy. Have a look round for somewhere for us to live and I'll be with you in no time."

I nodded, I didn't trust myself to speak.

It's just a new chapter in our lives, that's all, I tried to tell myself.

We stood and hugged, then Joe turned away and headed for the exit doors. Soon he and his new best friend, Jane the Sat Nav lady, would be driving the length of Spain to catch the ferry in Bilbao that would take them across the Bay of Biscay, into the English Channel, docking in Portsmouth. Then, together they'd navigate British roads.

My flight to Madrid flickered on the screen above my head. I concentrated on the tasks ahead, determined not to give in to emotions that threatened to engulf me.

I checked in, after paying to have my suitcase wrapped tightly in plastic. Maybe that would deter thieves if my luggage went missing again.

A thousand butterflies cartwheeled in my stomach as I climbed the steps and boarded the plane.

31

EPILOGUE

Foreign airports are always exciting, filled with promises of adventures ahead. Sydney Airport was no exception and, although it was becoming familiar to me, I was still excited.

It was ten o'clock at night when we touched down and I was groggy and light-headed from lack of sleep. My luggage hadn't been lost, thank goodness, and now I scanned the crowd, hoping to see Karly and Cam. Cam, being a head taller than most, was usually easy to spot. I knew Indy wouldn't be there as she was sleeping over with Cam's parents.

And there they were, the broad grins on their faces mirroring my own.

"Good journey?" asked Cam, when we'd all finished hugging.

"Yes, not too bad. Just long."

"Well, you won't have to do it again. You're home now!" said Karly.

"Yes! You're quite right! Australia is my home now!"

"And we've made you a special Welcome Pack," said Karly, handing me an envelope.

I grinned. Karly and I share the same sense of humour. I knew whatever was in the envelope would amuse me.

I ripped it open and took out the contents. The envelope contained a series of laminated cards, each with a picture and a message.

I read the first one out aloud.

This voucher entitles the holder to 1 x beach pool swim.

The picture was a photograph of Mona Vale ocean pool which I had fallen in love with on my last visit.

"How lovely!" I said.

"Read the next," said Karly.

This voucher entitles the holder to 1 x fish and chips on the beach.

"Oh, perfect!"

Each card had something wonderful written on it, ranging from gin and tonic to chocolate. Karly knows me well.

I squealed and laughed my way through the whole stack until only one card remained.

"Read it," said Karly.

This voucher entitles the holder to 1 x new grandchild.

The picture showed a pregnancy tester stick. For a split second, the world stopped spinning. I read it again, just to make sure, then looked up.

"Are you saying…"

"Yes!"

"You mean…"

"Yes!"

"You're…"

"Yes! We're pregnant! The baby is due in April!"

My jaw dropped.

"We've known for a while, but we wanted to tell you ourselves, in person."

"We haven't even told Indy yet."

"She's going to be a big sister!"

The news finally sank in. I shrieked, causing heads to turn. It was so totally unexpected, and the best welcome I could ever have dreamed of.

In that moment, I knew without a shadow of a doubt that Joe and I had made the right decision.

And what of Joe in the UK? Well, I'm pleased to say that he and Jane completed the journey without mishap, in spite of Jane developing the unnerving habit of flying off the dashboard and burying herself in his lap without warning.

Joe's radiotherapy treatment also went smoothly and the course finished before Christmas. Just three months had passed since our painful parting in Spain.

As the New Year fireworks exploded over Sydney harbour, Joe arrived in Australia.

For us, another joyous life-chapter was beginning.

This time, Down Under.

P.S. WHAT ABOUT MOTHER?

Thank you for the many wonderful Facebook messages and emails I've been receiving since *Turmoil* was published in December 2017. However, something has become clear from these.

I think I may have left a loose end trailing, concerning two old friends who didn't appear much in this book. What about Mother and Judith? Did they come to the wedding?

Yes, Mother came to the wedding, looking extremely glamorous as usual. She wore lilac, with a matching fascinator decorated with tiny beads and feathers. In her position as the bridegroom's grandfather's girlfriend, she sat with Alejandro Senior, at a table with Alejandro's extended family. Her gloved fingers held a long black cigarette holder, in which a 'herbal' cigarette smoked. I smiled when I remembered that time, years ago, when Mother had asked us to look after her tomato plants. How surprised we'd been when the penny dropped and we realised her smelly plants weren't tomatoes at all. Mother still knew how to enjoy herself, and blew a smoke ring into the air above her head.

Judith, her daughter, didn't attend the wedding as she lived in the next village, not El Hoyo. I don't believe the wedding would have been her kind of 'thing' anyway, she would have preferred to stay at home with all ten dogs and goodness knows how many cats.

January 2018

A REQUEST...

We authors absolutely rely on our readers' reviews. We love them even more than a glass of chilled wine on a summer's night beneath the stars.

Even more than chocolate.

If you enjoyed this book, I'd be so grateful if you left an Amazon review, even if it's simply one sentence.

THANK YOU!

SO WHAT HAPPENED NEXT?

EXCERPT FROM THE NEXT IN THE SERIES: "TWO OLD FOOLS DOWN UNDER"

I've always wanted a dog. I've had cats, all big personalities and all much missed. I remember Fortnum and her brother, Mason, who grew up with the children. Fortnum was a beautiful, delicate tabby with the heart of a lion, unlike her brother, Mason. He was huge, but cowered behind his little sister as she fought all the battles with the neighbouring feline community.

And there was Chox, the Siamese mix who enchanted us in Spain and ended up living in Germany.

There were always excellent reasons for us *not* to have a dog: we were working and out of the house all day. Or travelling too much and unable to give a dog the time or stability it deserved.

So I made myself a promise. One day, when the time was *exactly* right, we'd have a dog.

It was September 2015, and I had just landed in Australia clutching my precious, newly-granted Permanent Residence visa.

We no longer needed to travel. Our year working in Bahrain had cured my itchy feet and Joe was probably not well enough to explore the far-flung corners of the earth.

We'd stopped looking for greener pastures because we'd found them. Home is where the family is. Australia was where the family was and Australia was where we would put down our roots.

The possibility of owning a dog was suddenly within my reach for the first time in my life.

"You won't rush out and get a dog the moment you land in Australia, will you?" Joe had asked, watching me carefully.

"No! Of course not! I'm going to be far too busy catching up with little Indy, and house-hunting, to think about getting a dog."

But I lied.

"Good. When I've finished my treatment in the UK, and we've got a place of our own to live, then there'll be plenty of time to discuss whether we want a dog or not."

Read more in "Two Old Fools Down Under"

THE OLD FOOLS SERIES

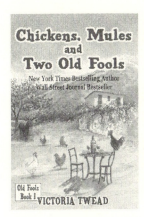  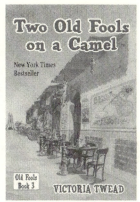

Book #1 **Chickens, Mules and Two Old Fools**
If Joe and Vicky had known what relocating to a tiny Spanish mountain village would REALLY be like, they might have hesitated...

Book #2 **Two Old Fools - Olé!**
Vicky and Joe have finished fixing up their house and look forward to peaceful days enjoying their retirement. Then the fish van arrives, and instead of delivering fresh fish, disgorges the Ufarte family.

Book #3 **Two Old Fools on a Camel**
Reluctantly, Vicky and Joe leave Spain to work for a year in the Middle East. Incredibly, the Arab revolution erupted, throwing them into violent events that made world headlines.
New York Times bestseller three times

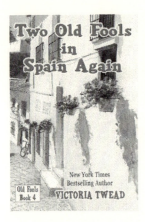 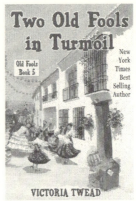 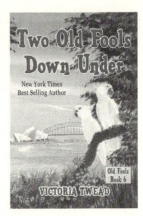

Book #4 Two Old Fools in Spain Again

Life refuses to stand still in tiny El Hoyo. Lola Ufarte's behaviour surprises nobody, but when a millionaire becomes a neighbour, the village turns into a battleground.

Book #5 Two Old Fools in Turmoil

When dark, sinister clouds loom, Victoria and Joe find themselves facing life-changing decisions. Happily, silver linings also abound. A fresh new face joins the cast of well-known characters but the return of a bad penny may be more than some can handle.

Book #6 Two Old Fools Down Under

When Vicky and Joe wave goodbye to their beloved Spanish village, they face their future in Australia with some trepidation. Now they must build a new life amongst strangers, snakes and spiders the size of saucers. Accompanied by their enthusiastic new puppy, Lola, adventures abound, both heartwarming and terrifying.

Two Old Fools in the Kitchen, Part 1 (Cookbook)

The *Old Fools' Kitchen* cookbooks were created in response to frequent requests from readers of the *Old Fools series* asking to see all the recipes collected together in one place.

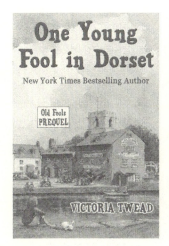 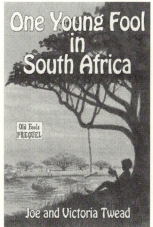

One Young Fool in Dorset (PREQUEL)
This light and charming story is the delightful prequel to Victoria
Twead's Old Fools series. Her childhood memories are vividly
portrayed, leaving the reader chuckling and enjoying a warm sense of
comfortable nostalgia.

One Young Fool in South Africa (PREQUEL)
Who is Joe Twead? What happened before Joe met Victoria and they
moved to a crazy Spanish mountain village? Joe vividly paints his
childhood memories despite constant heckling from Victoria at his
elbow.

THE SIXPENNY CROSS SERIES
SHORT FICTION, INSPIRED BY LIFE

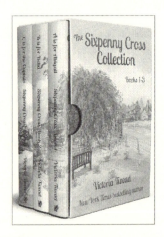

A is for Abigail

Abigail Martin has everything: beauty, money, a loving husband, and a fabulous house in the village of Sixpenny Cross. But Abigail is denied the one thing she craves... A baby.

B is for Bella

When two babies are born within weeks of each other in the village of Sixpenny Cross, one would expect the pair to become friends as they grow up. But nothing could be further from the truth.

C is for the Captain

Everyone knows ageing bachelors, the Captain and Sixpence, are inseparable. But when new barmaid, Babs, begins work at the Dew Drop Inn, will she enhance their twilight years, or will the consequences be catastrophic?

The Sixpenny Cross Collection: Books 1-3

D is for Dexter

MORE BOOKS BY VICTORIA TWEAD...

Dear Fran, Love Dulcie (letters collated by Victoria Twead)
An unforgettable glimpse of life and death in the hills and hollows of bygone Australia through the letters of two newly-weds.

How to Write a Bestselling Memoir
How does one write, publish and promote a memoir? How does one become a bestselling author?

Morgan and the Martians - A COMEDY PLAY FOR KIDS
Morgan is a bad boy. A VERY bad boy. When a bunch of Martians gives him a Shimmer Suit that makes him invisible, he wastes no time in wearing it to school and creating havoc. Well, wouldn't you?

Two Old Fools in the Kitchen, Part 1 (COOKBOOK)
The *Old Fools' Kitchen* cookbooks were created in response to frequent requests from readers of the *Old Fools series* asking to see all the recipes collected together in one place.

ABOUT THE AUTHOR

Victoria Twead is the New York Times bestselling author of *Chickens, Mules and Two Old Fools* and the subsequent books in the Old Fools series.

After living in a remote mountain village in Spain for eleven years, and owning probably the most dangerous cockerel in Europe, Victoria and Joe retired to Australia.

Another joyous life-chapter has begun.

For photographs and additional unpublished material to accompany this book, download the

Free Photo Book

from

www.victoriatwead.com/free-stuff

CONTACTS AND LINKS
CONNECT WITH VICTORIA

Email: TopHen@VictoriaTwead.com (emails welcome)

Website: www.VictoriaTwead.com

Old Fools' Updates Signup: www.VictoriaTwead.com

This includes the latest Old Fools' news, free books, book recommendations, and recipe. Guaranteed spam-free and sent out every few months.

Free Stuff: http://www.victoriatwead.com/Free-Stuff/

Facebook: https://www.facebook.com/VictoriaTwead (friend requests welcome)

Instagram: @victoria.twead

Twitter: @VictoriaTwead

Ant Press publishing: www.antpress.org

We Love Memoirs

Join me and other memoir authors and readers in the We Love Memoirs Facebook group, the friendliest group on Facebook.

www.facebook.com/groups/welovememoirs/

ACKNOWLEDGMENTS

Massive thanks to you, **Elle Gandy-Draper,** for generously allowing me to use Spanish recipes plucked from your new Spanish cookbook. If readers would like to see more, do head over to Spainbuddy.com where you'll find the recipe book, and a treasure trove of useful information for the Spanish expat.

Thanks again to **Nick Saltmer** who painted the fabulous cover picture. I've lost count how many covers you have designed for me, Nick, and I love them all.

Thanks also to **Julie Haigh** and **Pat Ellis** for your friendship and beta-reading talents. Skills like yours are essential for knocking any book into shape.

Big thanks and hugs to you, **Joe,** for your input and editing skills, and heartfelt thanks to my family for allowing me to write about you. **Joe, Karly, Cam, Indy,** my books would be so much duller without you.

Thank you Spain and El Hoyo for putting up with us for eleven years. To say you will always be in our hearts is a huge understatement.

Sincere thanks to all the wonderful **Facebook friends** I have made since I wrote my first book. Your loyalty and support often takes my breath away. Particular thanks to the members of the We Love Memoirs Facebook group. You are totes stonking amazebobs…

This memoir reflects my recollections of experiences over a period of time. In order to preserve the anonymity of the wonderful people I write about, some names have been changed, including the name of the village. Certain individuals are composites and dialogue and events have been recreated from memory and, in some cases, compressed to facilitate a natural narrative.

ANT PRESS BOOKS
AWESOME AUTHORS ~ AWESOME BOOKS

If you enjoyed this book, you may also enjoy these Ant Press titles:

MEMOIRS

Dear Fran, Love Dulcie: Life and Death in the Hills and Hollows of Bygone Australia collated by Victoria Twead

Chickens, Mules and Two Old Fools by Victoria Twead (Wall Street Journal Top 10 bestseller)
Two Old Fools ~ Olé! by Victoria Twead
Two Old Fools on a Camel by Victoria Twead (thrice New York Times bestseller)
Two Old Fools in Spain Again by Victoria Twead
Two Old Fools in Turmoil by Victoria Twead
Two Old Fools Down Under by Victoria Twead
One Young Fool in Dorset (Prequel) by Victoria Twead
One Young Fool in South Africa (Prequel) by Joe and Victoria Twead
Two Old Fools Boxset, Books 1-3 by Victoria Twead

Fat Dogs and French Estates ~ Part I by Beth Haslam
Fat Dogs and French Estates ~ Part II by Beth Haslam
Fat Dogs and French Estates ~ Part III by Beth Haslam
Fat Dogs and French Estates ~ Part IV by Beth Haslam
Fat Dogs and French Estates ~ Part V by Beth Haslam
Fat Dogs and French Estates ~ Boxset, Parts 1-3 by Beth Haslam

Fresh Eggs and Dog Beds 4: More Living the Dream in Rural Ireland by Nick Albert

Don't Do It Like This: How NOT to move to Spain by Joe Cawley, Victoria Twead and Alan Parks

Longing for Africa: Journeys Inspired by the Life of Jane Goodall. Part One: Ethiopia by Annie Schrank
Longing for Africa: Journeys Inspired by the Life of Jane Goodall. Part Two: Kenya by Annie Schrank

A Kiss Behind the Castanets: My Love Affair with Spain by Jean Roberts
Life Beyond the Castanets: My Love Affair with Spain by Jean Roberts

The Sunny Side of the Alps: From Scotland to Slovenia on a Shoestring by Roy Clark

FICTION

A is for Abigail by Victoria Twead (Sixpenny Cross 1)
B is for Bella by Victoria Twead (Sixpenny Cross 2)
C is for the Captain by Victoria Twead (Sixpenny Cross 3)
D is for Dexter by Victoria Twead
The Sixpenny Cross Collection, Vols 1-3 by Victoria Twead

NON FICTION

How to Write a Bestselling Memoir by Victoria Twead
Two Old Fools in the Kitchen, Part 1 by Victoria Twead

LARGE PRINT BOOKS

Chickens, Mules and Two Old Fools by Victoria Twead (Wall Street Journal Top 10 bestseller)
Two Old Fools ~ Olé! by Victoria Twead

Two Old Fools on a Camel by Victoria Twead (thrice New York Times bestseller)

Two Old Fools in Spain Again by Victoria Twead

Two Old Fools in Turmoil by Victoria Twead

Two Old Fools Down Under by Victoria Twead

One Young Fool in Dorset (The Prequel) by Victoria Twead

One Young Fool in South Africa (The Prequel) by Joe and Victoria Twead

Fat Dogs and French Estates ~ Part I by Beth Haslam

Fat Dogs and French Estates ~ Part II by Beth Haslam

Fat Dogs and French Estates ~ Part III by Beth Haslam

Fat Dogs and French Estates ~ Part IV by Beth Haslam

Fat Dogs and French Estates ~ Part V by Beth Haslam

A Kiss Behind the Castanets: My Love Affair with Spain by Jean Roberts

Horizon Fever 1: Explorer A E Filby's own account of his extraordinary expedition through Africa, 1931-1935 by A E Filby

Horizon Fever 2: Explorer AE Filby's own account of his extraordinary Australasian Adventures, 1921-1931 by A E Filby

A is for Abigail by Victoria Twead (Sixpenny Cross 1)

B is for Bella by Victoria Twead (Sixpenny Cross 2)

C is for the Captain by Victoria Twead (Sixpenny Cross 3)

How to Write a Bestselling Memoir by Victoria Twead

ANT PRESS ONLINE

Why not check out Ant Press's online presence and follow our social media accounts for news of forthcoming books and special offers?

Website: www.antpress.org
Email: admin@antpress.org
Facebook: www.facebook.com/AntPress
Instagram: www.instagram.com/publishwithantpress
Twitter: www.twitter.com/Ant_Press

HAVE YOU WRITTEN A BOOK?

Would you love to see your book published? Ant Press can help!
Take a look at www.antpress.org or contact Victoria directly.

Email: TopHen@VictoriaTwead.com